Assemble the Hyenas...
I FEEL A PUN COMING ON!

A Frank and Ernest® Book

by Bob Thaves

TOPPER BOOKS
AN IMPRINT OF PHAROS BOOKS • A SCRIPPS HOWARD COMPANY
NEW YORK

D1522581

First published in 1991.

Frank and Ernest Comics: © and ® 1983 through 1990
Newspaper Enterprise Association, Inc.

LIBRARY OF CONGRESS CATALOGING-IN-PUBLICATION DATA

Thaves, Bob.
[Frank and Ernest.   Selections]
Assemble the hyenas—I feel a pun coming on! : a Frank and Ernest
book / by Bob Thaves.
p.   cm.
Selections from the comic strip Frank and Ernest.
ISBN 0-88687-529-3 $6.95
1. American wit and humor. Pictorial.   I. Frank and Ernest.
II. Title.
NC1429.T44A4 1991
741.5'973—dc20   91-6896
CIP

Pharos ISBN: 0-88687-631-1

Printed in the United States of America

TOPPER BOOKS
An Imprint of Pharos Books
A Scripps Howard Company
200 Park Avenue
NY, NY 10166

10 9 8 7 6 5 4 3 2 1

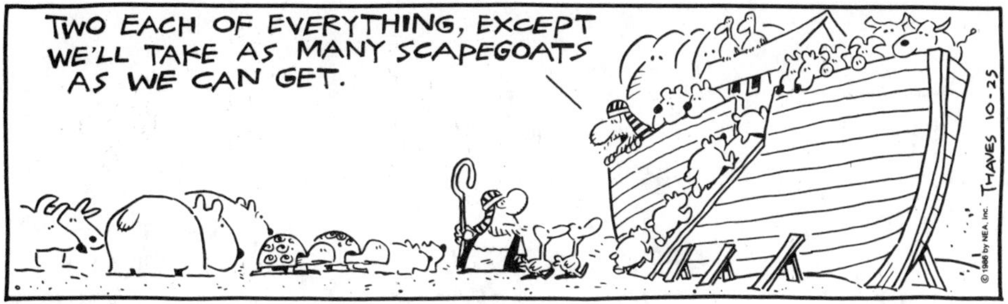
TWO EACH OF EVERYTHING, EXCEPT WE'LL TAKE AS MANY SCAPEGOATS AS WE CAN GET.
THAVES 10-25
© 1986 by NEA, Inc.

When *Frank and Ernest* first came into our lives few of us realized how their importance to us would grow as life on Earth became more complex. Now that we know that its complexion isn't likely to improve, the importance of being Ernest and/or Frank in trying to understand life has never been greater.

What better place to start than with the Ark? As Shakespeare, that well-known forerunner of Bob Thaves, observed, "There is a tide in the affairs of men which, taken at the Flood..."

After you have pondered the wisdom in these pages we feel sure that you will understand why Bob Thaves has been named Punster of the Year by the International Save the Pun Foundation and why its members hope that there will be many more books to come from this master in the art of word-play!

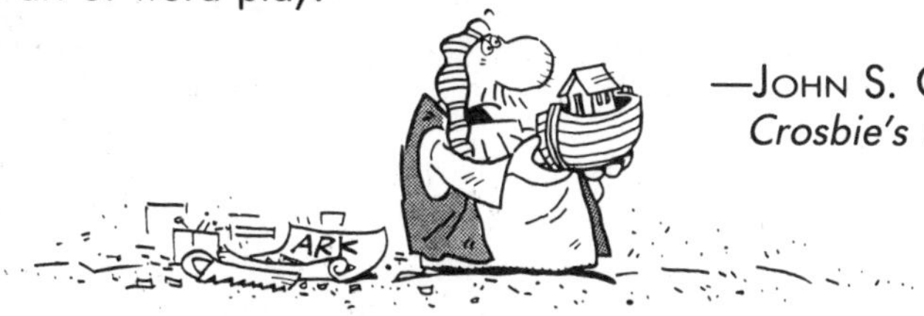
ARK

—John S. Crosbie,
Crosbie's Dictionary of Puns

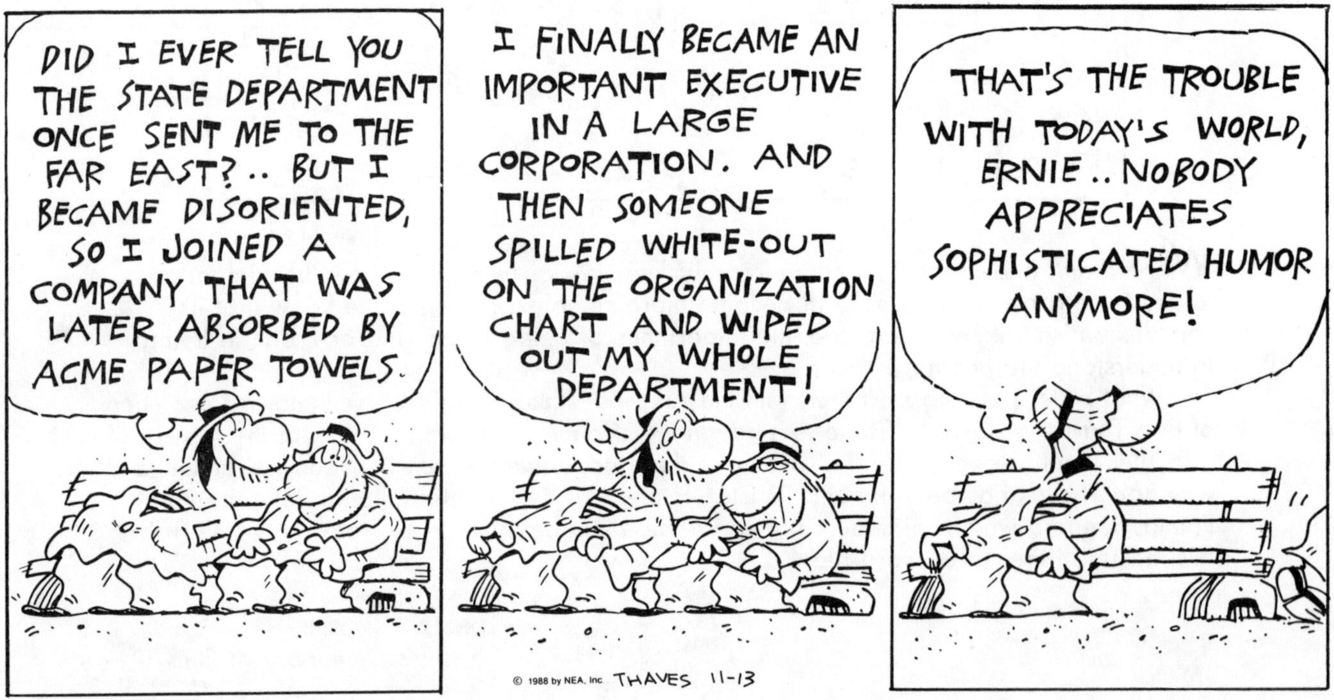
DID I EVER TELL YOU THE STATE DEPARTMENT ONCE SENT ME TO THE FAR EAST? .. BUT I BECAME DISORIENTED, SO I JOINED A COMPANY THAT WAS LATER ABSORBED BY ACME PAPER TOWELS.
I FINALLY BECAME AN IMPORTANT EXECUTIVE IN A LARGE CORPORATION. AND THEN SOMEONE SPILLED WHITE-OUT ON THE ORGANIZATION CHART AND WIPED OUT MY WHOLE DEPARTMENT!
THAT'S THE TROUBLE WITH TODAY'S WORLD, ERNIE .. NOBODY APPRECIATES SOPHISTICATED HUMOR ANYMORE!
© 1988 by NEA, Inc. THAVES 11-13

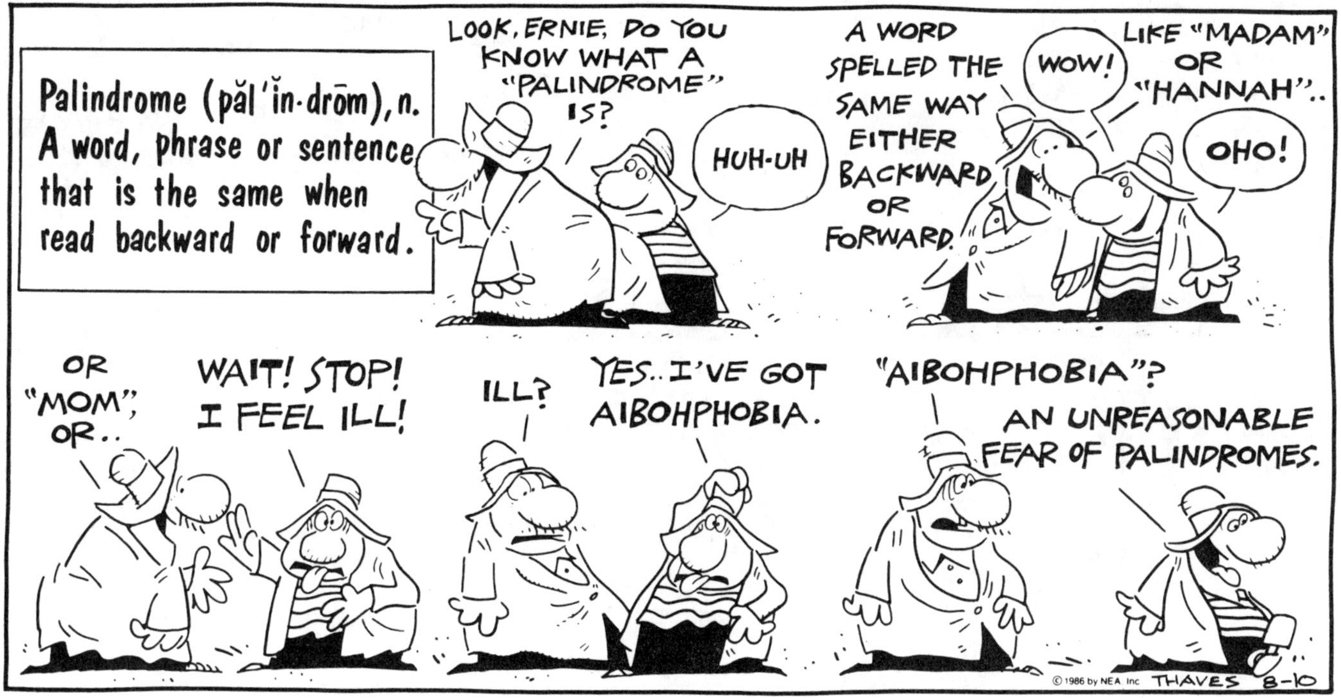

Palindrome (păl´ĭn·drōm), n. A word, phrase or sentence that is the same when read backward or forward.
LOOK, ERNIE, DO YOU KNOW WHAT A "PALINDROME" IS?
HUH-UH
A WORD SPELLED THE SAME WAY EITHER BACKWARD OR FORWARD.
WOW!
LIKE "MADAM" OR "HANNAH"..
OHO!
OR "MOM", OR..
WAIT! STOP! I FEEL ILL!
ILL?
YES.. I'VE GOT AIBOHPHOBIA.
"AIBOHPHOBIA"?
AN UNREASONABLE FEAR OF PALINDROMES.
© 1986 by NEA, Inc.
THAVES 8-10

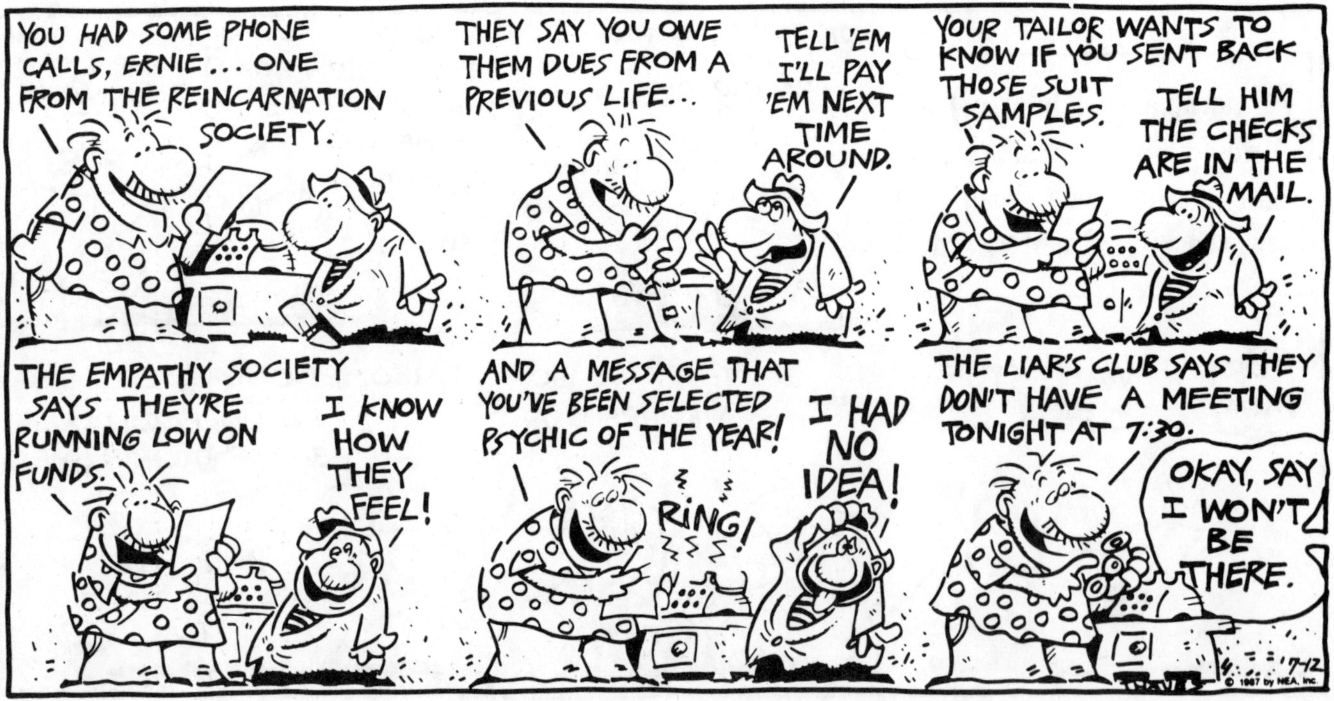
YOU HAD SOME PHONE CALLS, ERNIE... ONE FROM THE REINCARNATION SOCIETY.
THEY SAY YOU OWE THEM DUES FROM A PREVIOUS LIFE...
TELL 'EM I'LL PAY 'EM NEXT TIME AROUND.
YOUR TAILOR WANTS TO KNOW IF YOU SENT BACK THOSE SUIT SAMPLES.
TELL HIM THE CHECKS ARE IN THE MAIL.
THE EMPATHY SOCIETY SAYS THEY'RE RUNNING LOW ON FUNDS.
I KNOW HOW THEY FEEL!
AND A MESSAGE THAT YOU'VE BEEN SELECTED PSYCHIC OF THE YEAR!
RING!
I HAD NO IDEA!
THE LIAR'S CLUB SAYS THEY DON'T HAVE A MEETING TONIGHT AT 7:30.
OKAY, SAY I WON'T BE THERE.
7-12
© 1987 by NEA, Inc.

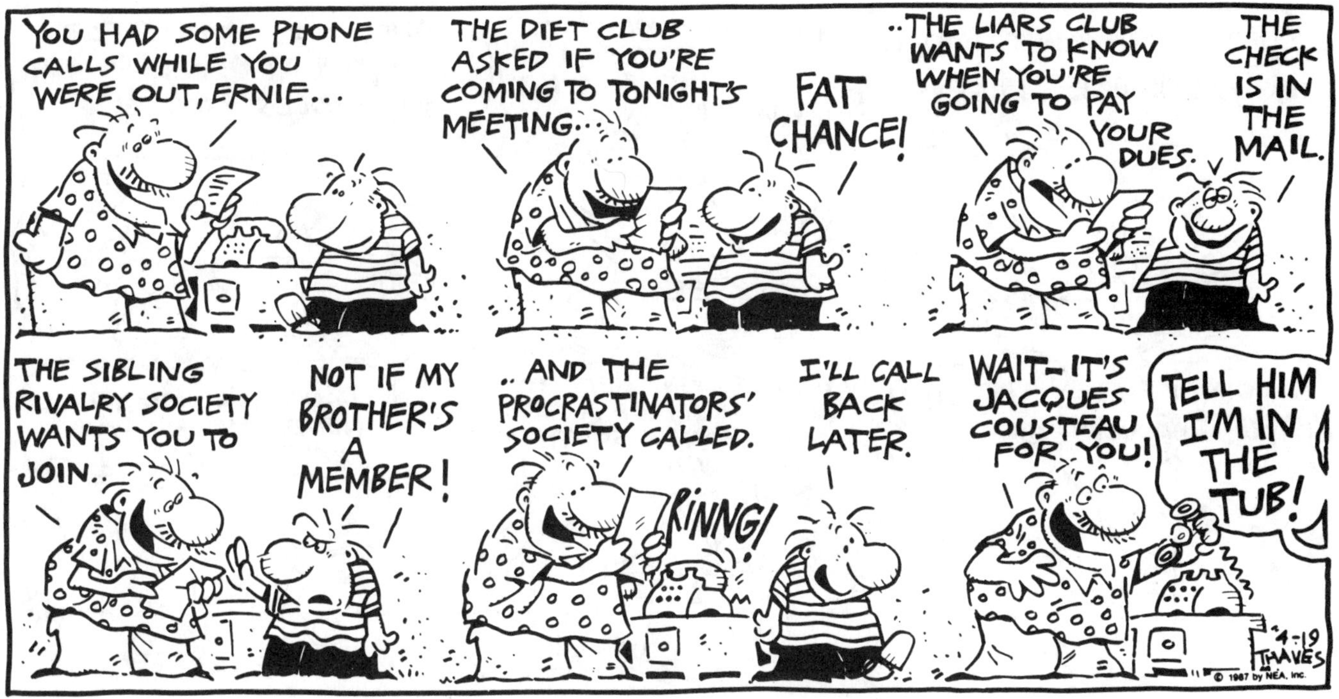
YOU HAD SOME PHONE CALLS WHILE YOU WERE OUT, ERNIE...
THE DIET CLUB ASKED IF YOU'RE COMING TO TONIGHT'S MEETING...
FAT CHANCE!
..THE LIARS CLUB WANTS TO KNOW WHEN YOU'RE GOING TO PAY YOUR DUES.
THE CHECK IS IN THE MAIL.
THE SIBLING RIVALRY SOCIETY WANTS YOU TO JOIN..
NOT IF MY BROTHER'S A MEMBER!
.. AND THE PROCRASTINATORS' SOCIETY CALLED.
RINNG!
I'LL CALL BACK LATER.
WAIT- IT'S JACQUES COUSTEAU FOR YOU!
TELL HIM I'M IN THE TUB!
4-19
THAVES
© 1987 by NEA, Inc.

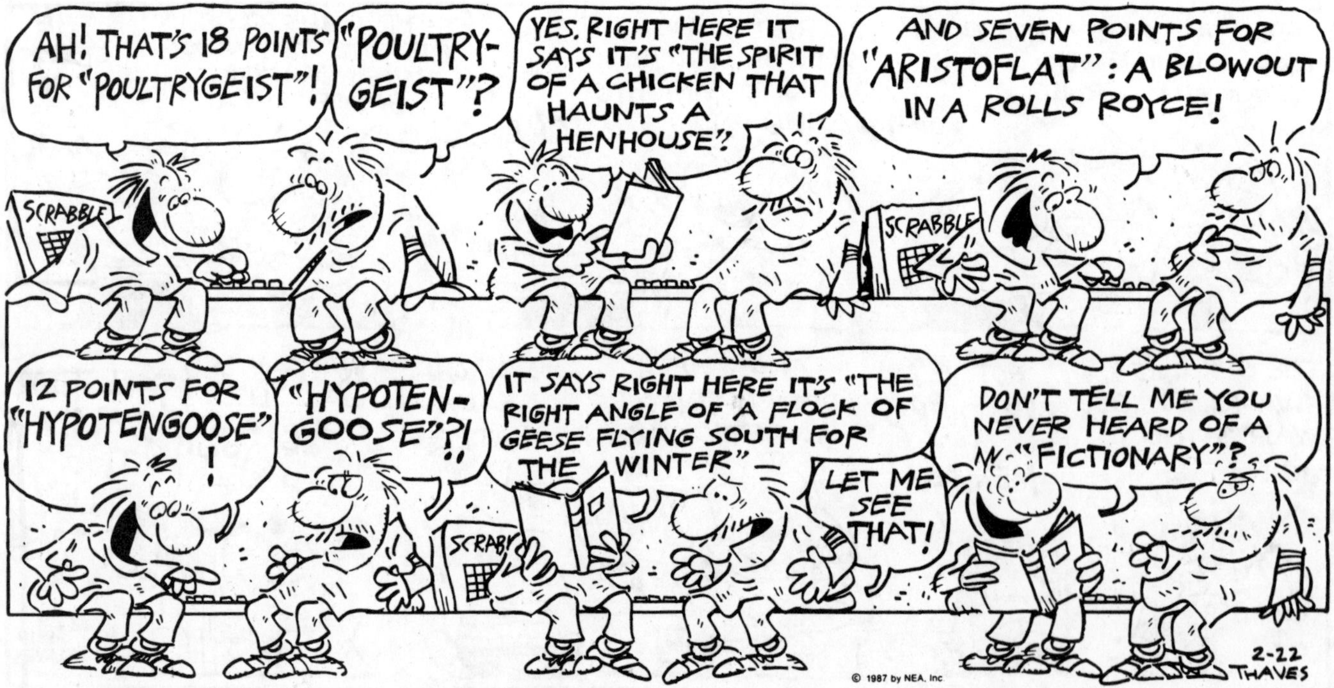
AH! THAT'S 18 POINTS FOR "POULTRYGEIST"!
"POULTRY-GEIST"?
YES. RIGHT HERE IT SAYS IT'S "THE SPIRIT OF A CHICKEN THAT HAUNTS A HENHOUSE"!
AND SEVEN POINTS FOR "ARISTOFLAT": A BLOWOUT IN A ROLLS ROYCE!
12 POINTS FOR "HYPOTENGOOSE"!
"HYPOTEN-GOOSE"?!
IT SAYS RIGHT HERE IT'S "THE RIGHT ANGLE OF A FLOCK OF GEESE FLYING SOUTH FOR THE WINTER"
LET ME SEE THAT!
DON'T TELL ME YOU NEVER HEARD OF A "FICTIONARY"?
SCRABBLE
2-22
THAVES
© 1987 by NEA, Inc

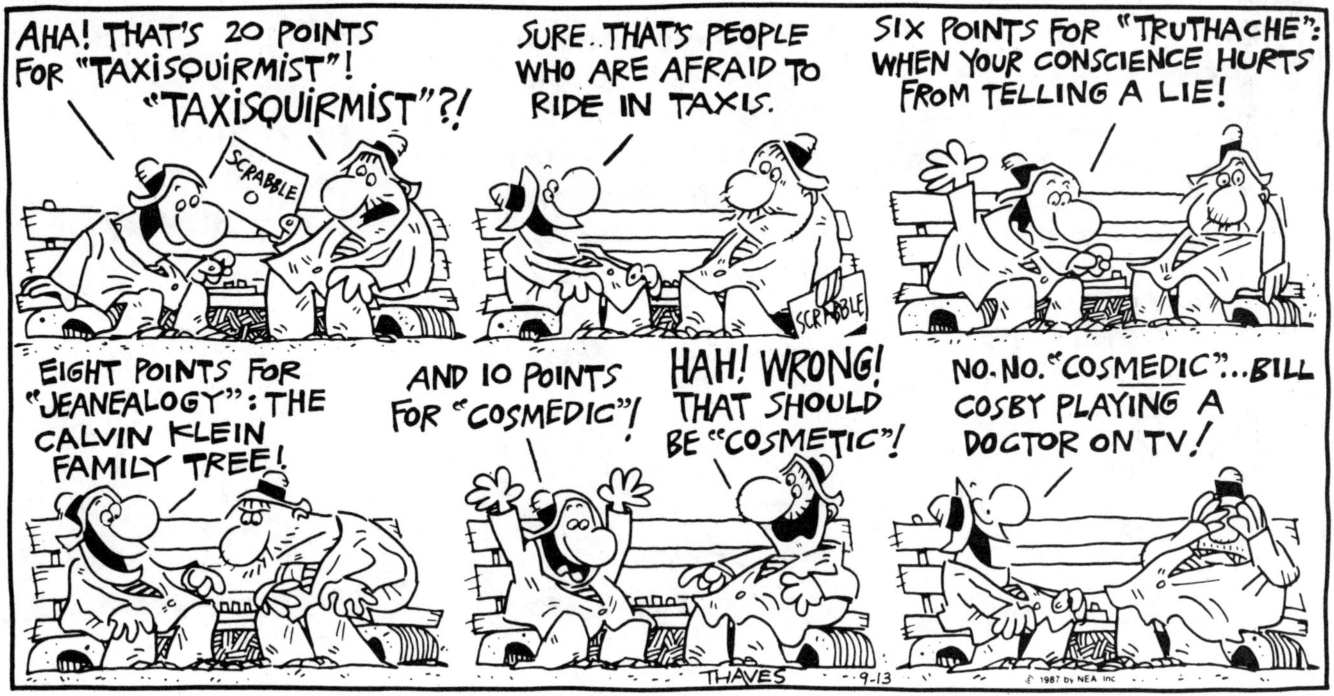
AHA! THAT'S 20 POINTS FOR "TAXISQUIRMIST"!
"TAXISQUIRMIST"?!
SCRABBLE
SURE..THAT'S PEOPLE WHO ARE AFRAID TO RIDE IN TAXIS.
SCRABBLE
SIX POINTS FOR "TRUTHACHE": WHEN YOUR CONSCIENCE HURTS FROM TELLING A LIE!
EIGHT POINTS FOR "JEANEALOGY": THE CALVIN KLEIN FAMILY TREE!
AND 10 POINTS FOR "COSMEDIC"!
HAH! WRONG! THAT SHOULD BE "COSMETIC"!
NO..NO.."COSMEDIC"...BILL COSBY PLAYING A DOCTOR ON TV!
THAVES
9-13
© 1987 by NEA Inc

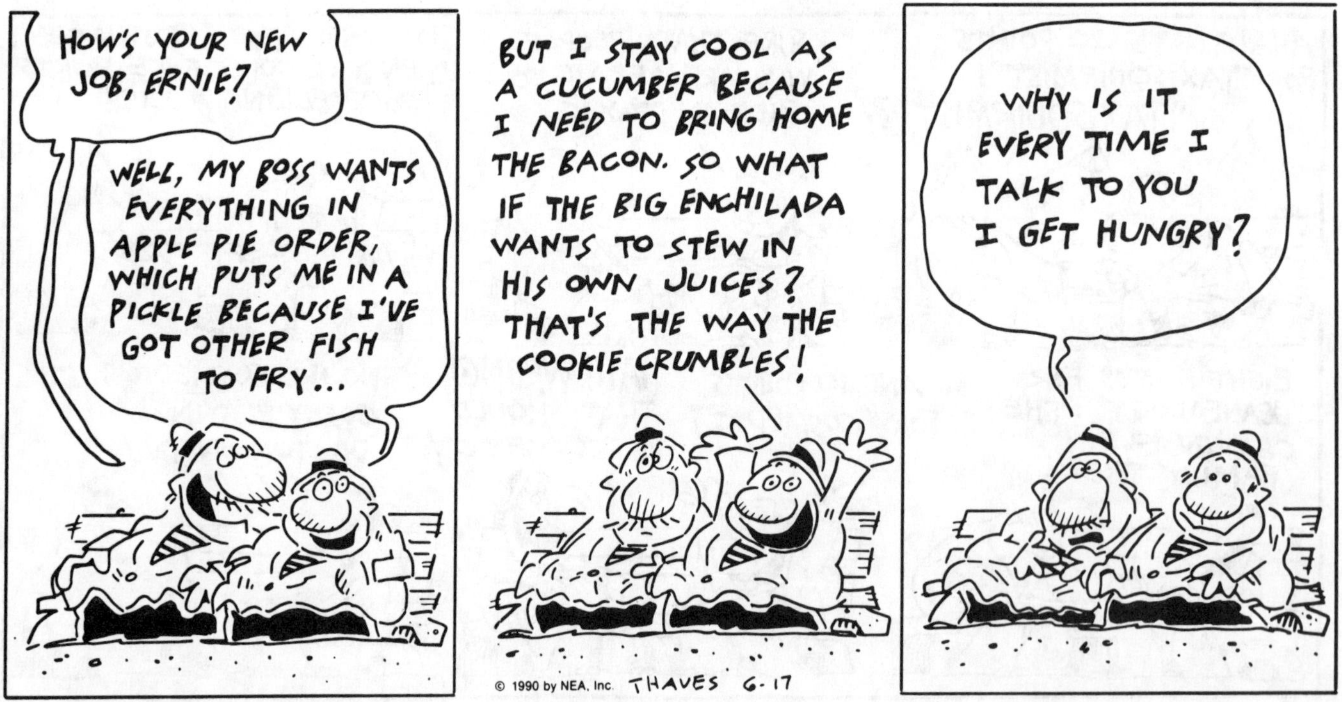
HOW'S YOUR NEW JOB, ERNIE?
WELL, MY BOSS WANTS EVERYTHING IN APPLE PIE ORDER, WHICH PUTS ME IN A PICKLE BECAUSE I'VE GOT OTHER FISH TO FRY...
BUT I STAY COOL AS A CUCUMBER BECAUSE I NEED TO BRING HOME THE BACON. SO WHAT IF THE BIG ENCHILADA WANTS TO STEW IN HIS OWN JUICES? THAT'S THE WAY THE COOKIE CRUMBLES!
© 1990 by NEA, Inc.
THAVES 6-17
WHY IS IT EVERY TIME I TALK TO YOU I GET HUNGRY?

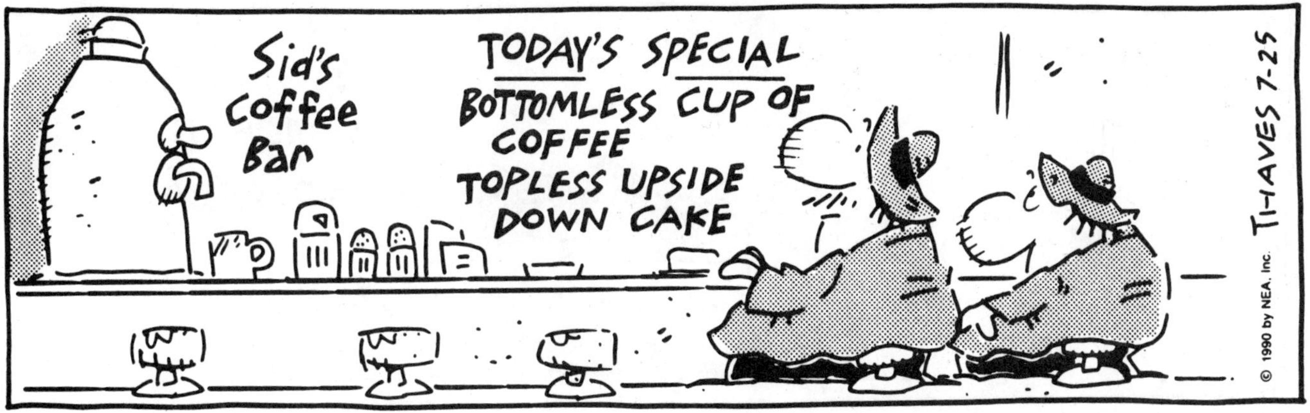
Sid's Coffee Bar
TODAY'S SPECIAL
BOTTOMLESS CUP OF COFFEE
TOPLESS UPSIDE DOWN CAKE
THAVES 7-25
© 1990 by NEA, Inc.

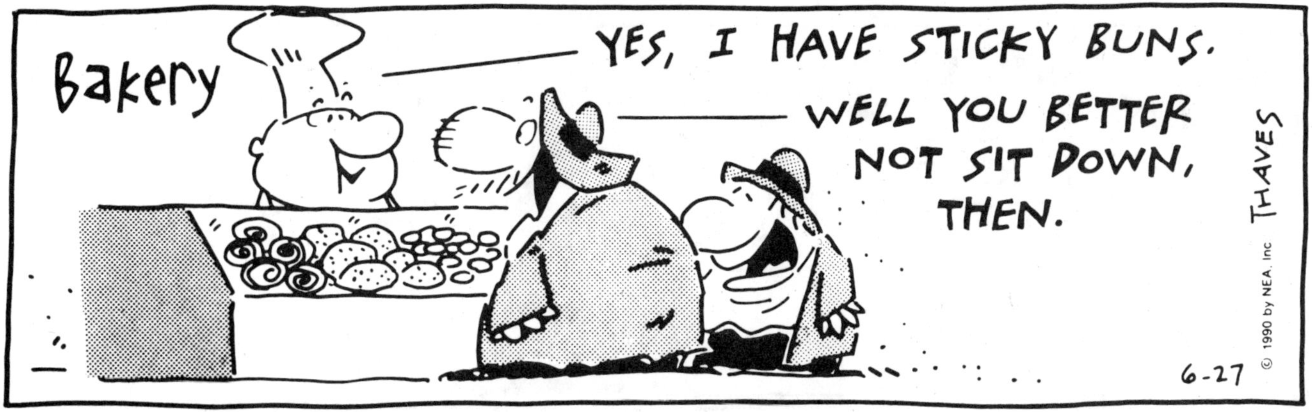
Bakery
YES, I HAVE STICKY BUNS.
WELL YOU BETTER NOT SIT DOWN, THEN.
THAVES
© 1990 by NEA, Inc.
6-27

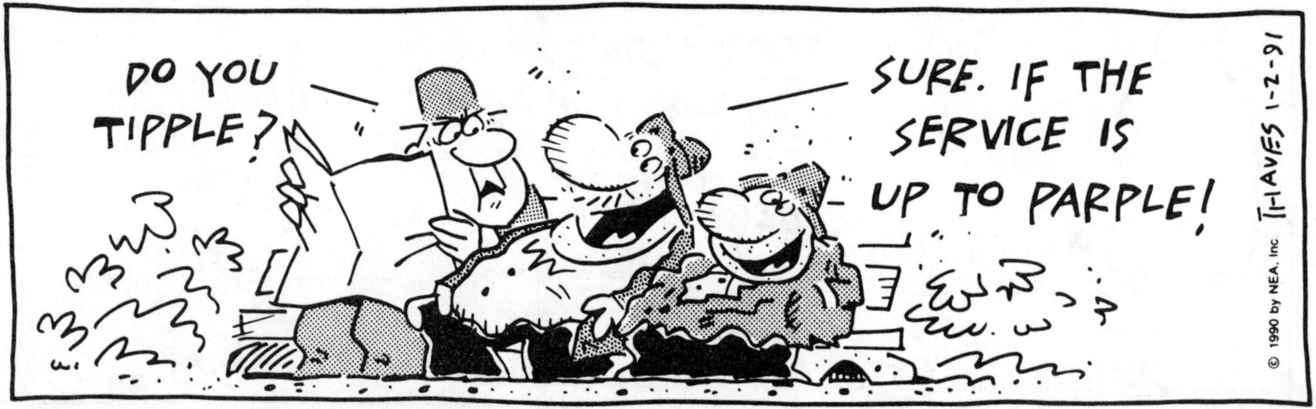
DO YOU TIPPLE?
SURE. IF THE SERVICE IS UP TO PARPLE!
THAVES 1-2-91
© 1990 by NEA, Inc.

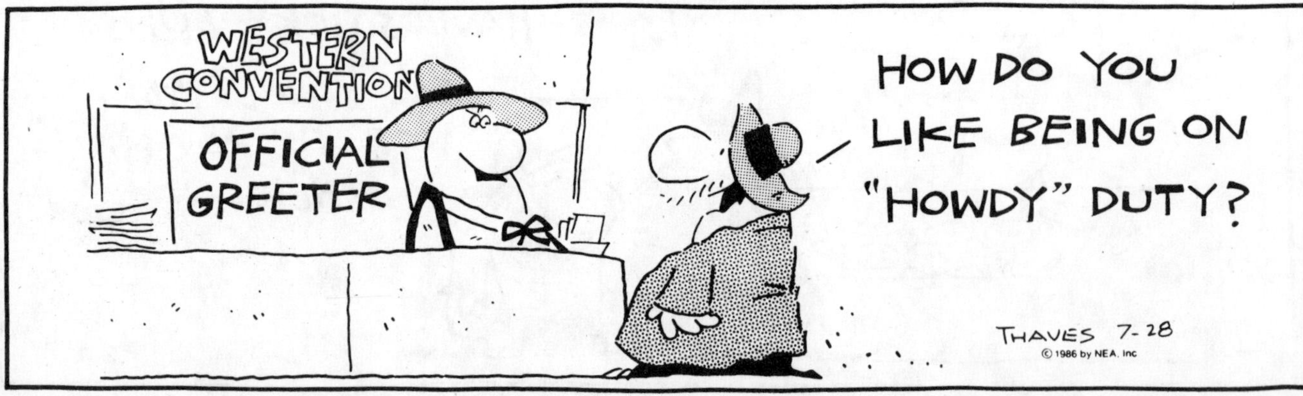
WESTERN CONVENTION
OFFICIAL GREETER
HOW DO YOU LIKE BEING ON "HOWDY" DUTY?
THAVES 7-28
© 1986 by NEA, Inc

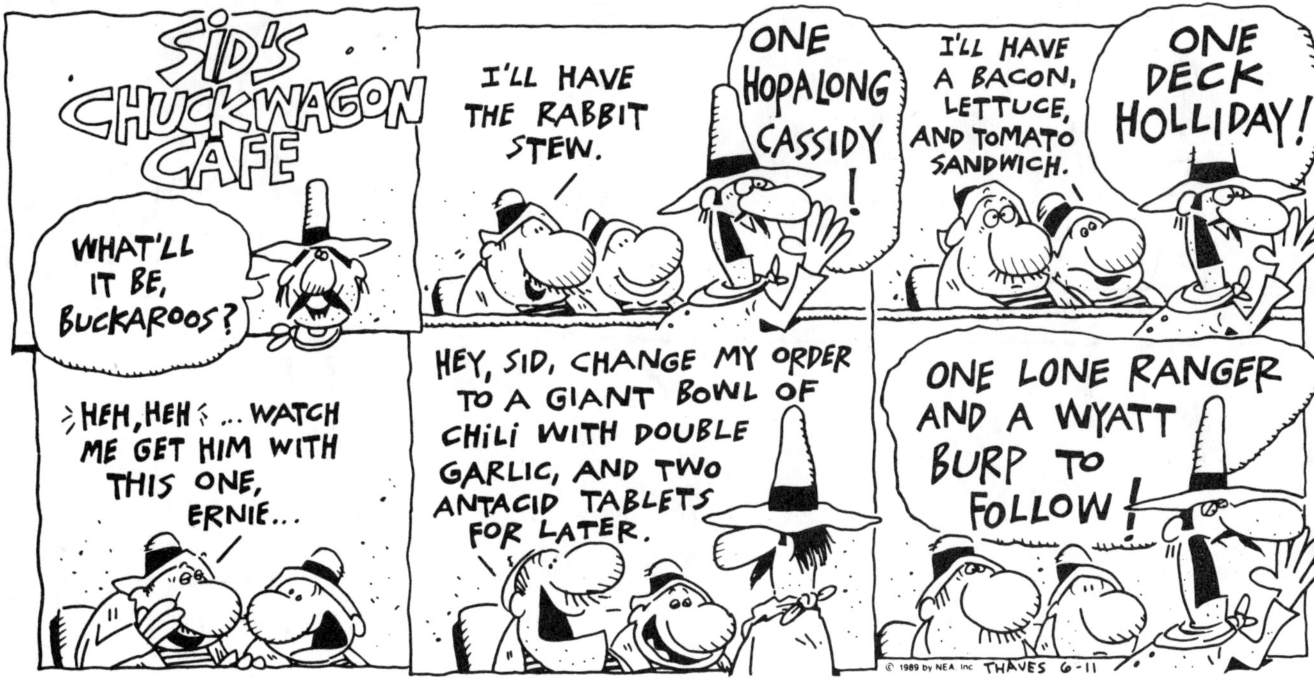
SID'S CHUCKWAGON CAFE
WHAT'LL IT BE, BUCKAROOS?
I'LL HAVE THE RABBIT STEW.
ONE HOPALONG CASSIDY!
I'LL HAVE A BACON, LETTUCE, AND TOMATO SANDWICH.
ONE DECK HOLLIDAY!
HEH, HEH ... WATCH ME GET HIM WITH THIS ONE, ERNIE...
HEY, SID, CHANGE MY ORDER TO A GIANT BOWL OF CHILI WITH DOUBLE GARLIC, AND TWO ANTACID TABLETS FOR LATER.
ONE LONE RANGER AND A WYATT BURP TO FOLLOW!
© 1989 by NEA, Inc THAVES 6-11

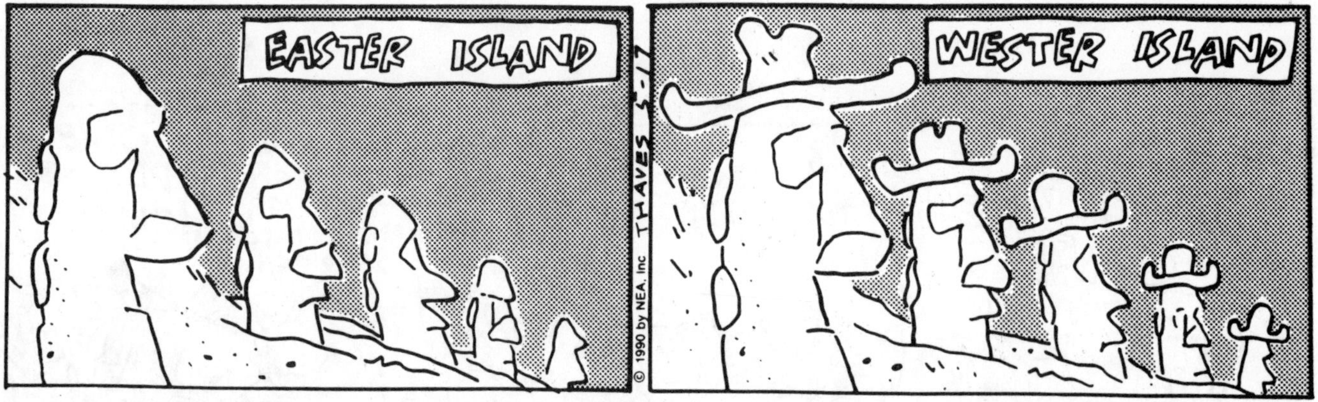
EASTER ISLAND
© 1990 by NEA, Inc THAVES 5-17
WESTER ISLAND

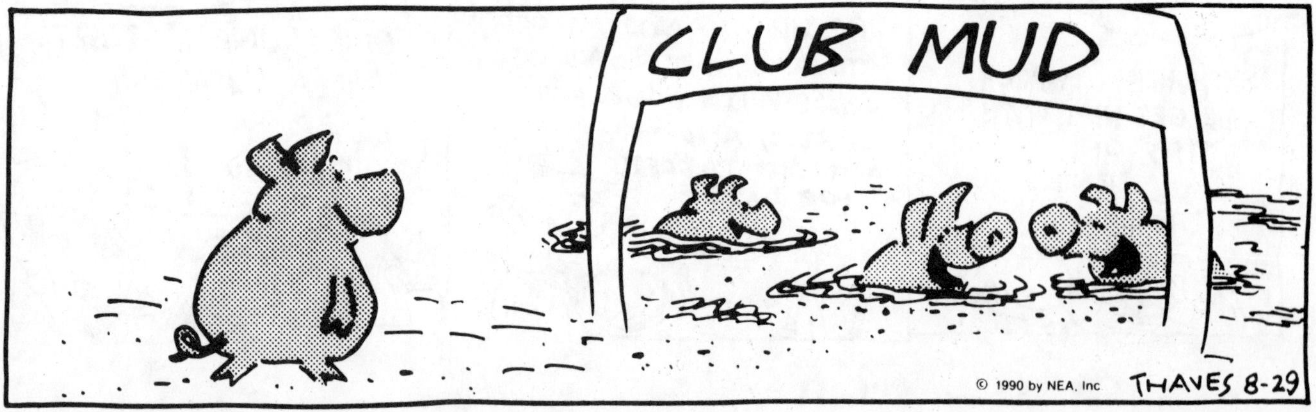
CLUB MUD
© 1990 by NEA, Inc
THAVES 8-29

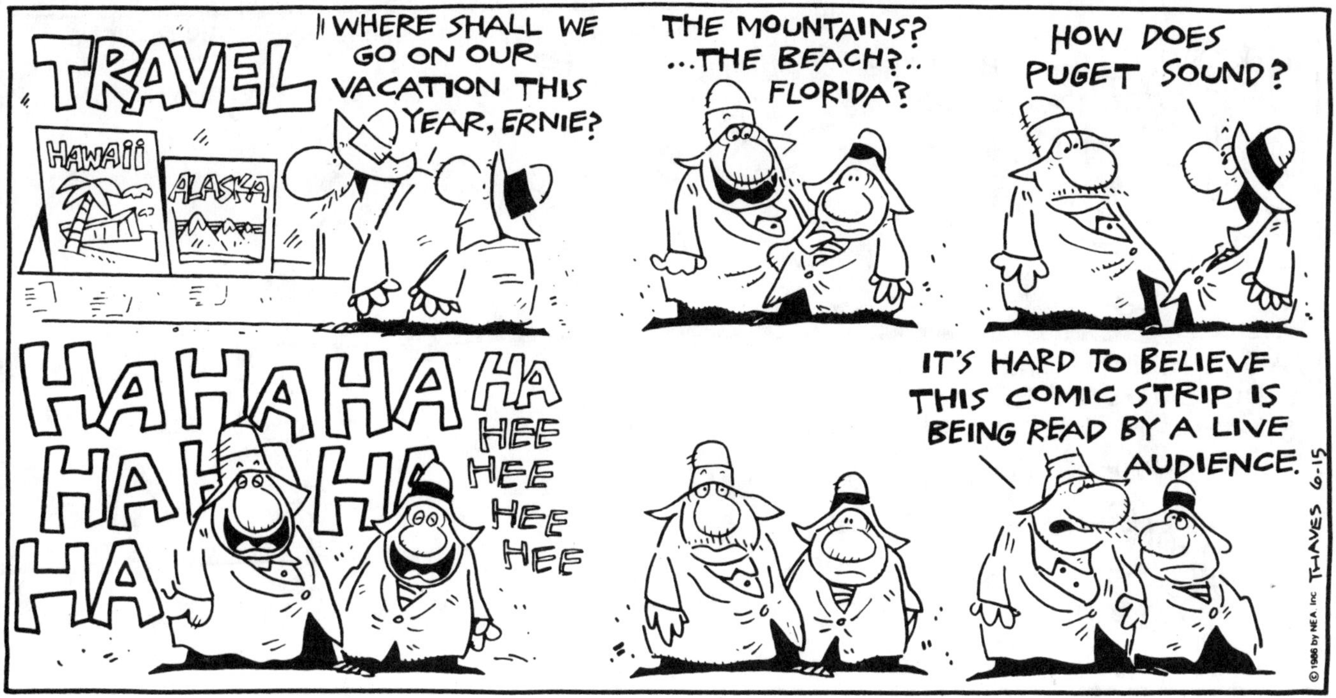
TRAVEL
HAWAII
ALASKA
WHERE SHALL WE GO ON OUR VACATION THIS YEAR, ERNIE?
THE MOUNTAINS? ...THE BEACH?.. FLORIDA?
HOW DOES PUGET SOUND?
HAHAHA HA HAHAHA HA HA
HEE HEE HEE HEE
IT'S HARD TO BELIEVE THIS COMIC STRIP IS BEING READ BY A LIVE AUDIENCE.
THAVES 6-15
© 1986 by NEA, Inc

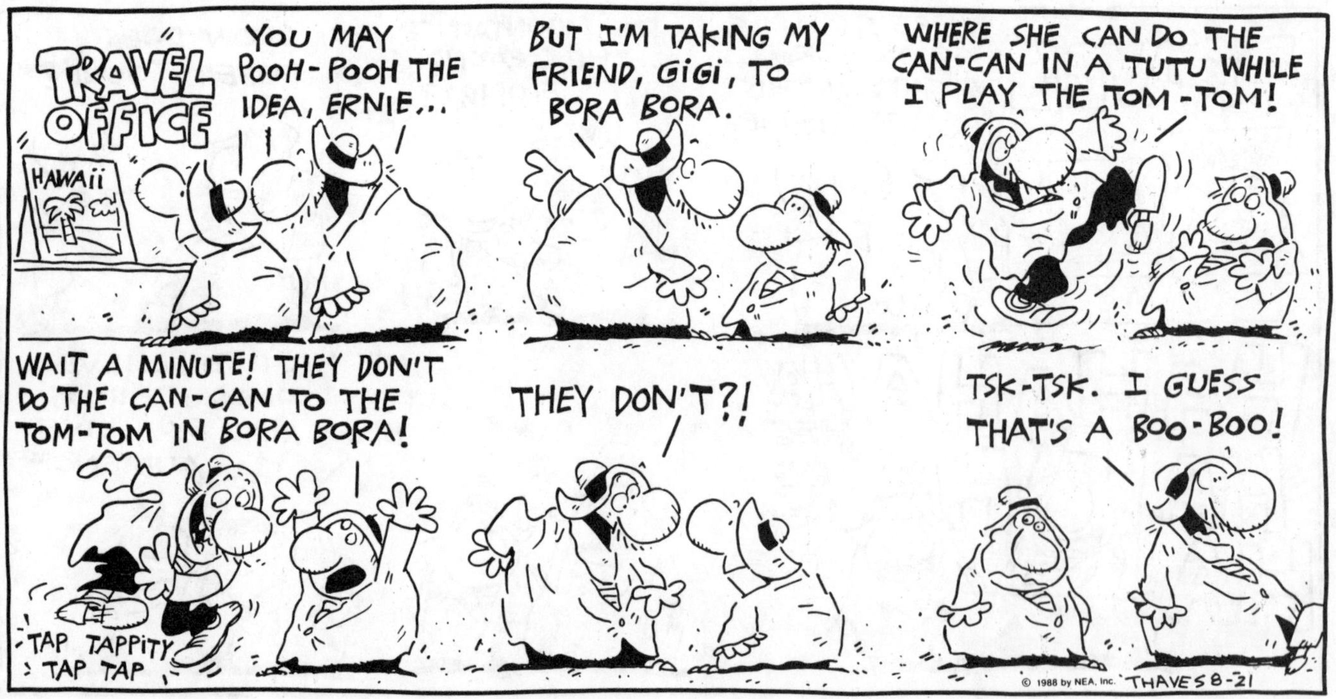
TRAVEL OFFICE
HAWAii
YOU MAY POOH-POOH THE IDEA, ERNIE...
BUT I'M TAKING MY FRIEND, GIGI, TO BORA BORA.
WHERE SHE CAN DO THE CAN-CAN IN A TUTU WHILE I PLAY THE TOM-TOM!
WAIT A MINUTE! THEY DON'T DO THE CAN-CAN TO THE TOM-TOM IN BORA BORA!
TAP TAPPITY TAP TAP
THEY DON'T?!
TSK-TSK. I GUESS THAT'S A BOO-BOO!
© 1988 by NEA, Inc.
THAVES 8-21

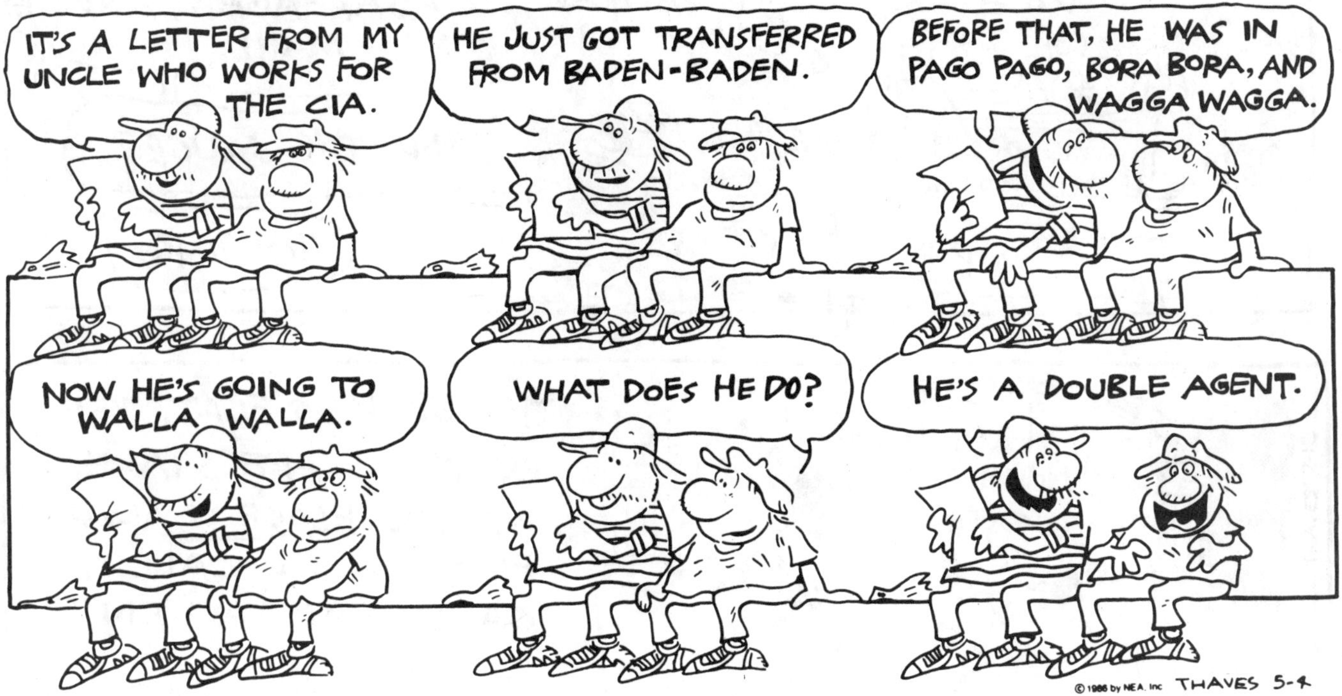
IT'S A LETTER FROM MY UNCLE WHO WORKS FOR THE CIA.
HE JUST GOT TRANSFERRED FROM BADEN-BADEN.
BEFORE THAT, HE WAS IN PAGO PAGO, BORA BORA, AND WAGGA WAGGA.
NOW HE'S GOING TO WALLA WALLA.
WHAT DOES HE DO?
HE'S A DOUBLE AGENT.
© 1986 by NEA, Inc
THAVES 5-4

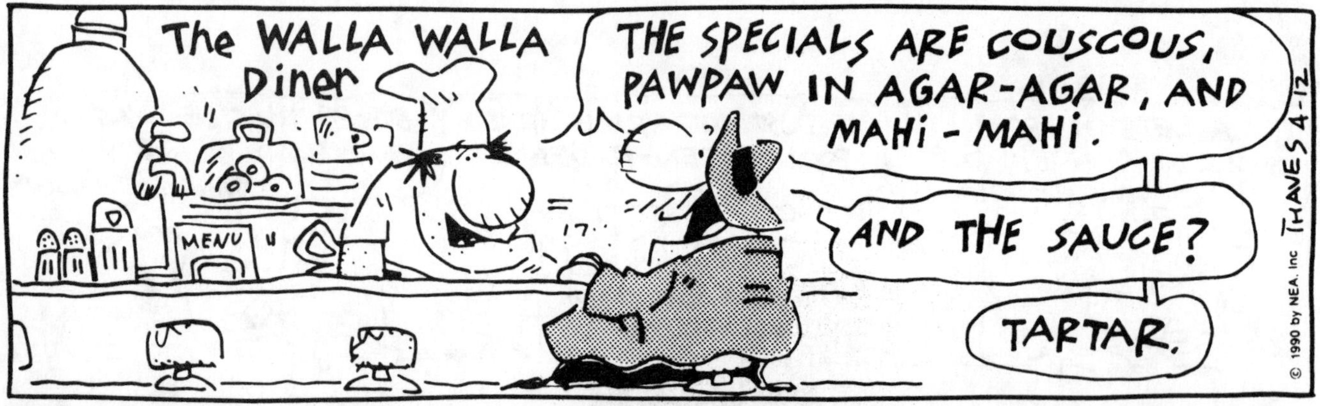
The WALLA WALLA Diner
MENU
THE SPECIALS ARE COUSCOUS, PAWPAW IN AGAR-AGAR, AND MAHI-MAHI.
AND THE SAUCE?
TARTAR.
© 1990 by NEA, Inc
THAVES 4-12

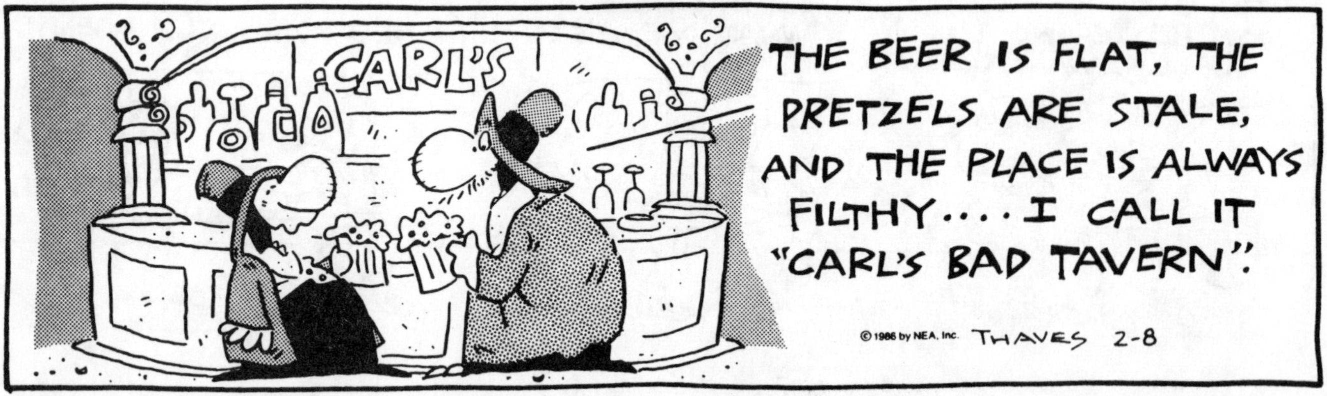
CARL'S
THE BEER IS FLAT, THE PRETZELS ARE STALE, AND THE PLACE IS ALWAYS FILTHY.... I CALL IT "CARL'S BAD TAVERN".
© 1986 by NEA, Inc.
THAVES 2-8

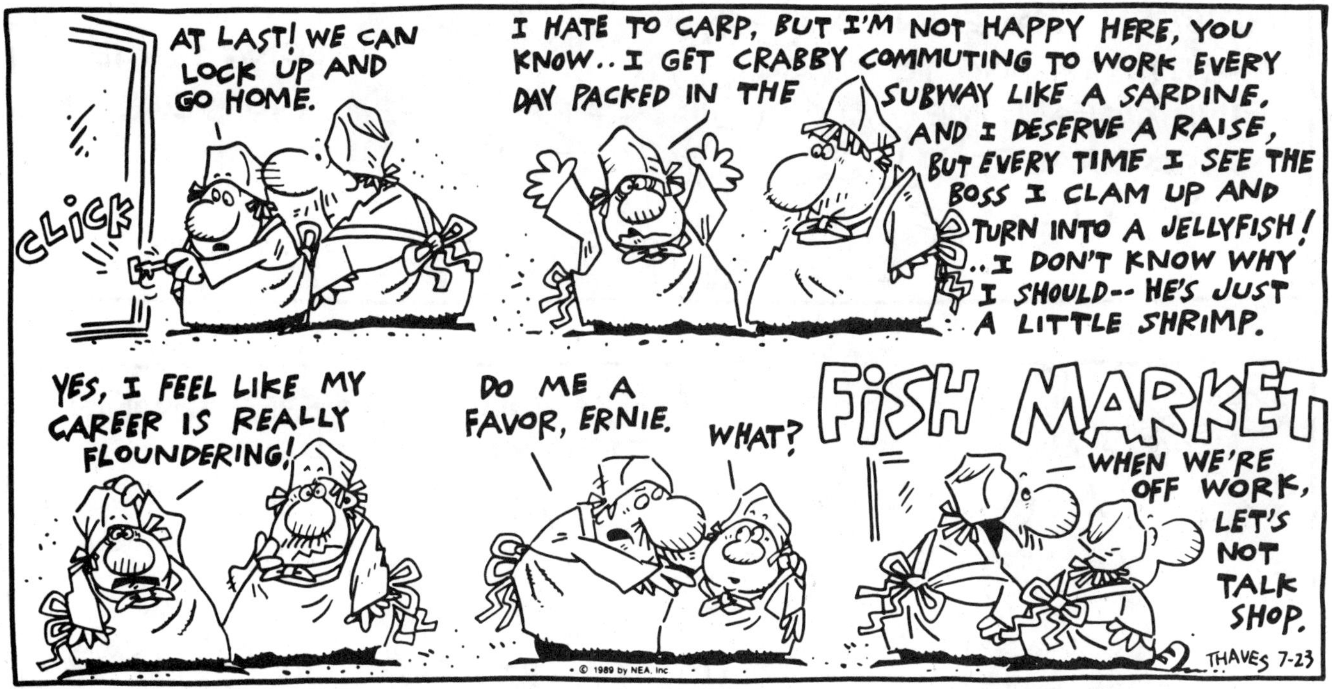
AT LAST! WE CAN LOCK UP AND GO HOME.
CLICK
I HATE TO CARP, BUT I'M NOT HAPPY HERE, YOU KNOW.. I GET CRABBY COMMUTING TO WORK EVERY DAY PACKED IN THE SUBWAY LIKE A SARDINE, AND I DESERVE A RAISE, BUT EVERY TIME I SEE THE BOSS I CLAM UP AND TURN INTO A JELLYFISH! .. I DON'T KNOW WHY I SHOULD-- HE'S JUST A LITTLE SHRIMP.
YES, I FEEL LIKE MY CAREER IS REALLY FLOUNDERING!
DO ME A FAVOR, ERNIE.
WHAT?
FISH MARKET
WHEN WE'RE OFF WORK, LET'S NOT TALK SHOP.
© 1989 by NEA, Inc
THAVES 7-23

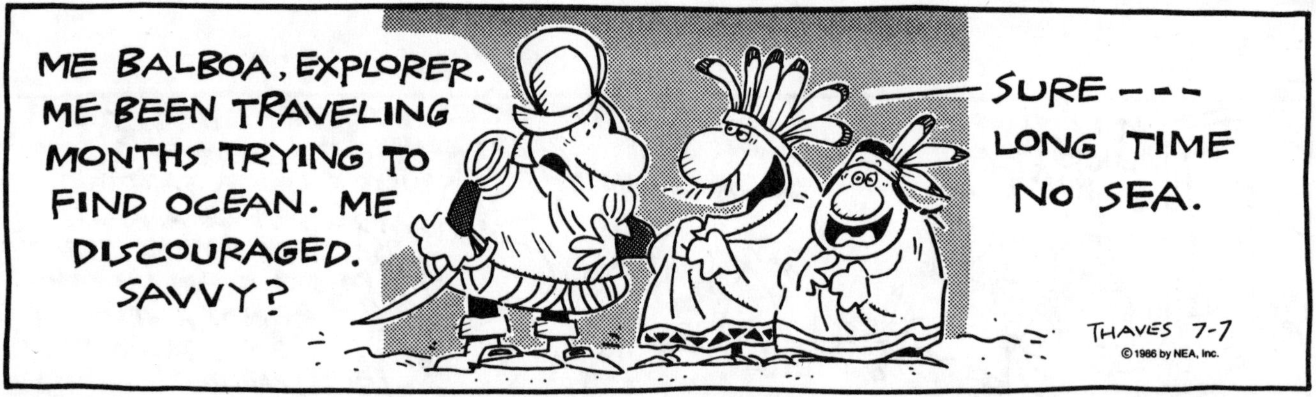
ME BALBOA, EXPLORER. ME BEEN TRAVELING MONTHS TRYING TO FIND OCEAN. ME DISCOURAGED. SAVVY?
SURE --- LONG TIME NO SEA.
THAVES 7-7
© 1986 by NEA, Inc.

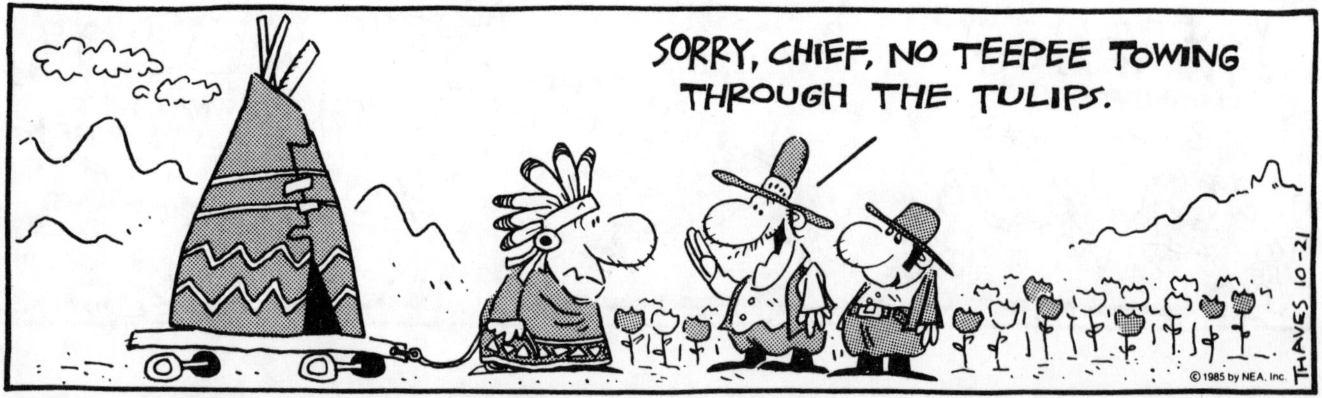
SORRY, CHIEF, NO TEEPEE TOWING THROUGH THE TULIPS.
THAVES 10-21
© 1985 by NEA, Inc.

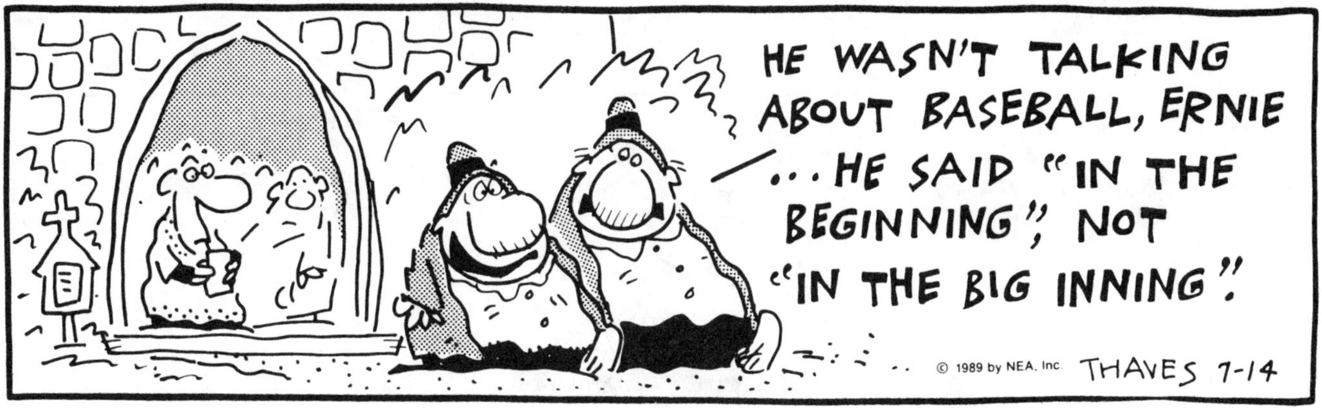
HE WASN'T TALKING ABOUT BASEBALL, ERNIE ...HE SAID "IN THE BEGINNING", NOT "IN THE BIG INNING"!
© 1989 by NEA, Inc.
THAVES 7-14

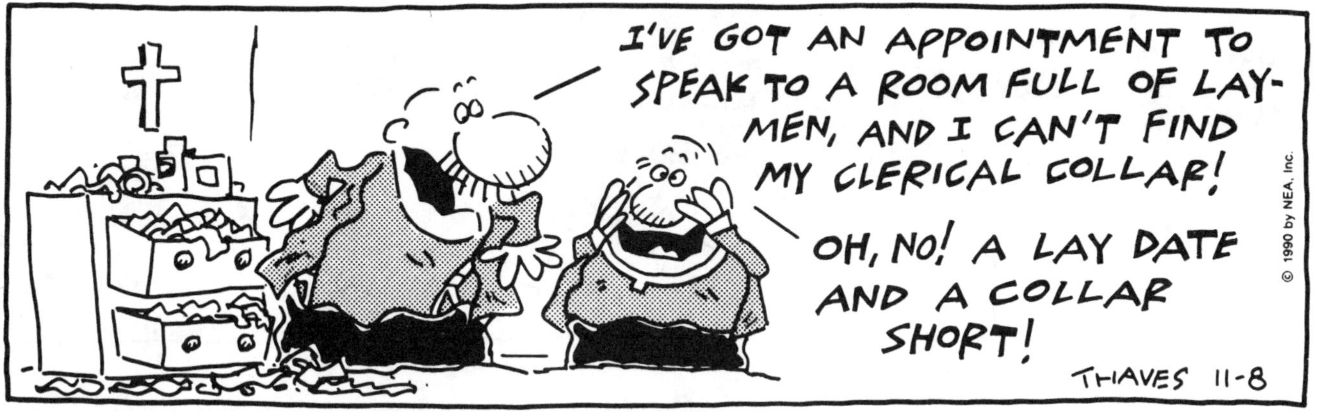
I'VE GOT AN APPOINTMENT TO SPEAK TO A ROOM FULL OF LAY-MEN, AND I CAN'T FIND MY CLERICAL COLLAR!
OH, NO! A LAY DATE AND A COLLAR SHORT!
© 1990 by NEA, Inc.
THAVES 11-8

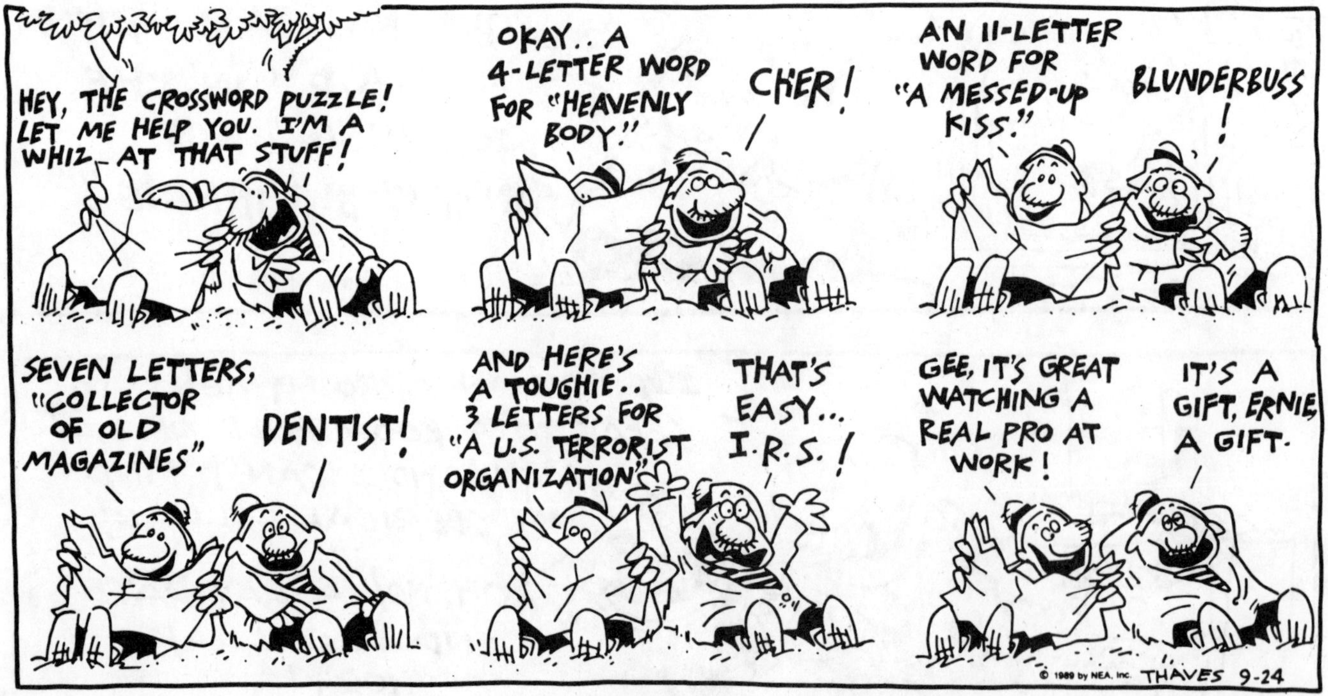
HEY, THE CROSSWORD PUZZLE! LET ME HELP YOU. I'M A WHIZ AT THAT STUFF!
OKAY.. A 4-LETTER WORD FOR "HEAVENLY BODY."
CHER!
AN 11-LETTER WORD FOR "A MESSED-UP KISS."
BLUNDERBUSS!
SEVEN LETTERS, "COLLECTOR OF OLD MAGAZINES".
DENTIST!
AND HERE'S A TOUGHIE.. 3 LETTERS FOR "A U.S. TERRORIST ORGANIZATION"
THAT'S EASY... I.R.S.!
GEE, IT'S GREAT WATCHING A REAL PRO AT WORK!
IT'S A GIFT, ERNIE, A GIFT.
© 1989 by NEA, Inc.
THAVES 9-24

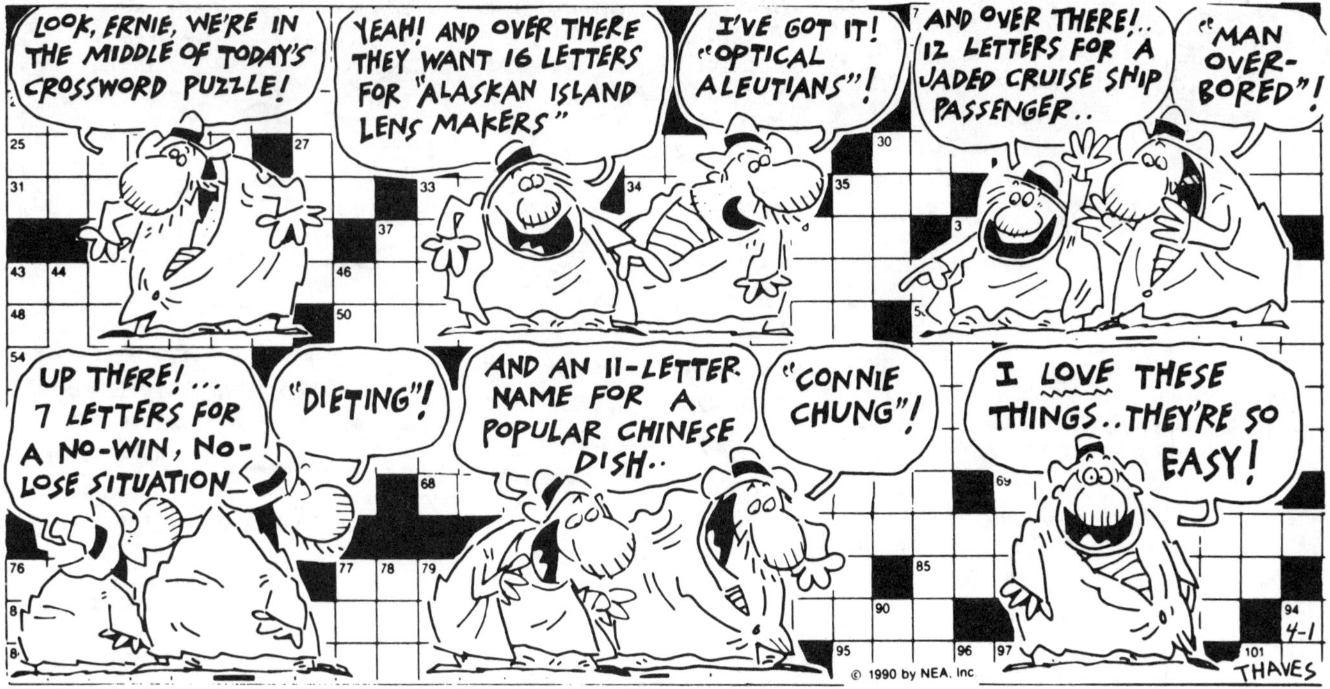
LOOK, ERNIE, WE'RE IN THE MIDDLE OF TODAY'S CROSSWORD PUZZLE!
YEAH! AND OVER THERE THEY WANT 16 LETTERS FOR "ALASKAN ISLAND LENS MAKERS"
I'VE GOT IT! "OPTICAL ALEUTIANS"!
AND OVER THERE!.. 12 LETTERS FOR A JADED CRUISE SHIP PASSENGER..
"MAN OVER-BORED"!
UP THERE!... 7 LETTERS FOR A NO-WIN, NO-LOSE SITUATION
"DIETING"!
AND AN 11-LETTER NAME FOR A POPULAR CHINESE DISH..
"CONNIE CHUNG"!
I LOVE THESE THINGS.. THEY'RE SO EASY!
4-1
© 1990 by NEA, Inc
THAVES

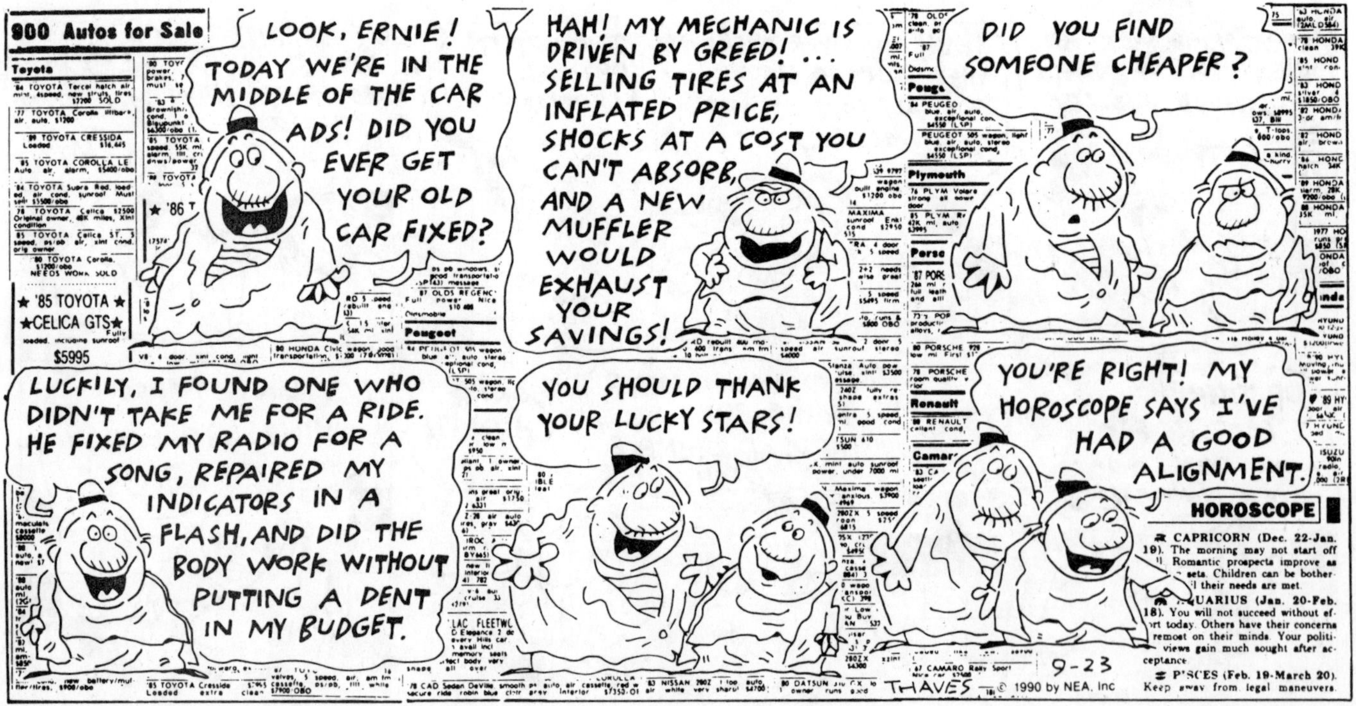

900 Autos for Sale
LOOK, ERNIE! TODAY WE'RE IN THE MIDDLE OF THE CAR ADS! DID YOU EVER GET YOUR OLD CAR FIXED?
HAH! MY MECHANIC IS DRIVEN BY GREED! ... SELLING TIRES AT AN INFLATED PRICE, SHOCKS AT A COST YOU CAN'T ABSORB, AND A NEW MUFFLER WOULD EXHAUST YOUR SAVINGS!
DID YOU FIND SOMEONE CHEAPER?
LUCKILY, I FOUND ONE WHO DIDN'T TAKE ME FOR A RIDE. HE FIXED MY RADIO FOR A SONG, REPAIRED MY INDICATORS IN A FLASH, AND DID THE BODY WORK WITHOUT PUTTING A DENT IN MY BUDGET.
YOU SHOULD THANK YOUR LUCKY STARS!
YOU'RE RIGHT! MY HOROSCOPE SAYS I'VE HAD A GOOD ALIGNMENT.
HOROSCOPE
9-23
THAVES
© 1990 by NEA, Inc

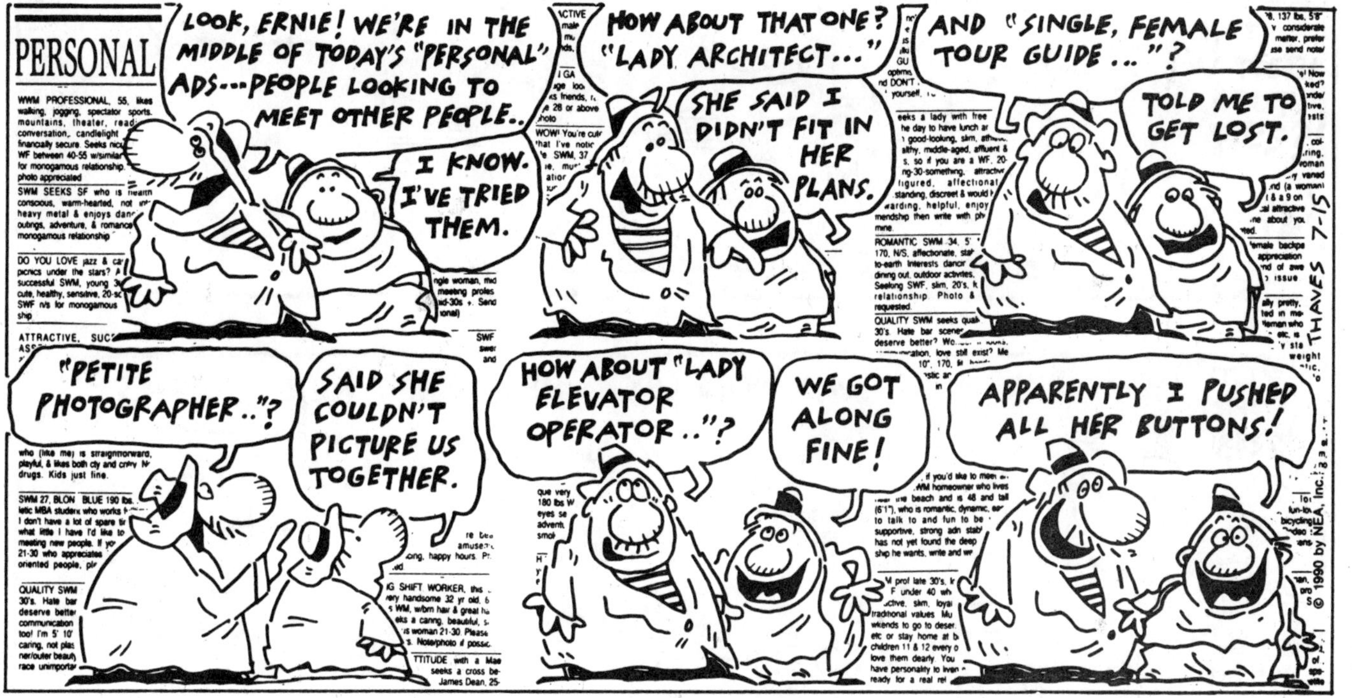
PERSONAL
LOOK, ERNIE! WE'RE IN THE MIDDLE OF TODAY'S "PERSONAL" ADS---PEOPLE LOOKING TO MEET OTHER PEOPLE..
I KNOW. I'VE TRIED THEM.
HOW ABOUT THAT ONE? "LADY ARCHITECT..."
SHE SAID I DIDN'T FIT IN HER PLANS.
AND "SINGLE, FEMALE TOUR GUIDE..."?
TOLD ME TO GET LOST.
THAVES 7-15
"PETITE PHOTOGRAPHER.."?
SAID SHE COULDN'T PICTURE US TOGETHER.
HOW ABOUT "LADY ELEVATOR OPERATOR.."?
WE GOT ALONG FINE!
APPARENTLY I PUSHED ALL HER BUTTONS!
© 1990 by NEA, Inc.

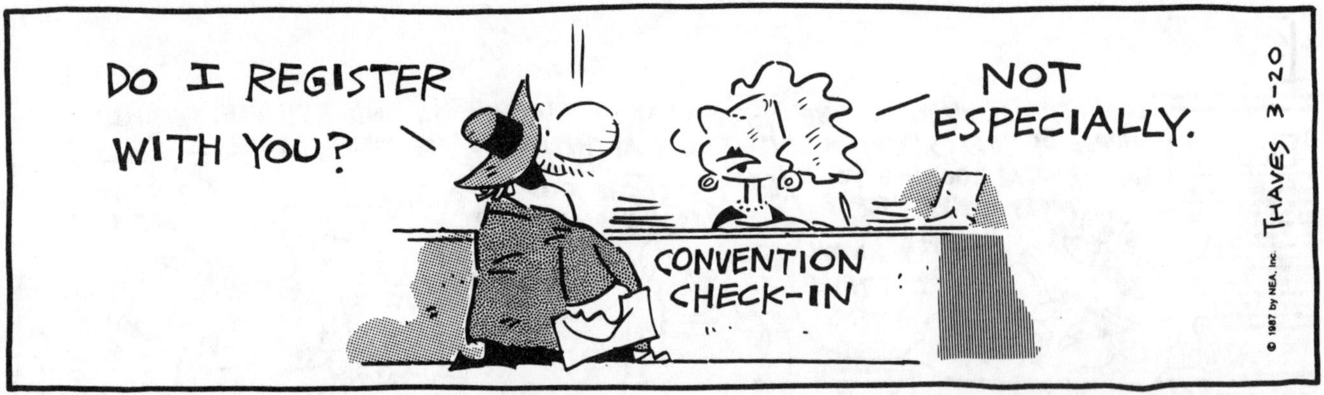
DO I REGISTER WITH YOU?
NOT ESPECIALLY.
CONVENTION CHECK-IN
THAVES 3-20
© 1987 by NEA, Inc

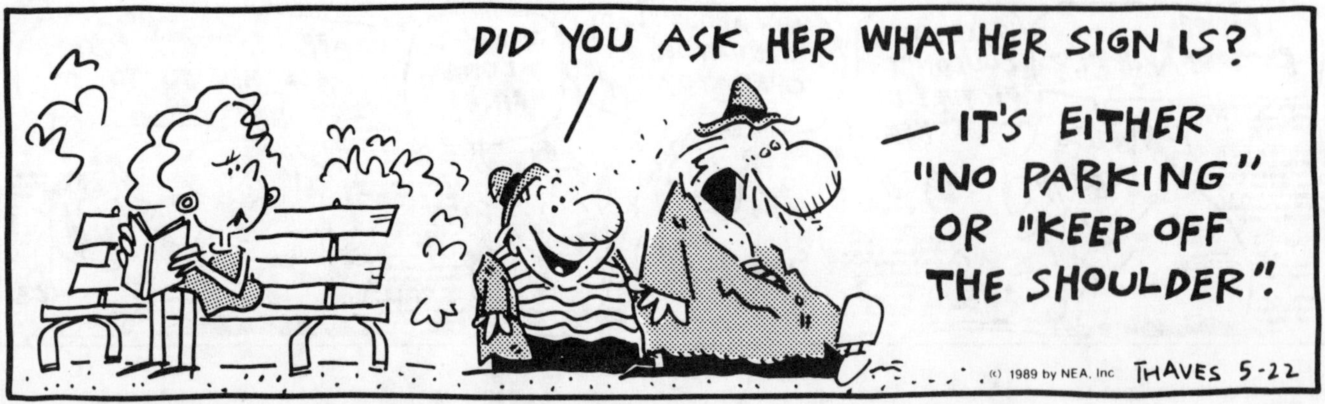
DID YOU ASK HER WHAT HER SIGN IS?
IT'S EITHER "NO PARKING" OR "KEEP OFF THE SHOULDER".
(c) 1989 by NEA, Inc
THAVES 5-22

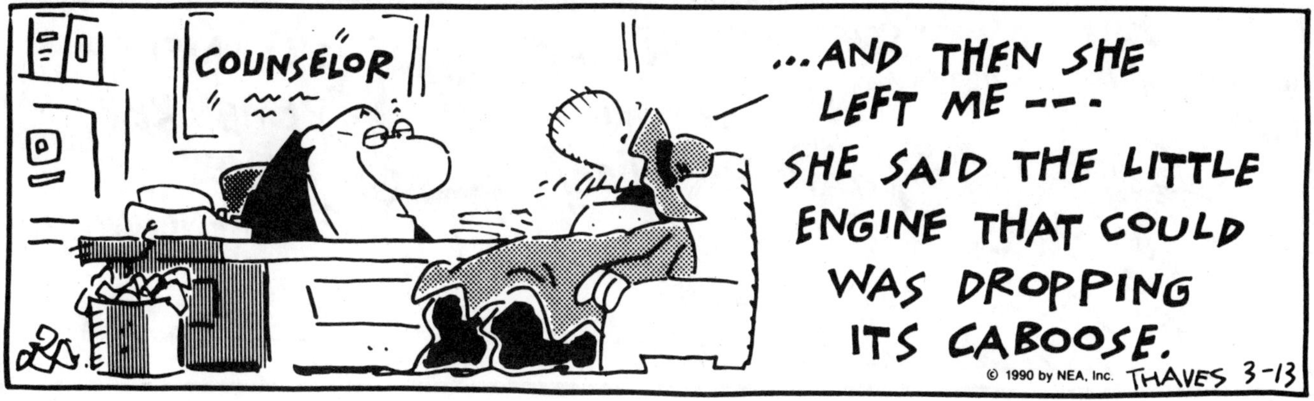

COUNSELOR
...AND THEN SHE LEFT ME ---. SHE SAID THE LITTLE ENGINE THAT COULD WAS DROPPING ITS CABOOSE.
© 1990 by NEA, Inc. THAVES 3-13

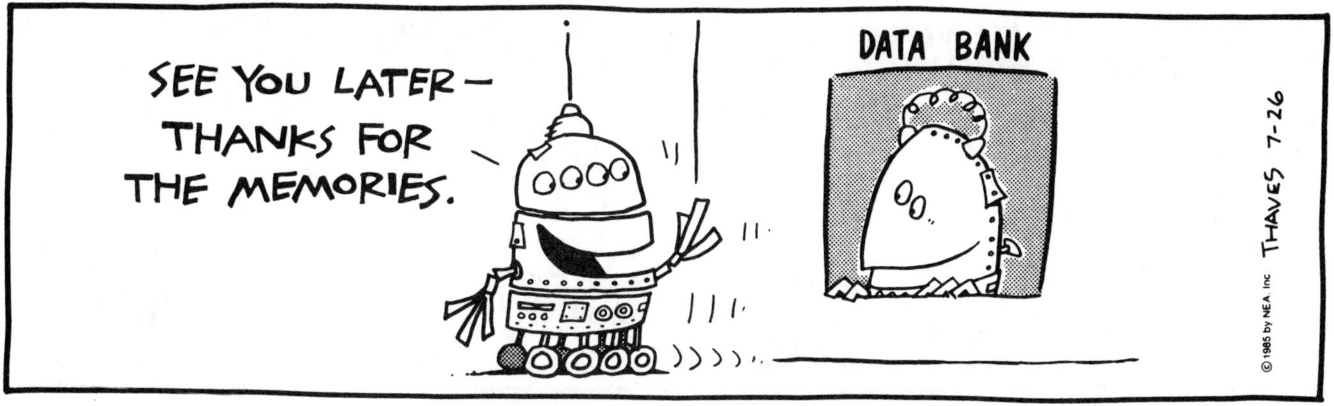

SEE YOU LATER— THANKS FOR THE MEMORIES.
DATA BANK
THAVES 7-26
© 1985 by NEA, Inc

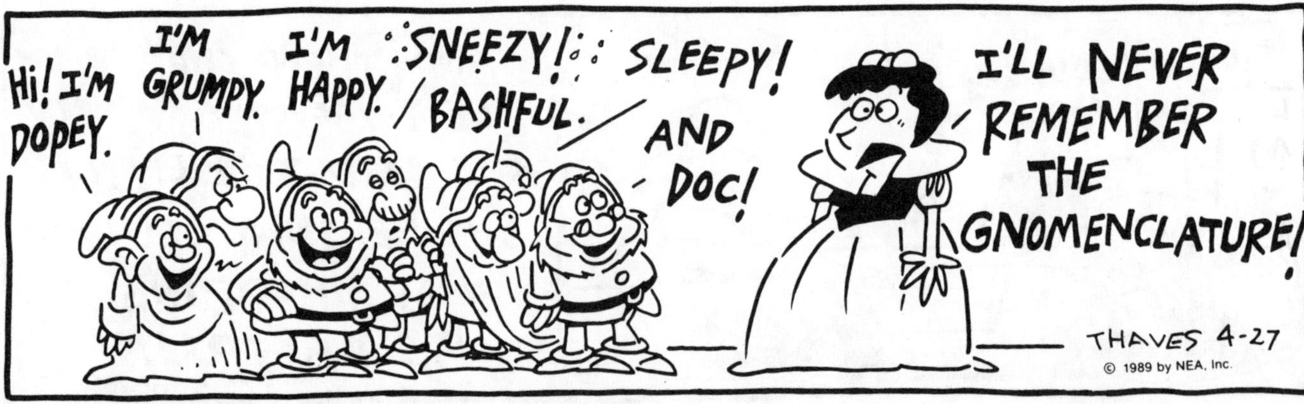

HI! I'M DOPEY.
I'M GRUMPY.
I'M HAPPY.
SNEEZY!
BASHFUL.
SLEEPY!
AND DOC!
I'LL NEVER REMEMBER THE GNOMENCLATURE!
THAVES 4-27
© 1989 by NEA, Inc.

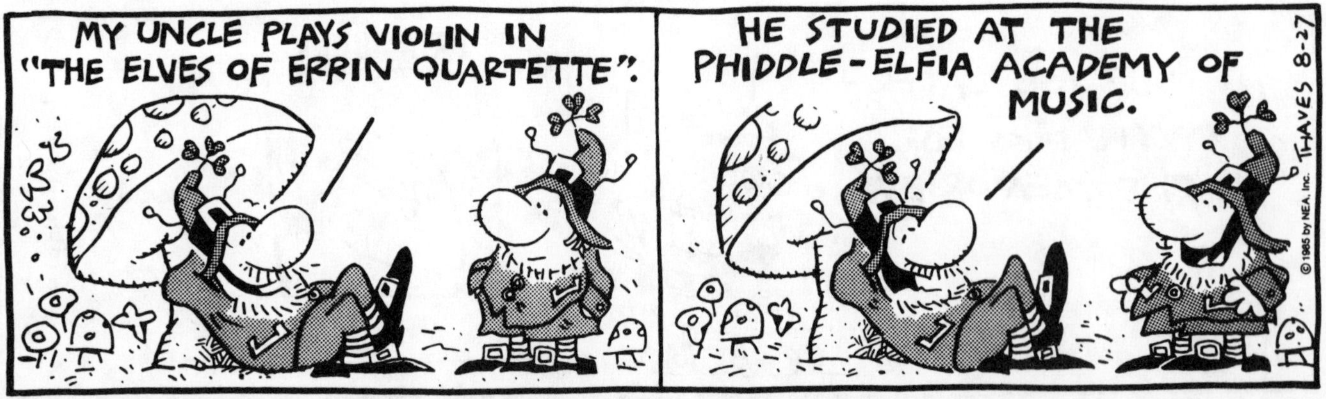

MY UNCLE PLAYS VIOLIN IN "THE ELVES OF ERRIN QUARTETTE".
HE STUDIED AT THE PHIDDLE-ELFIA ACADEMY OF MUSIC.
THAVES 8-27
© 1985 by NEA, Inc.

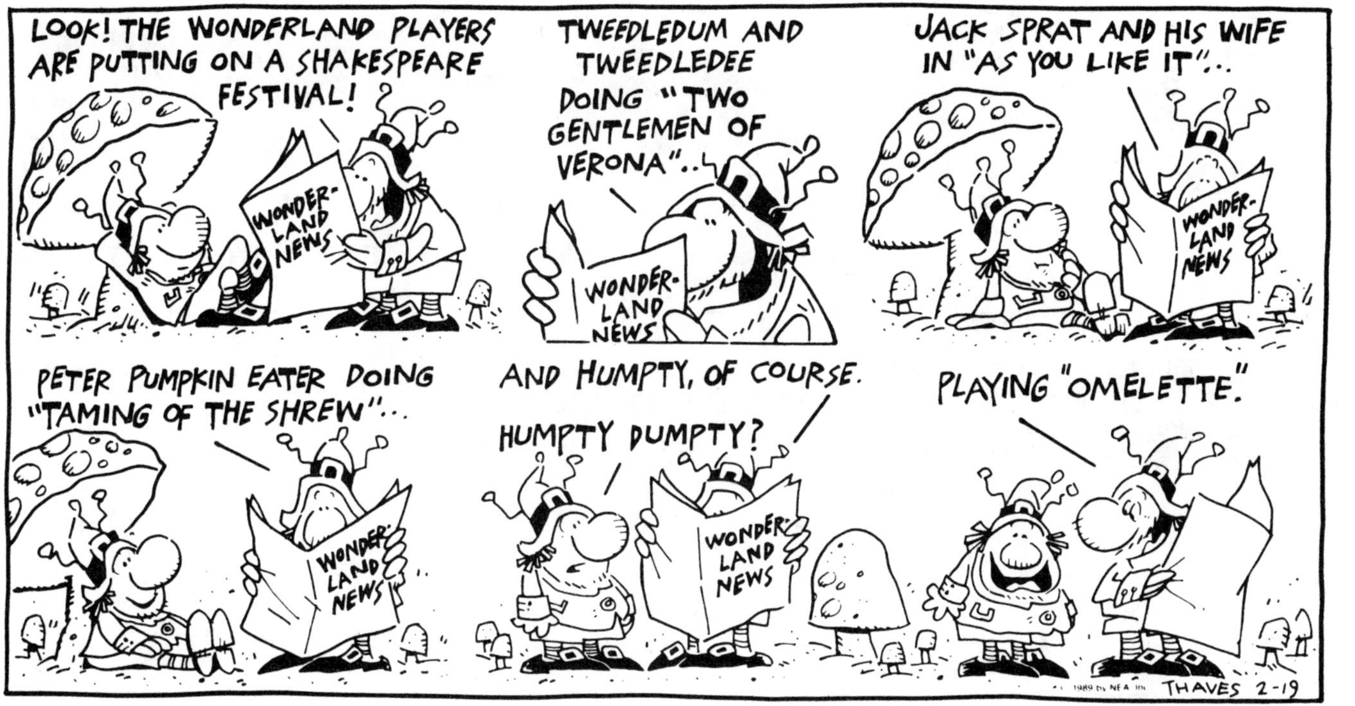
LOOK! THE WONDERLAND PLAYERS ARE PUTTING ON A SHAKESPEARE FESTIVAL!
WONDER-LAND NEWS
TWEEDLEDUM AND TWEEDLEDEE DOING "TWO GENTLEMEN OF VERONA"...
WONDER-LAND NEWS
JACK SPRAT AND HIS WIFE IN "AS YOU LIKE IT"...
WONDER-LAND NEWS
PETER PUMPKIN EATER DOING "TAMING OF THE SHREW"...
WONDER-LAND NEWS
AND HUMPTY, OF COURSE.
HUMPTY DUMPTY?
WONDER-LAND NEWS
PLAYING "OMELETTE."
THAVES 2-19

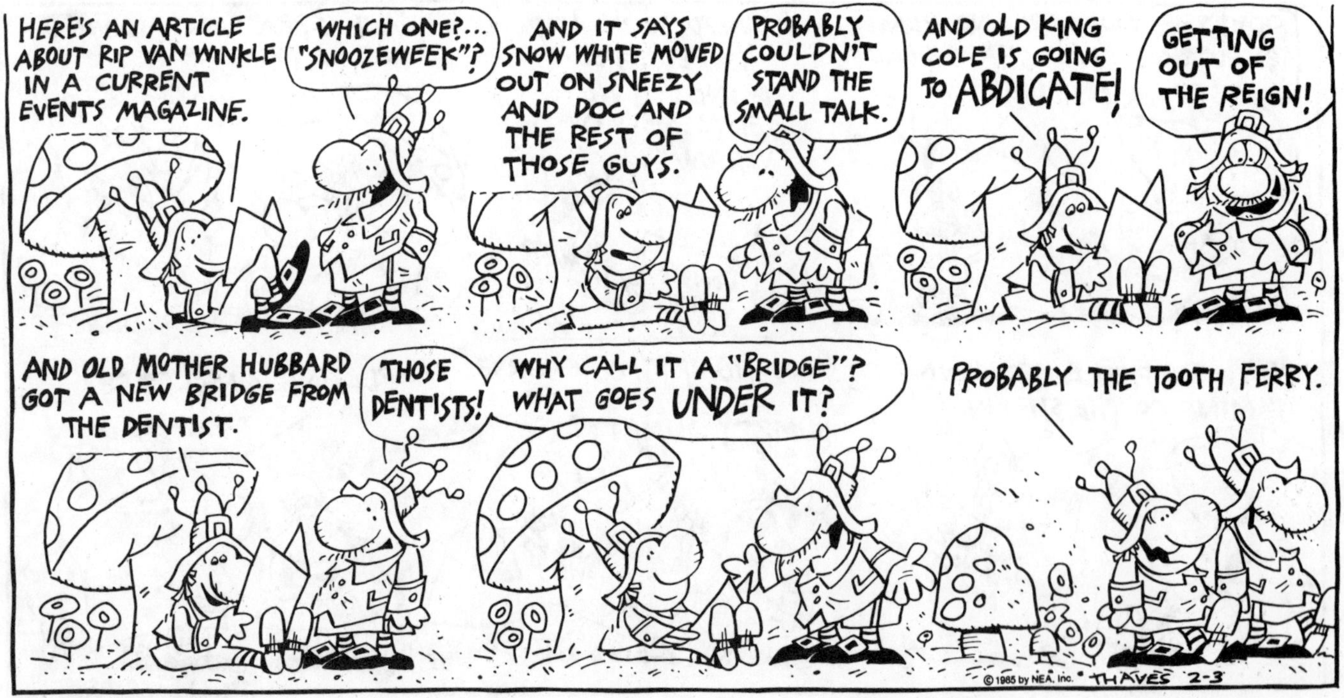
HERE'S AN ARTICLE ABOUT RIP VAN WINKLE IN A CURRENT EVENTS MAGAZINE.
WHICH ONE?... "SNOOZEWEEK"?
AND IT SAYS SNOW WHITE MOVED OUT ON SNEEZY AND DOC AND THE REST OF THOSE GUYS.
PROBABLY COULDN'T STAND THE SMALL TALK.
AND OLD KING COLE IS GOING TO ABDICATE!
GETTING OUT OF THE REIGN!
AND OLD MOTHER HUBBARD GOT A NEW BRIDGE FROM THE DENTIST.
THOSE DENTISTS!
WHY CALL IT A "BRIDGE"? WHAT GOES UNDER IT?
PROBABLY THE TOOTH FERRY.
© 1985 by NEA, Inc. THAVES 2-3
FRANK + ERNEST

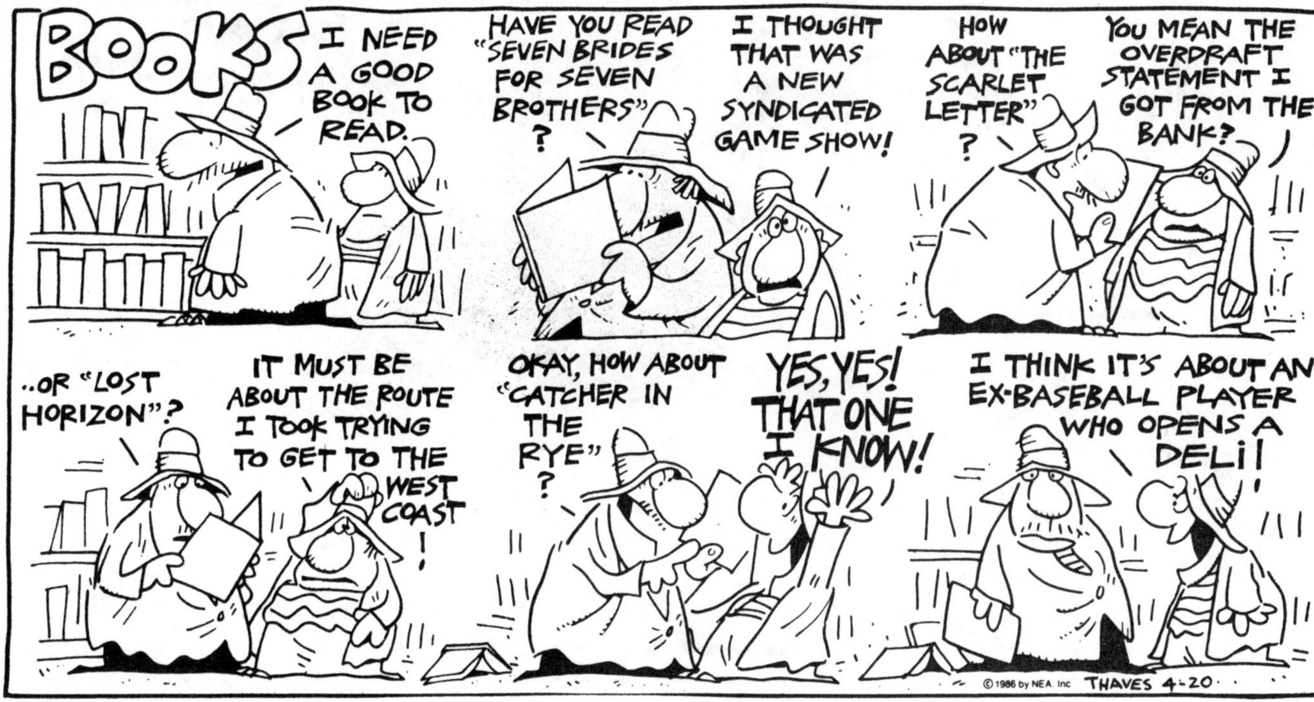
BOOKS
I NEED A GOOD BOOK TO READ.
HAVE YOU READ "SEVEN BRIDES FOR SEVEN BROTHERS"?
I THOUGHT THAT WAS A NEW SYNDICATED GAME SHOW!
HOW ABOUT "THE SCARLET LETTER"?
YOU MEAN THE OVERDRAFT STATEMENT I GOT FROM THE BANK?
..OR "LOST HORIZON"?
IT MUST BE ABOUT THE ROUTE I TOOK TRYING TO GET TO THE WEST COAST!
OKAY, HOW ABOUT "CATCHER IN THE RYE"?
YES, YES! THAT ONE I KNOW!
I THINK IT'S ABOUT AN EX-BASEBALL PLAYER WHO OPENS A DELI!
© 1986 by NEA. Inc
THAVES 4-20

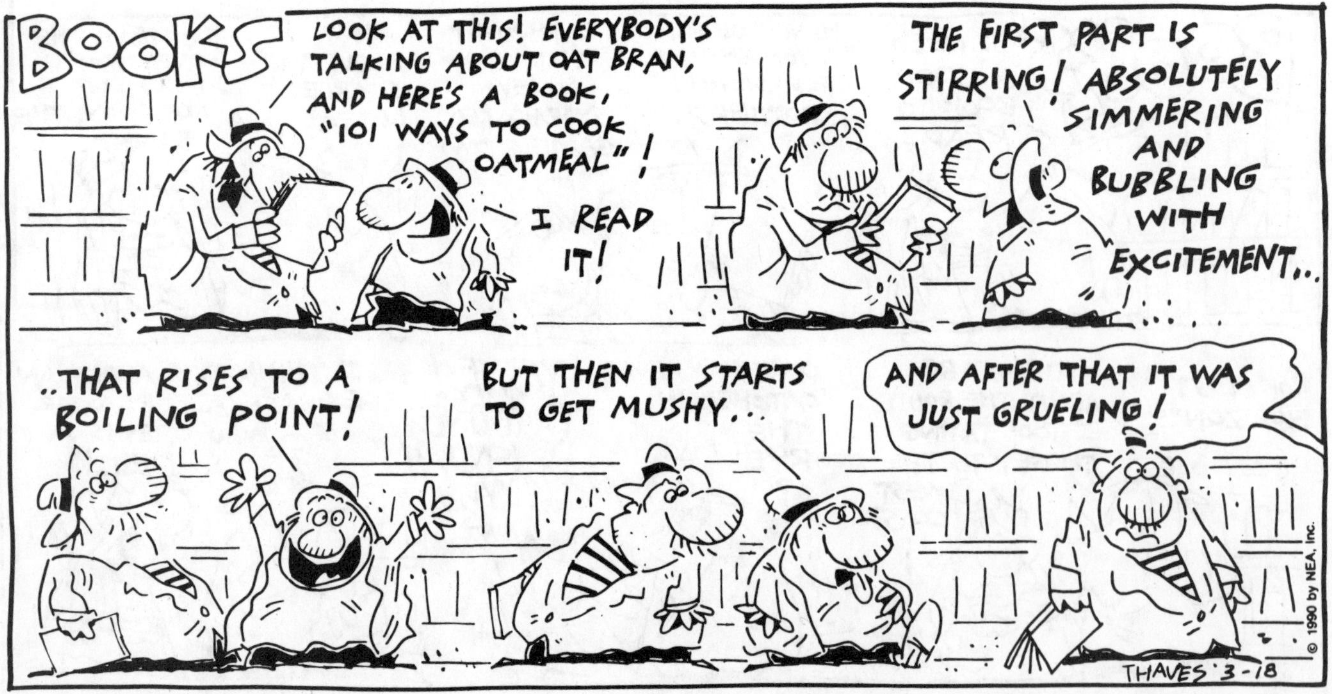
BOOKS
LOOK AT THIS! EVERYBODY'S TALKING ABOUT OAT BRAN, AND HERE'S A BOOK, "101 WAYS TO COOK OATMEAL"!
I READ IT!
THE FIRST PART IS STIRRING! ABSOLUTELY SIMMERING AND BUBBLING WITH EXCITEMENT...
..THAT RISES TO A BOILING POINT!
BUT THEN IT STARTS TO GET MUSHY...
AND AFTER THAT IT WAS JUST GRUELING!
THAVES 3-18
© 1990 by NEA, Inc.

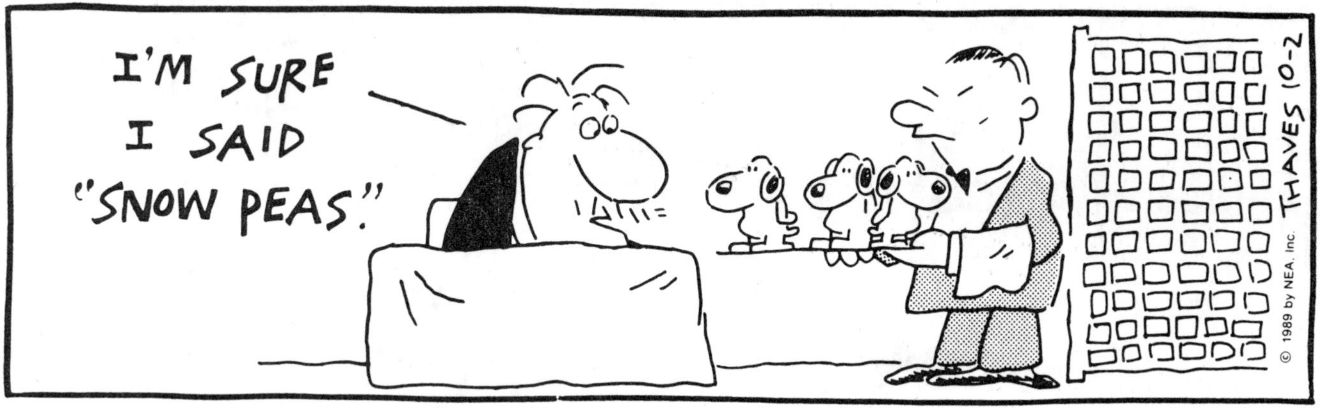
I'M SURE I SAID "SNOW PEAS."
© 1989 by NEA, Inc.
THAVES 10-2

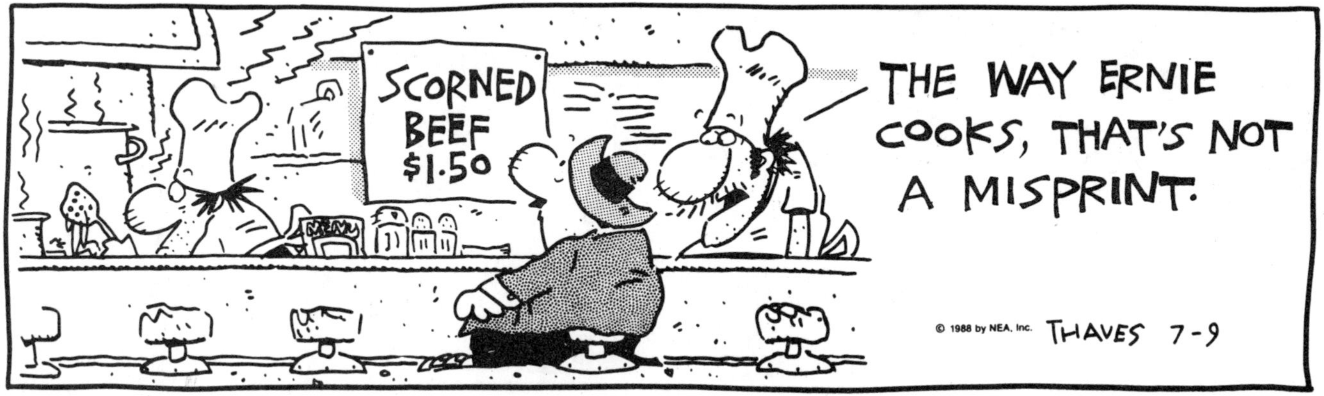
SCORNED BEEF $1.50
MENU
THE WAY ERNIE COOKS, THAT'S NOT A MISPRINT.
© 1988 by NEA, Inc.
THAVES 7-9

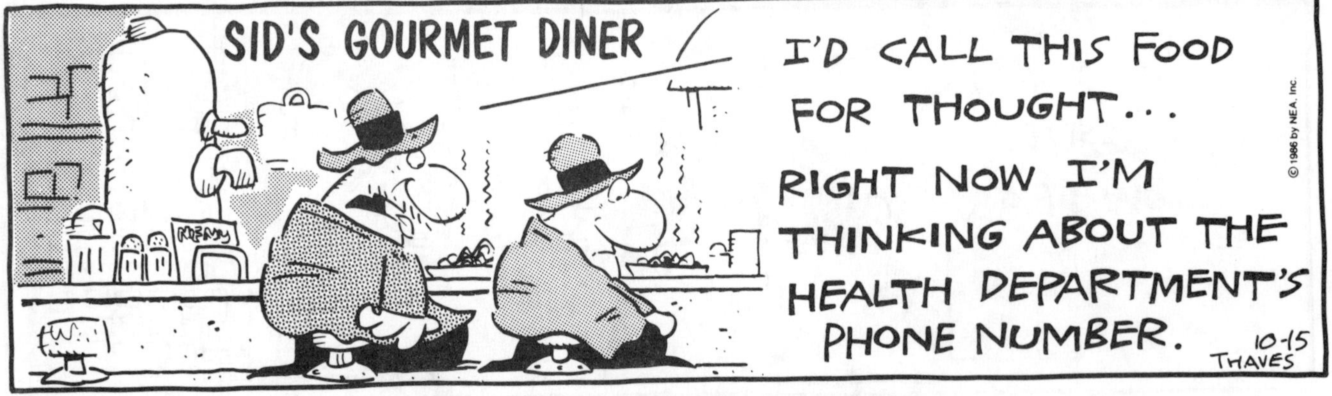
SID'S GOURMET DINER
I'D CALL THIS FOOD FOR THOUGHT... RIGHT NOW I'M THINKING ABOUT THE HEALTH DEPARTMENT'S PHONE NUMBER.
© 1986 by NEA, Inc.
10-15
THAVES

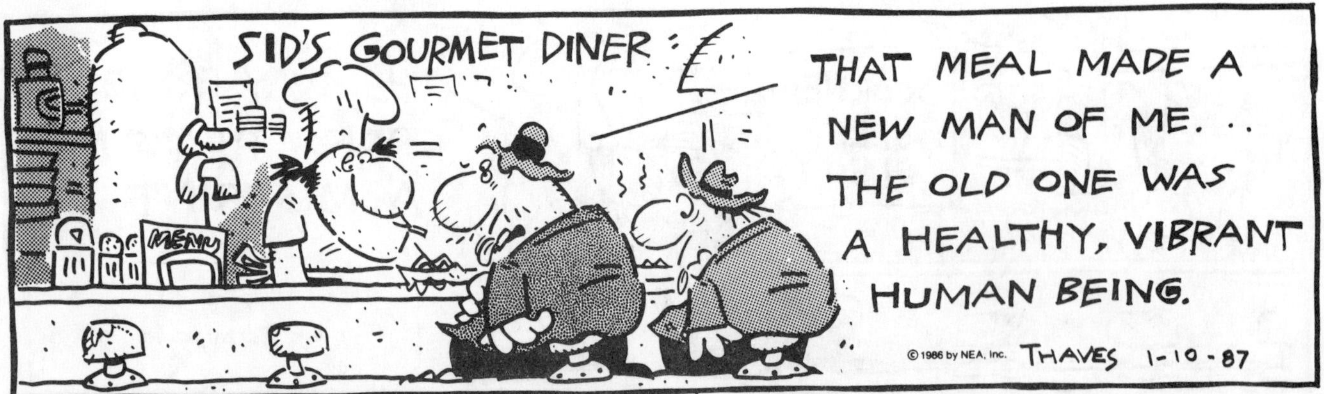
SID'S GOURMET DINER
MENU
THAT MEAL MADE A NEW MAN OF ME... THE OLD ONE WAS A HEALTHY, VIBRANT HUMAN BEING.
© 1986 by NEA, Inc.
THAVES 1-10-87

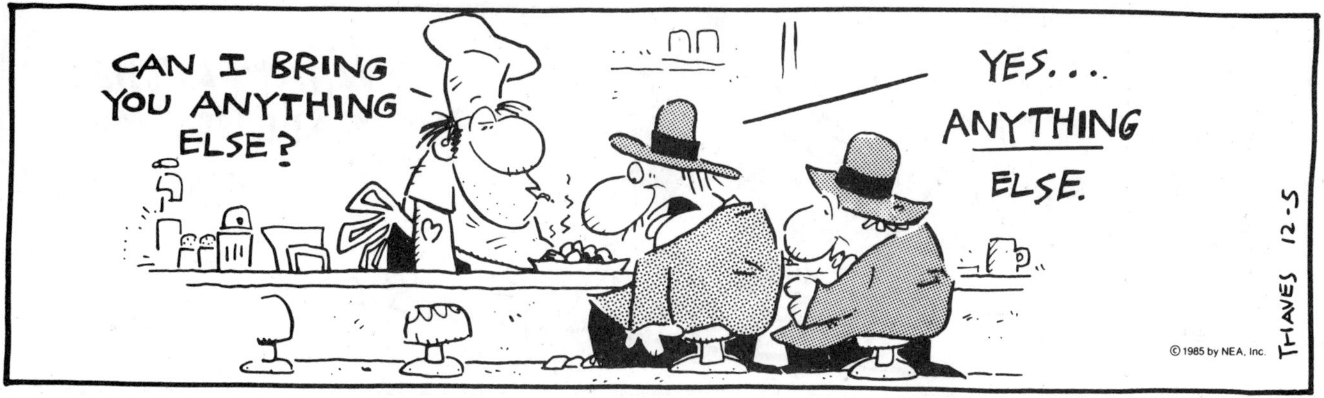
CAN I BRING YOU ANYTHING ELSE?
YES.... ANYTHING ELSE.
© 1985 by NEA, Inc.
THAVES 12-5

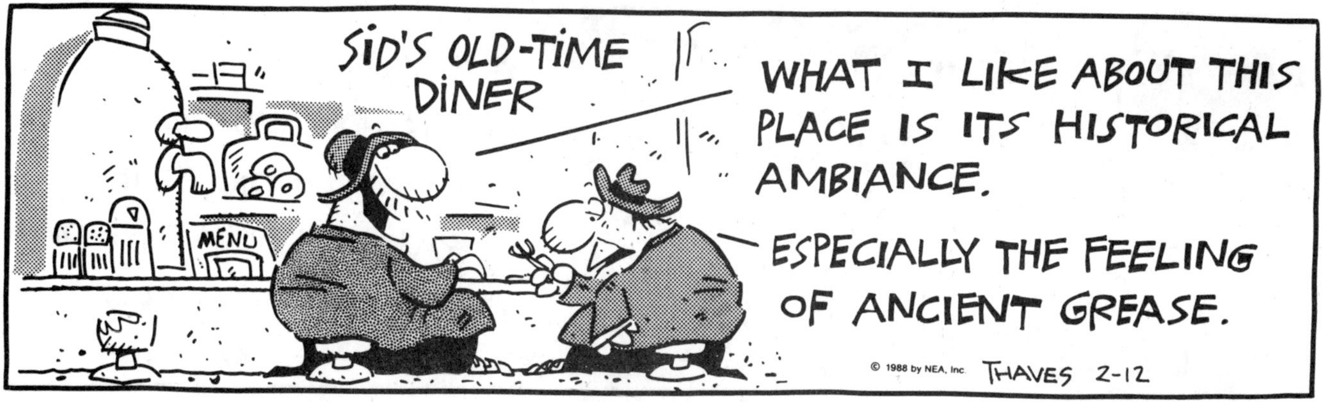
SID'S OLD-TIME DINER
WHAT I LIKE ABOUT THIS PLACE IS ITS HISTORICAL AMBIANCE.
ESPECIALLY THE FEELING OF ANCIENT GREASE.
MENU
© 1988 by NEA, Inc.
THAVES 2-12

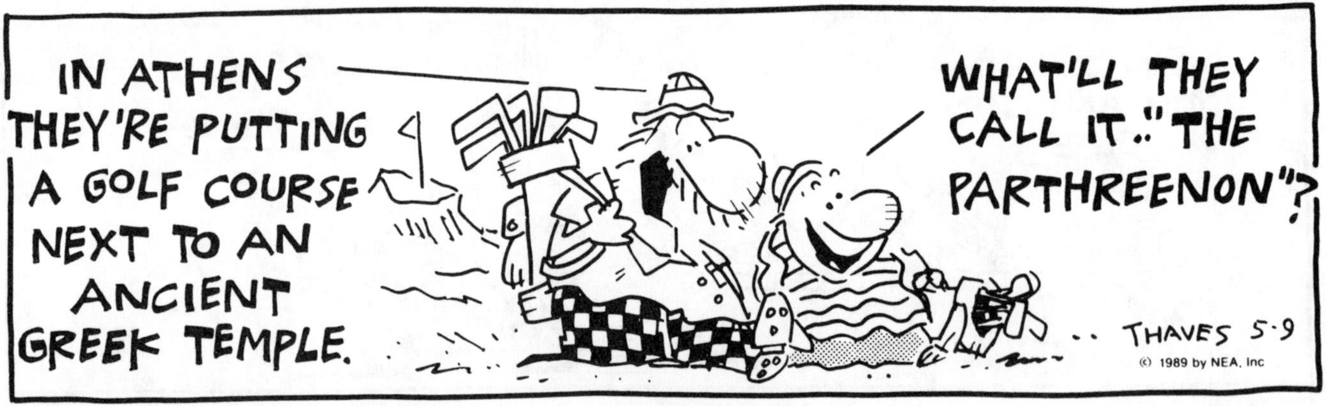
IN ATHENS THEY'RE PUTTING A GOLF COURSE NEXT TO AN ANCIENT GREEK TEMPLE.
WHAT'LL THEY CALL IT.."THE PARTHREENON"?
THAVES 5-9
© 1989 by NEA, Inc

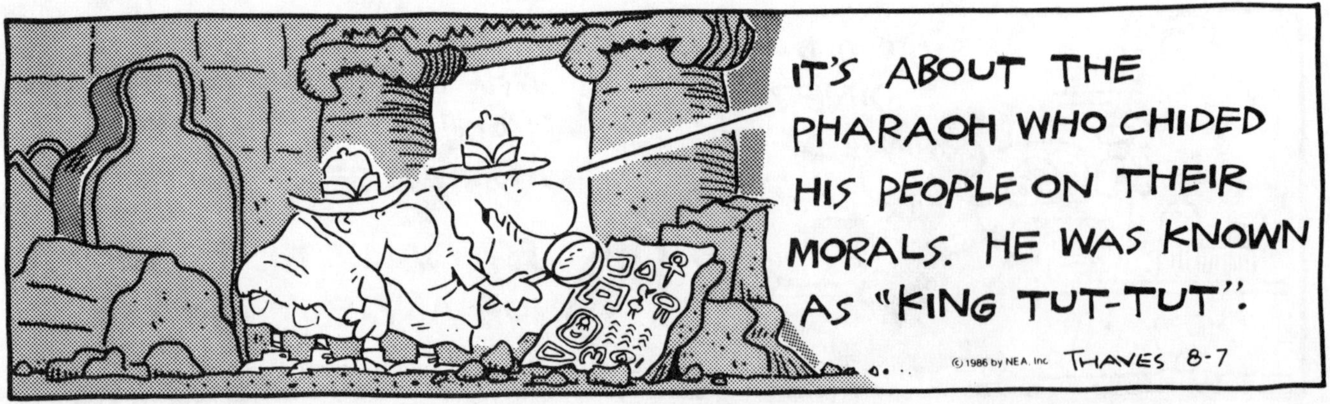
IT'S ABOUT THE PHARAOH WHO CHIDED HIS PEOPLE ON THEIR MORALS. HE WAS KNOWN AS "KING TUT-TUT".
© 1986 by NEA, Inc
THAVES 8-7

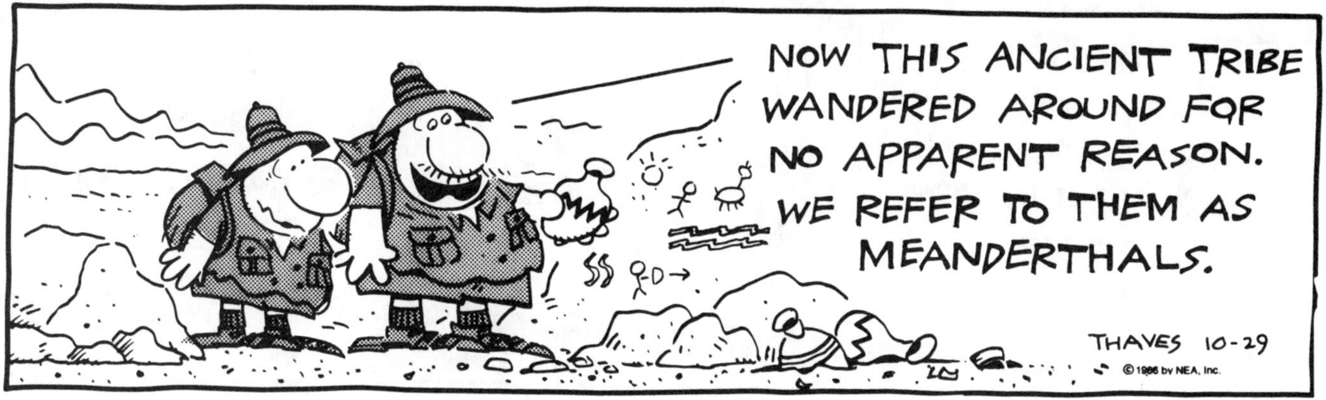
NOW THIS ANCIENT TRIBE WANDERED AROUND FOR NO APPARENT REASON. WE REFER TO THEM AS MEANDERTHALS.
THAVES 10-29
© 1988 by NEA, Inc.

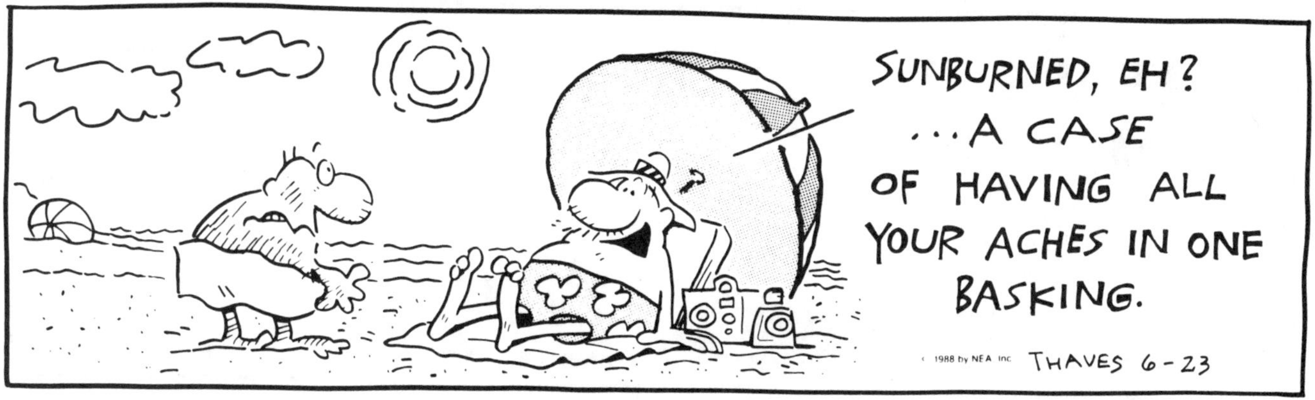
SUNBURNED, EH? ...A CASE OF HAVING ALL YOUR ACHES IN ONE BASKING.
© 1988 by NEA Inc.
THAVES 6-23

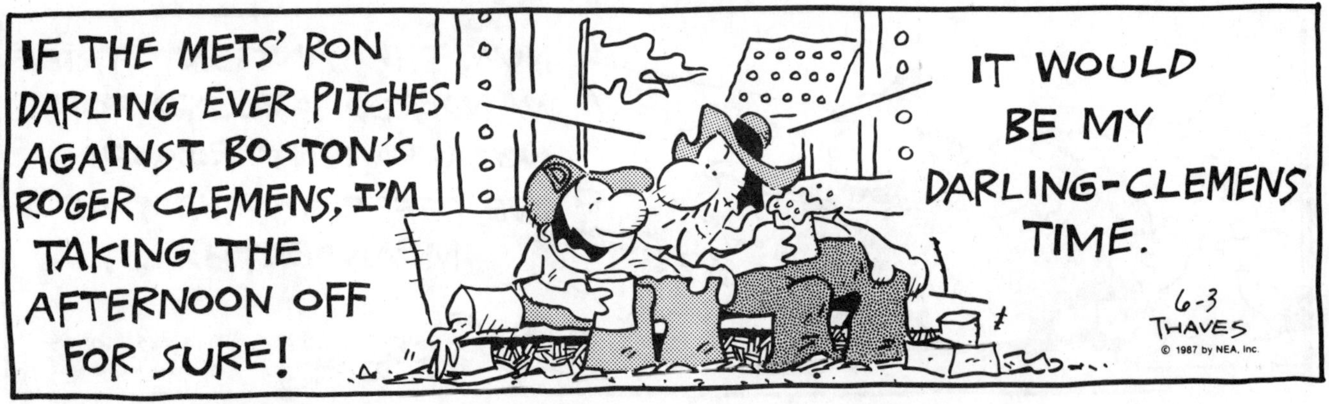
IF THE METS' RON DARLING EVER PITCHES AGAINST BOSTON'S ROGER CLEMENS, I'M TAKING THE AFTERNOON OFF FOR SURE!
IT WOULD BE MY DARLING-CLEMENS TIME.
6-3
THAVES
© 1987 by NEA, Inc.

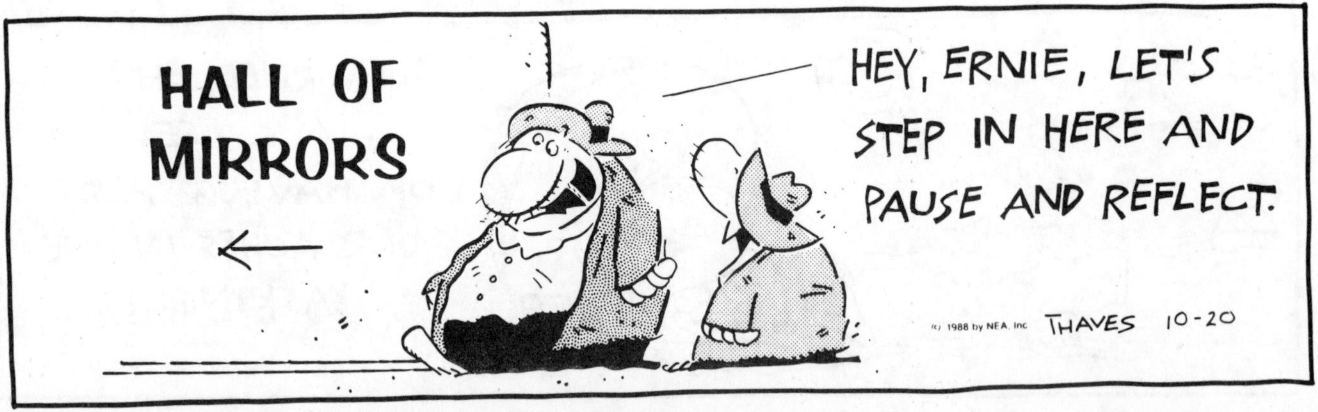
HALL OF MIRRORS
HEY, ERNIE, LET'S STEP IN HERE AND PAUSE AND REFLECT.
(c) 1988 by NEA, Inc
THAVES 10-20

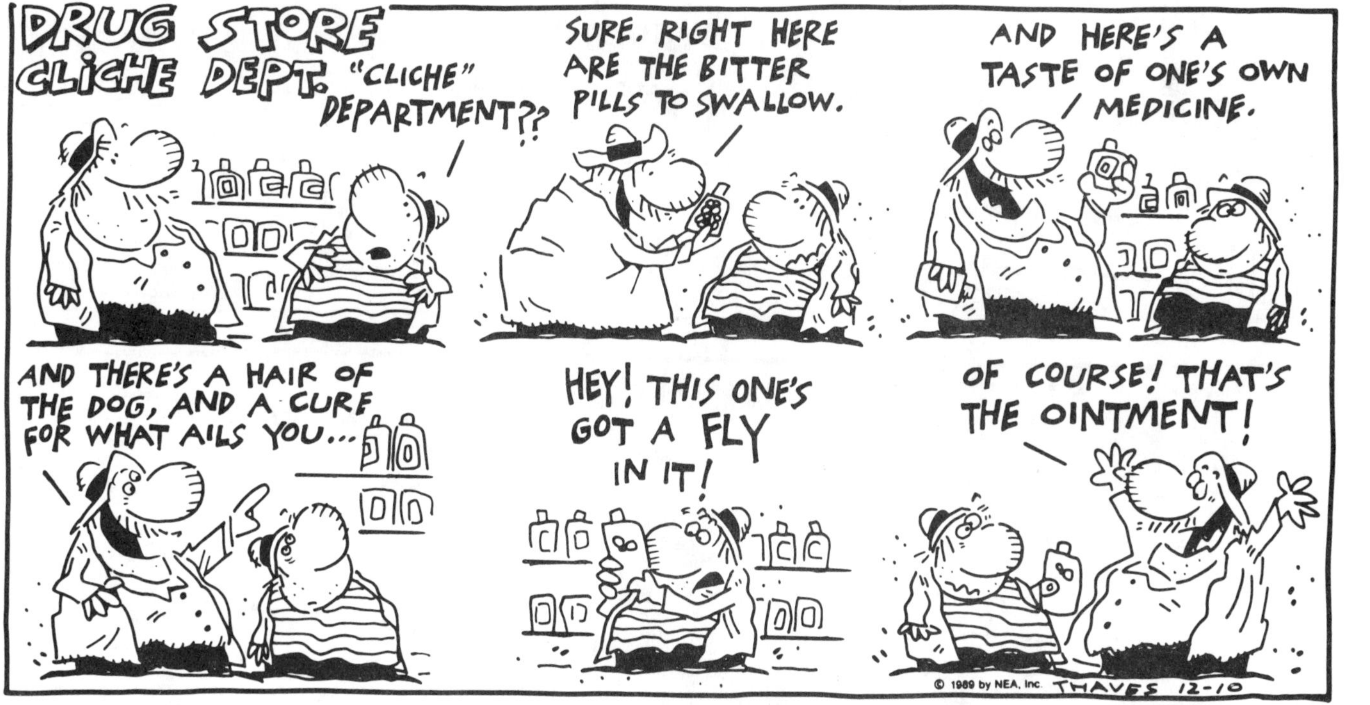
DRUG STORE CLICHE DEPT.
"CLICHE" DEPARTMENT??
SURE. RIGHT HERE ARE THE BITTER PILLS TO SWALLOW.
AND HERE'S A TASTE OF ONE'S OWN MEDICINE.
AND THERE'S A HAIR OF THE DOG, AND A CURE FOR WHAT AILS YOU...
HEY! THIS ONE'S GOT A FLY IN IT!
OF COURSE! THAT'S THE OINTMENT!
© 1989 by NEA, Inc.
THAVES 12-10

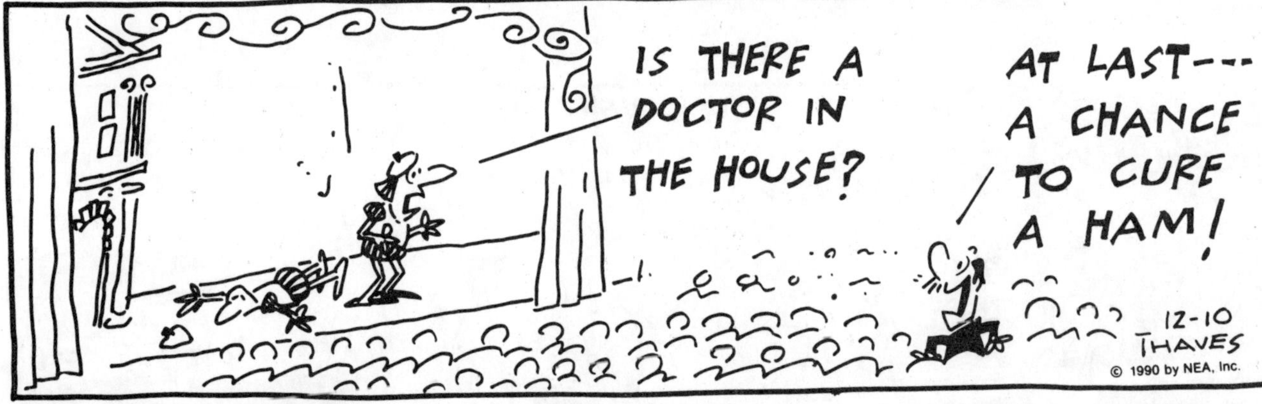
IS THERE A DOCTOR IN THE HOUSE?
AT LAST--- A CHANCE TO CURE A HAM!
12-10 THAVES
© 1990 by NEA, Inc.

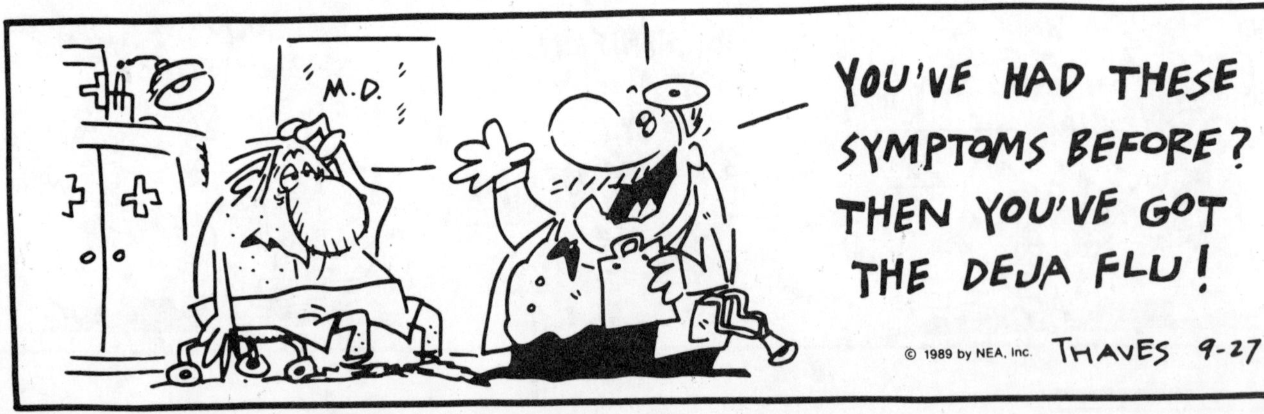
M.D.
YOU'VE HAD THESE SYMPTOMS BEFORE? THEN YOU'VE GOT THE DEJA FLU!
© 1989 by NEA, Inc.
THAVES 9-27

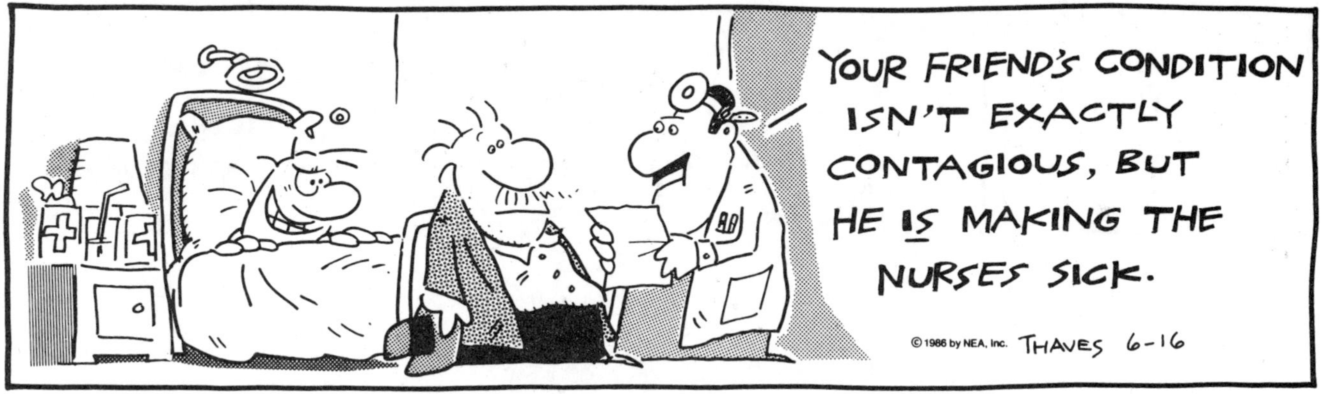
YOUR FRIEND'S CONDITION ISN'T EXACTLY CONTAGIOUS, BUT HE IS MAKING THE NURSES SICK.
© 1986 by NEA, Inc. THAVES 6-16

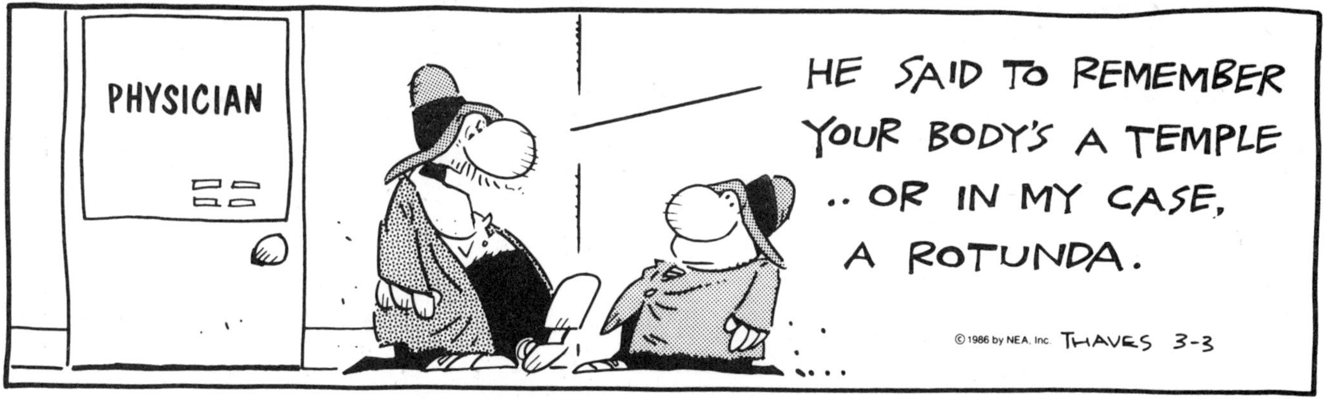
PHYSICIAN
HE SAID TO REMEMBER YOUR BODY'S A TEMPLE .. OR IN MY CASE, A ROTUNDA.
© 1986 by NEA, Inc. THAVES 3-3

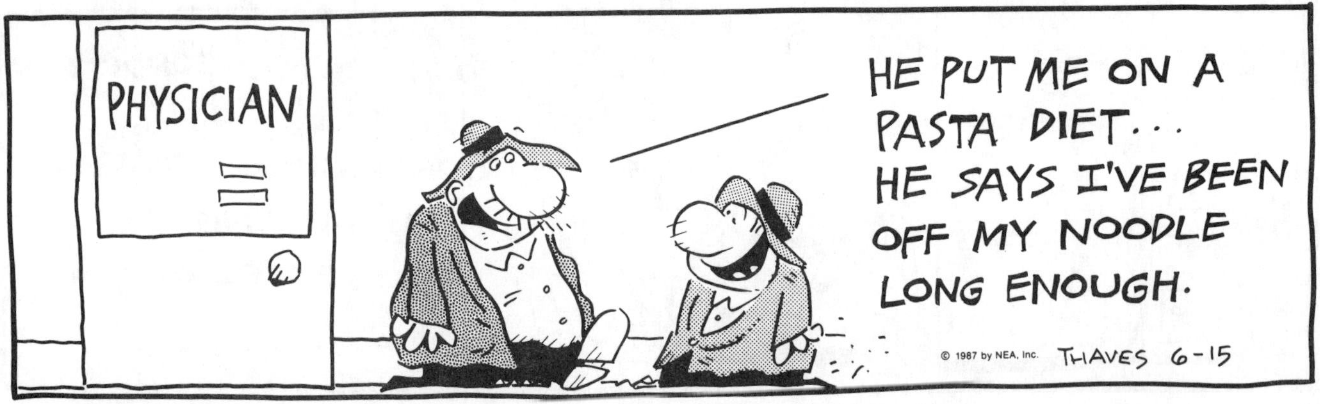
PHYSICIAN
HE PUT ME ON A PASTA DIET... HE SAYS I'VE BEEN OFF MY NOODLE LONG ENOUGH.
© 1987 by NEA, Inc.
THAVES 6-15

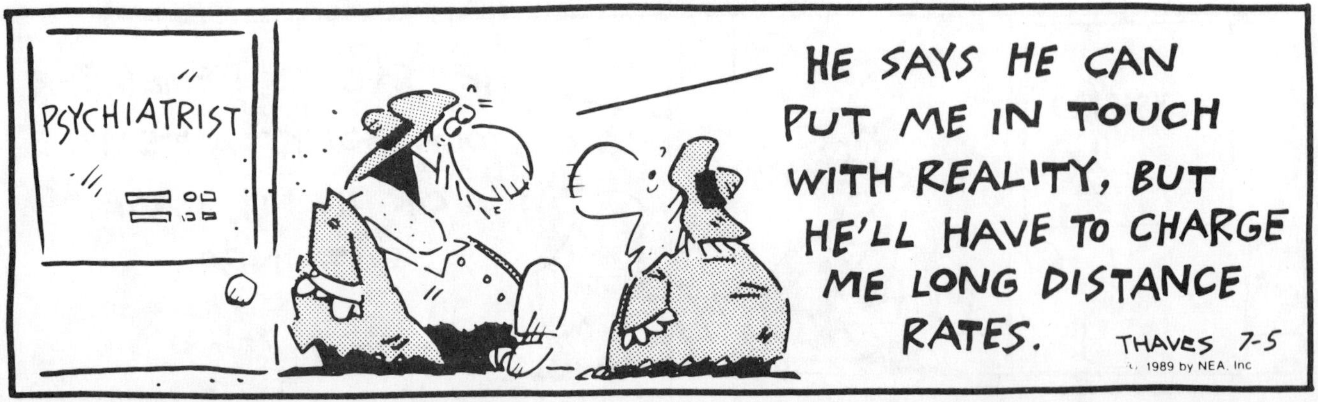
PSYCHIATRIST
HE SAYS HE CAN PUT ME IN TOUCH WITH REALITY, BUT HE'LL HAVE TO CHARGE ME LONG DISTANCE RATES.
THAVES 7-5
1989 by NEA, Inc

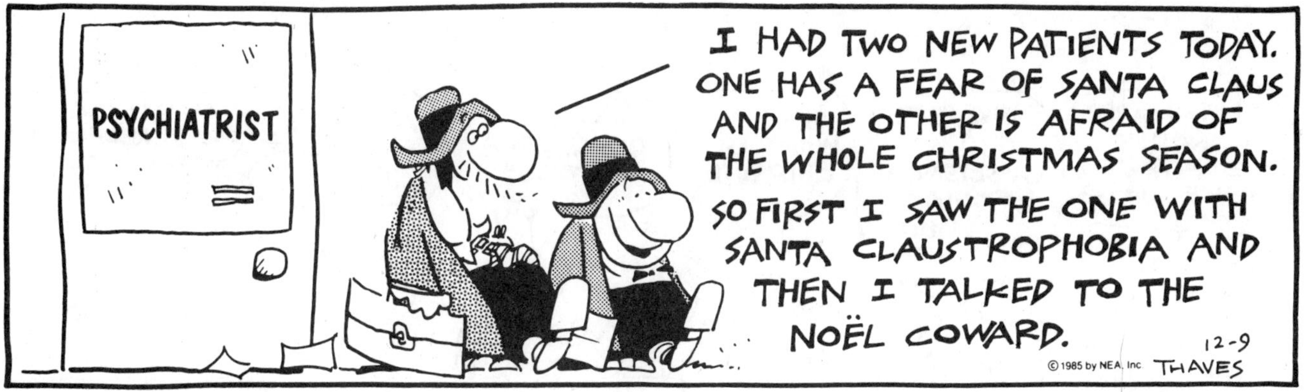
PSYCHIATRIST
I HAD TWO NEW PATIENTS TODAY. ONE HAS A FEAR OF SANTA CLAUS AND THE OTHER IS AFRAID OF THE WHOLE CHRISTMAS SEASON.
SO FIRST I SAW THE ONE WITH SANTA CLAUSTROPHOBIA AND THEN I TALKED TO THE NOËL COWARD.
12-9
© 1985 by NEA, Inc. THAVES

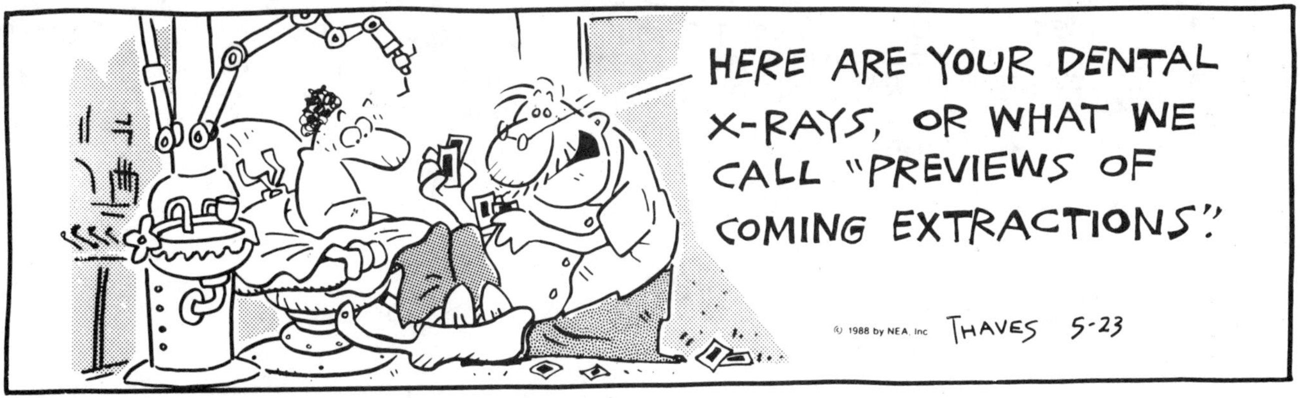
HERE ARE YOUR DENTAL X-RAYS, OR WHAT WE CALL "PREVIEWS OF COMING EXTRACTIONS."
© 1988 by NEA, Inc. THAVES 5-23

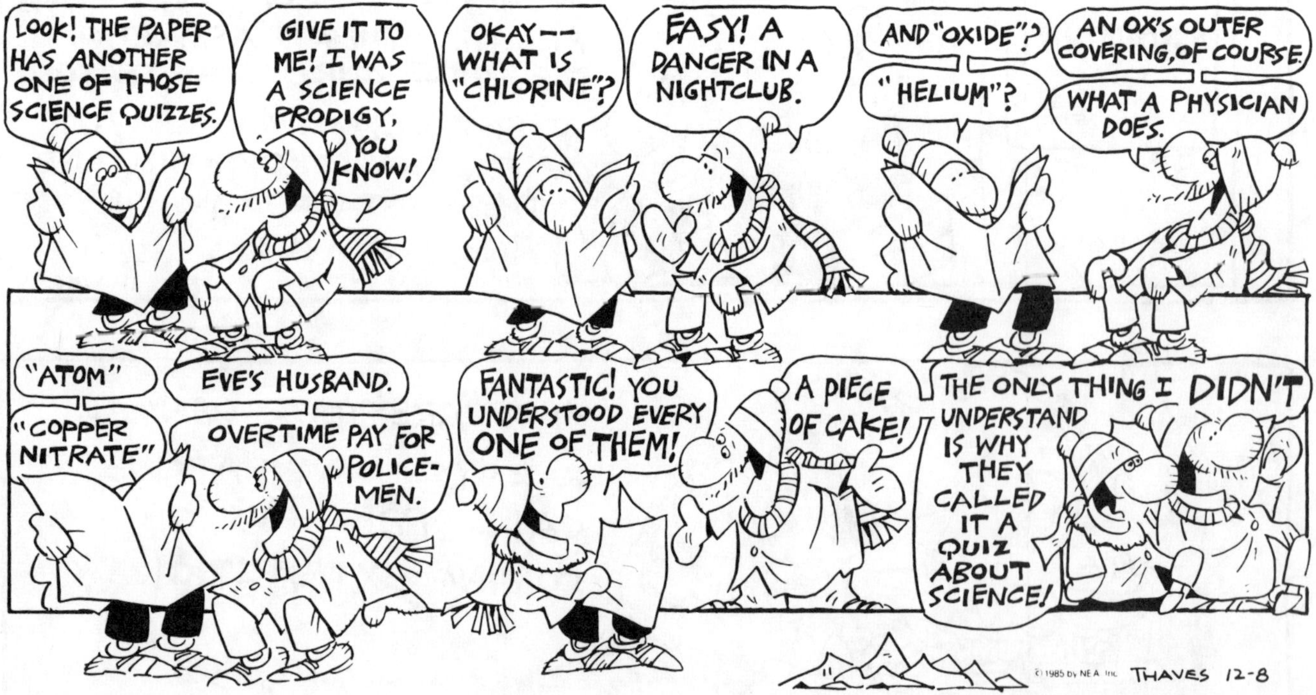
LOOK! THE PAPER HAS ANOTHER ONE OF THOSE SCIENCE QUIZZES.
GIVE IT TO ME! I WAS A SCIENCE PRODIGY, YOU KNOW!
OKAY -- WHAT IS "CHLORINE"?
EASY! A DANCER IN A NIGHTCLUB.
AND "OXIDE"?
AN OX'S OUTER COVERING, OF COURSE.
"HELIUM"?
WHAT A PHYSICIAN DOES.
"ATOM"
EVE'S HUSBAND.
"COPPER NITRATE"
OVERTIME PAY FOR POLICE-MEN.
FANTASTIC! YOU UNDERSTOOD EVERY ONE OF THEM!
A PIECE OF CAKE!
THE ONLY THING I DIDN'T UNDERSTAND IS WHY THEY CALLED IT A QUIZ ABOUT SCIENCE!
© 1985 by NEA, Inc.
THAVES 12-8

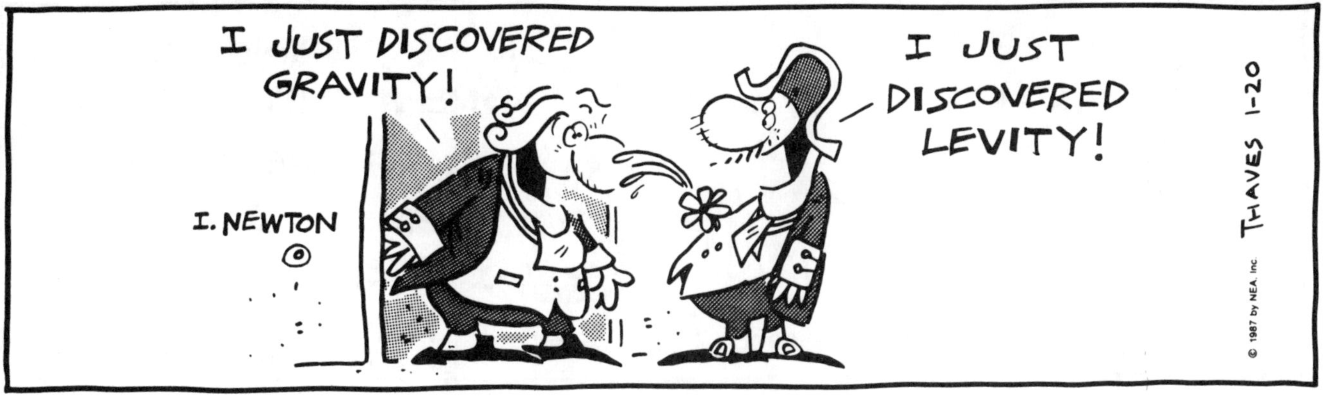
I JUST DISCOVERED GRAVITY!
I. NEWTON
I JUST DISCOVERED LEVITY!
THAVES 1-20
© 1987 by NEA, Inc.

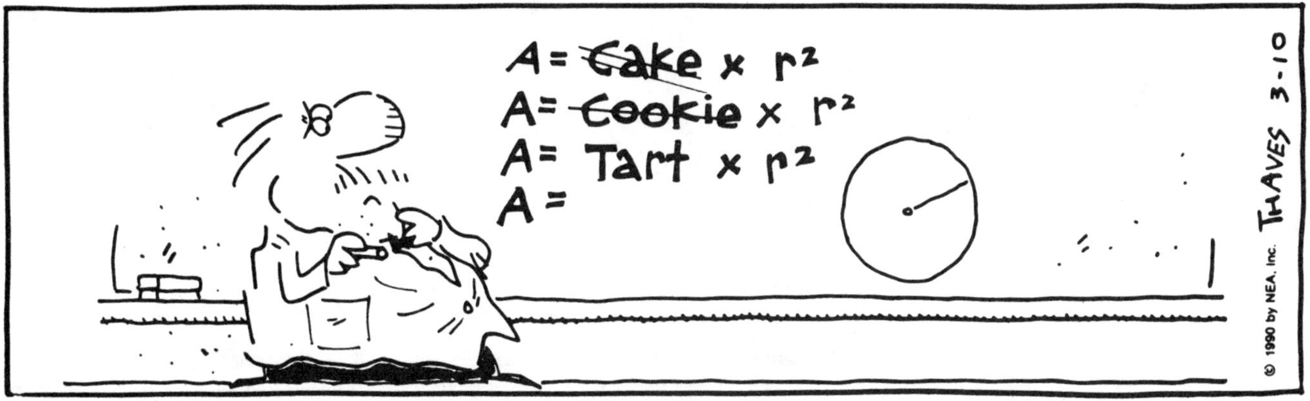
A= Cake x r²
A= Cookie x r²
A= Tart x r²
A=
THAVES 3-10
© 1990 by NEA, Inc.

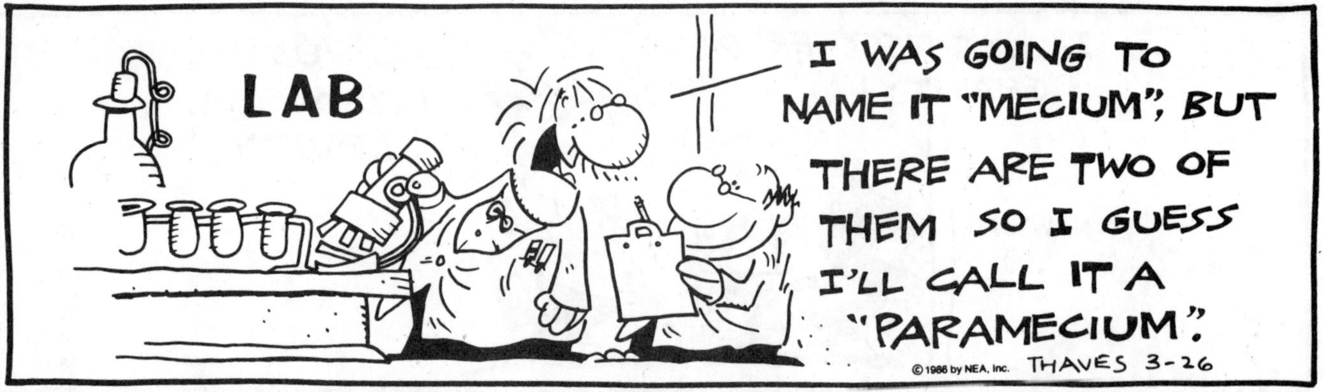
LAB
I WAS GOING TO NAME IT "MECIUM", BUT THERE ARE TWO OF THEM SO I GUESS I'LL CALL IT A "PARAMECIUM".
© 1986 by NEA, Inc. THAVES 3-26

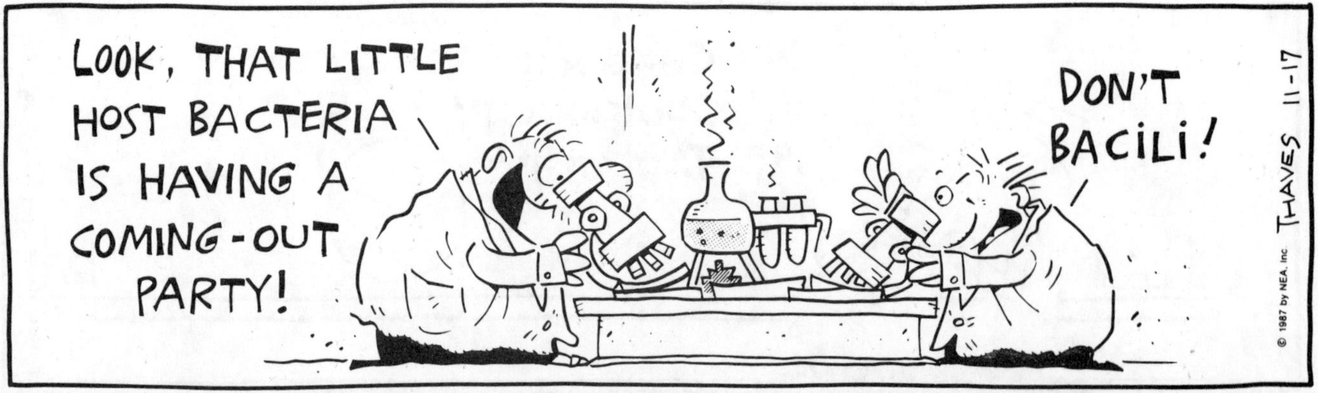
LOOK, THAT LITTLE HOST BACTERIA IS HAVING A COMING-OUT PARTY!
DON'T BACILI!
THAVES 11-17
© 1987 by NEA, Inc.

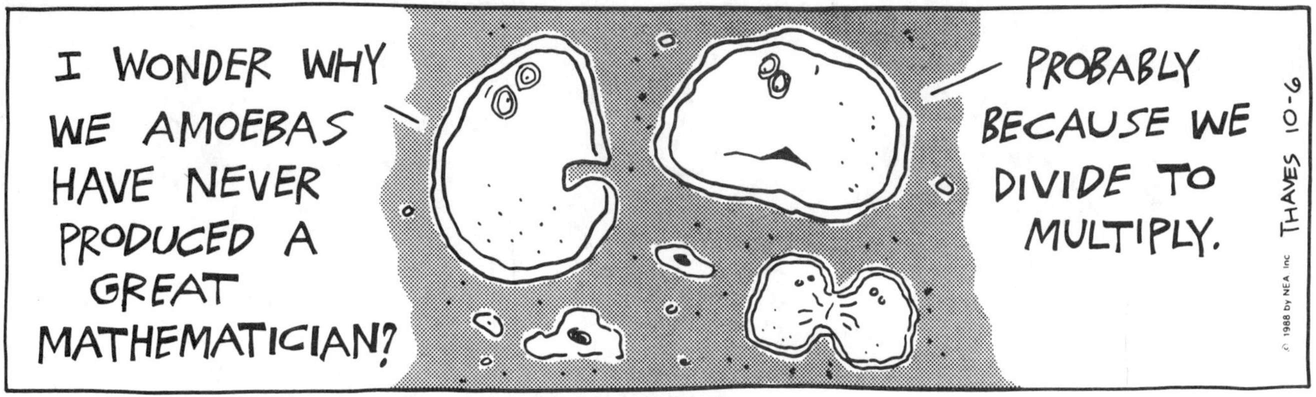
I WONDER WHY WE AMOEBAS HAVE NEVER PRODUCED A GREAT MATHEMATICIAN?
PROBABLY BECAUSE WE DIVIDE TO MULTIPLY.
© 1988 by NEA, Inc
THAVES 10-6

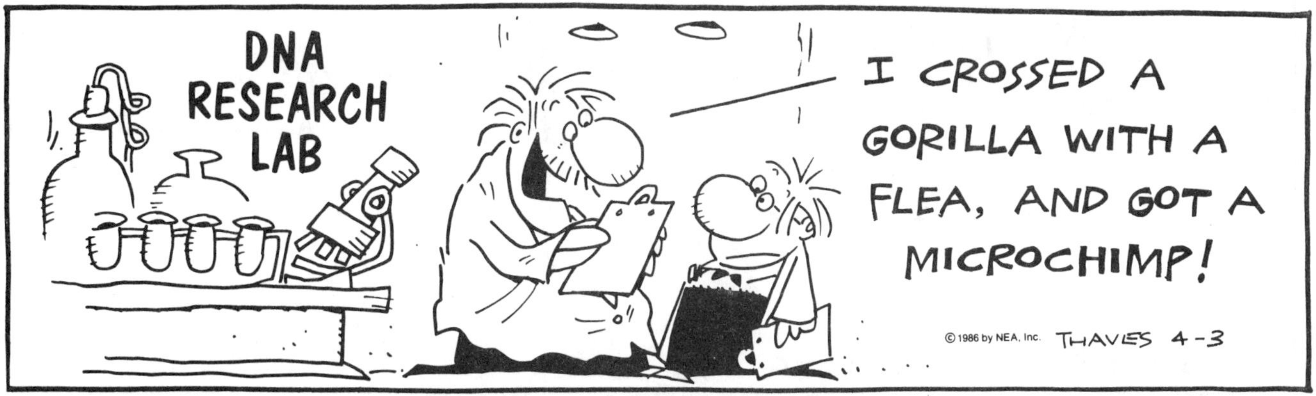
DNA RESEARCH LAB
I CROSSED A GORILLA WITH A FLEA, AND GOT A MICROCHIMP!
© 1986 by NEA, Inc.
THAVES 4-3

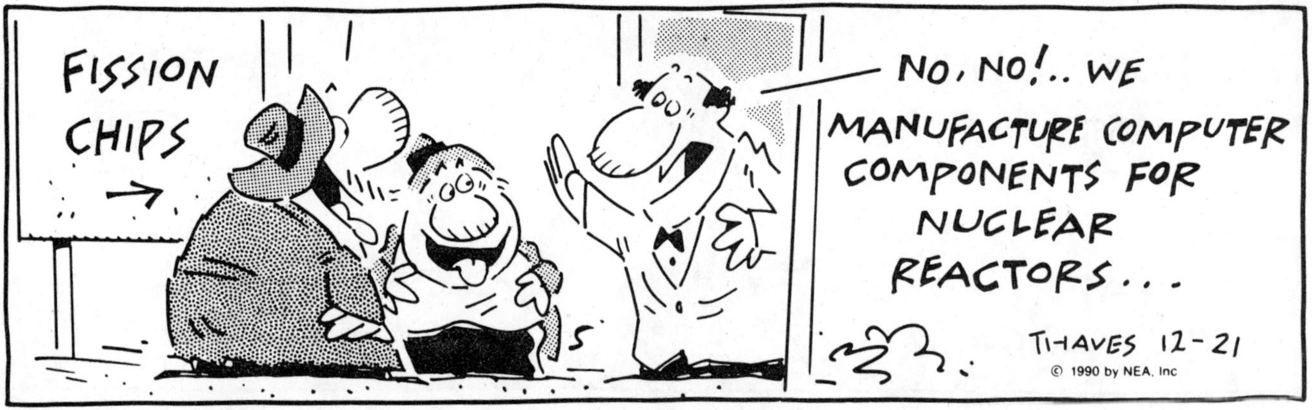
FISSION CHIPS
NO, NO!.. WE MANUFACTURE COMPUTER COMPONENTS FOR NUCLEAR REACTORS...
THAVES 12-21
© 1990 by NEA, Inc

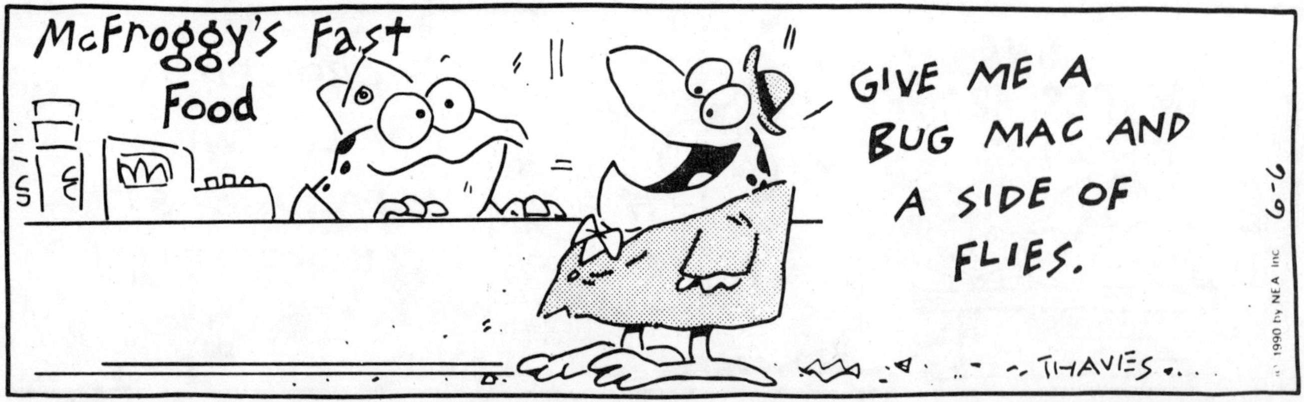
McFroggy's Fast Food
GIVE ME A BUG MAC AND A SIDE OF FLIES.
THAVES
6-6
© 1990 by NEA, Inc

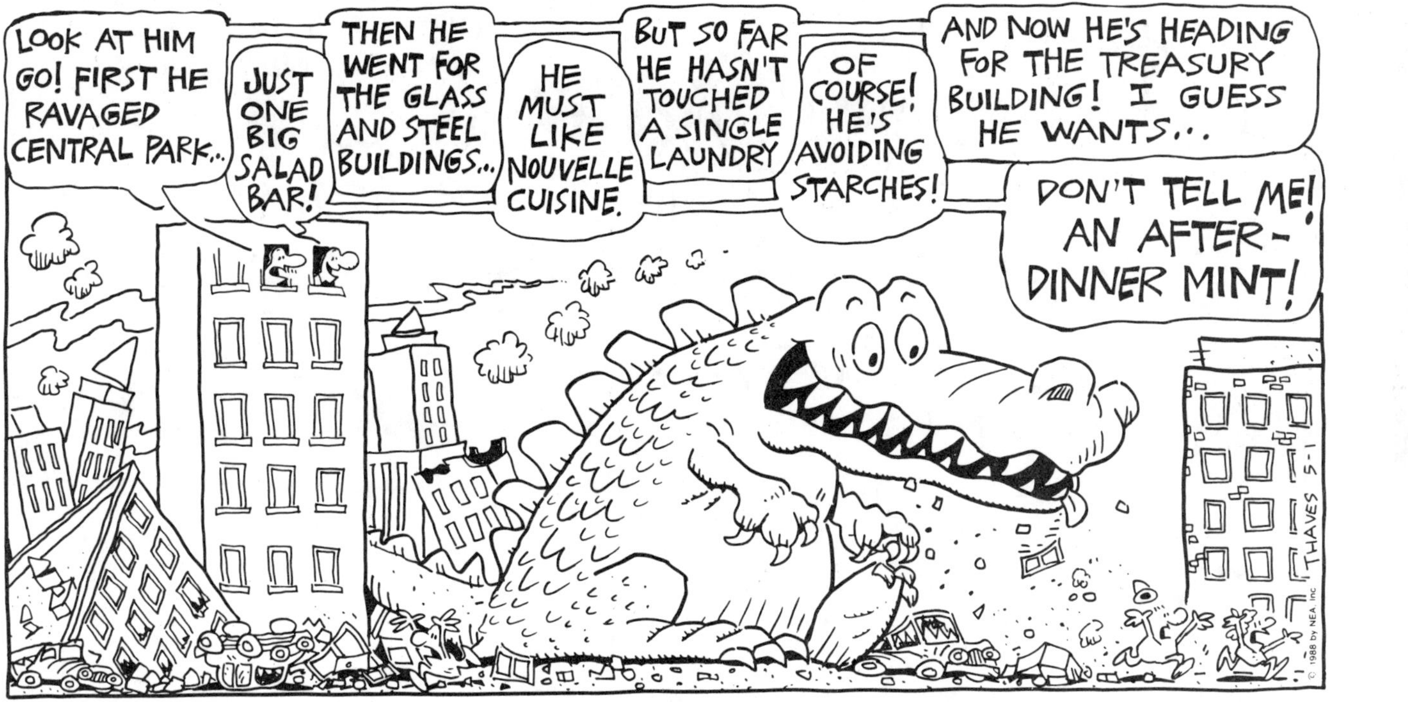
LOOK AT HIM GO! FIRST HE RAVAGED CENTRAL PARK...
JUST ONE BIG SALAD BAR!
THEN HE WENT FOR THE GLASS AND STEEL BUILDINGS...
HE MUST LIKE NOUVELLE CUISINE.
BUT SO FAR HE HASN'T TOUCHED A SINGLE LAUNDRY
OF COURSE! HE'S AVOIDING STARCHES!
AND NOW HE'S HEADING FOR THE TREASURY BUILDING! I GUESS HE WANTS...
DON'T TELL ME! AN AFTER-DINNER MINT!
THAVES 5-1
© 1988 by NEA, Inc.

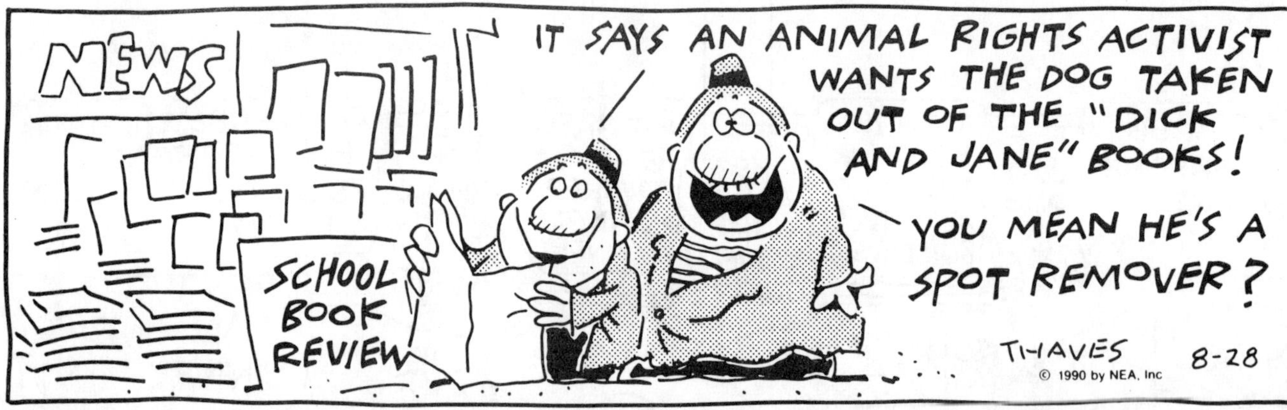
NEWS
SCHOOL BOOK REVIEW
IT SAYS AN ANIMAL RIGHTS ACTIVIST WANTS THE DOG TAKEN OUT OF THE "DICK AND JANE" BOOKS!
YOU MEAN HE'S A SPOT REMOVER?
THAVES
© 1990 by NEA, Inc
8-28

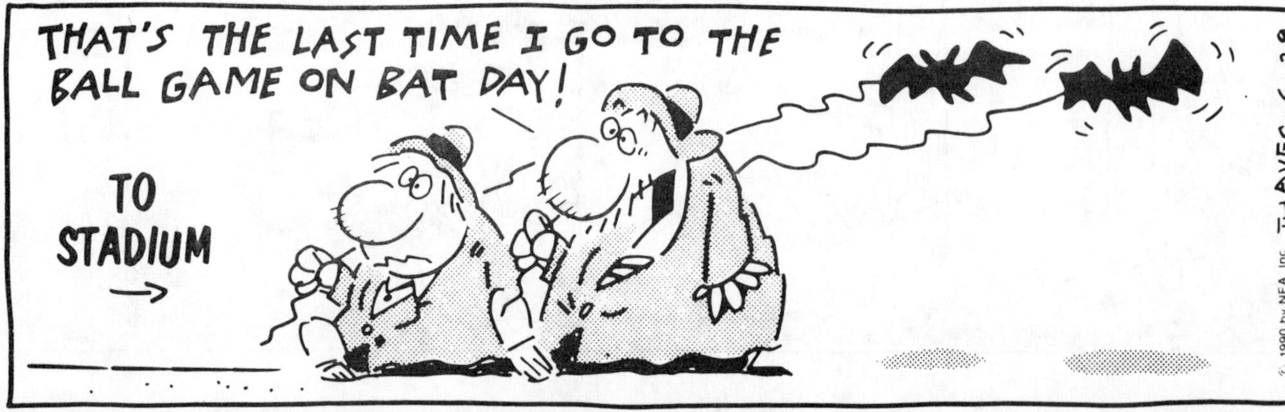
THAT'S THE LAST TIME I GO TO THE BALL GAME ON BAT DAY!
TO STADIUM →
THAVES 6-28
© 1990 by NEA, Inc

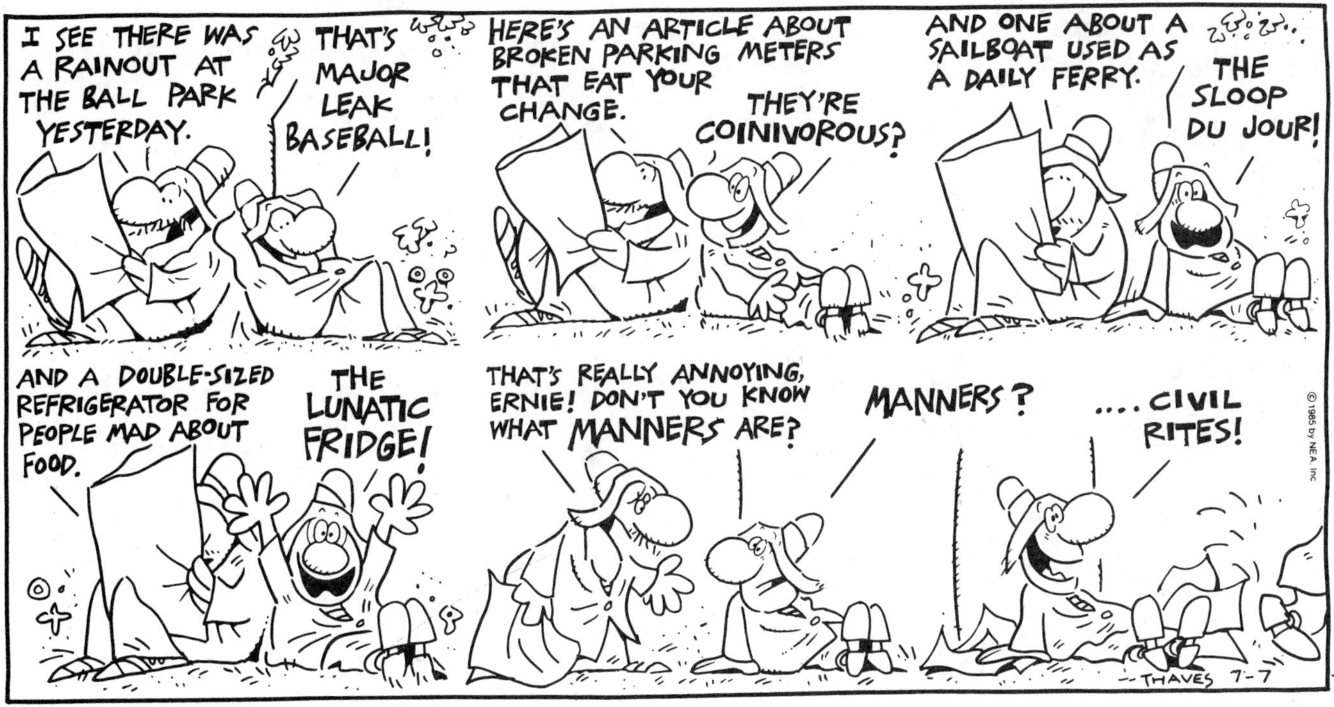
I SEE THERE WAS A RAINOUT AT THE BALL PARK YESTERDAY.
THAT'S MAJOR LEAK BASEBALL!
HERE'S AN ARTICLE ABOUT BROKEN PARKING METERS THAT EAT YOUR CHANGE.
THEY'RE COINIVOROUS?
AND ONE ABOUT A SAILBOAT USED AS A DAILY FERRY.
THE SLOOP DU JOUR!
AND A DOUBLE-SIZED REFRIGERATOR FOR PEOPLE MAD ABOUT FOOD.
THE LUNATIC FRIDGE!
THAT'S REALLY ANNOYING, ERNIE! DON'T YOU KNOW WHAT MANNERS ARE?
MANNERS?
....CIVIL RITES!
© 1985 by NEA, Inc
THAVES 7-7

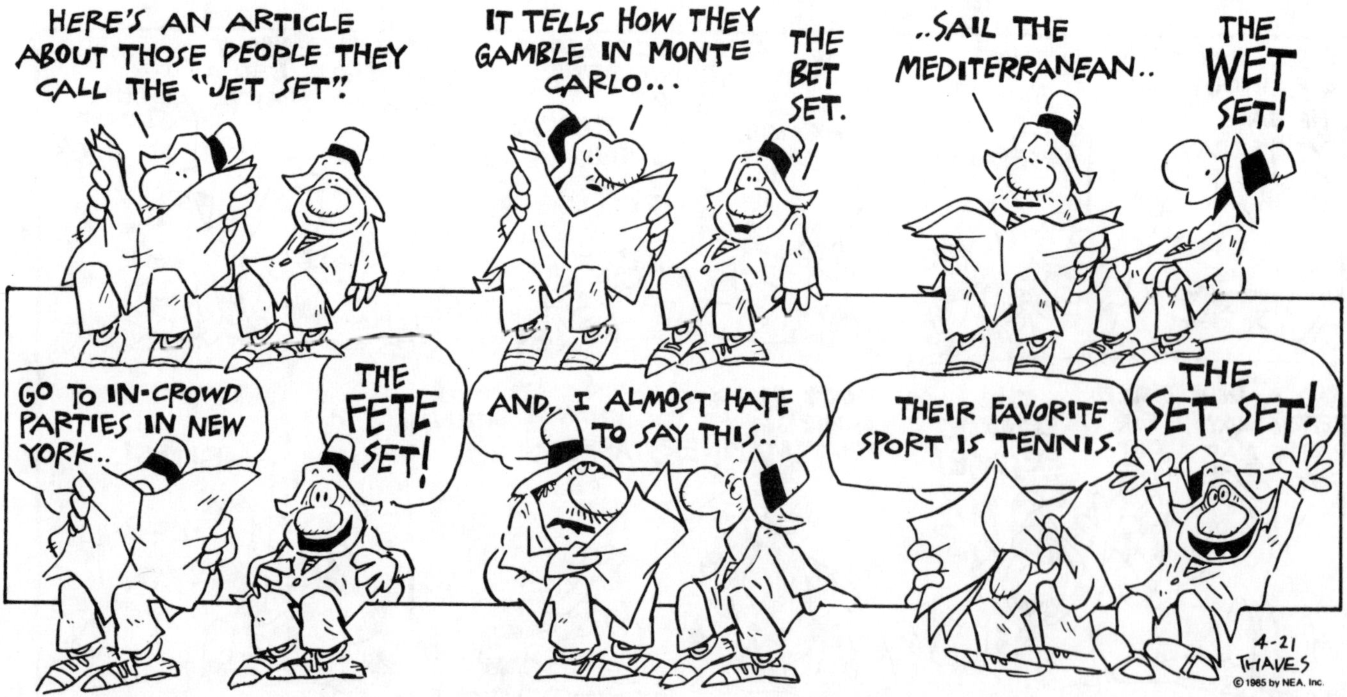
HERE'S AN ARTICLE ABOUT THOSE PEOPLE THEY CALL THE "JET SET".
IT TELLS HOW THEY GAMBLE IN MONTE CARLO...
THE BET SET.
..SAIL THE MEDITERRANEAN..
THE WET SET!
GO TO IN-CROWD PARTIES IN NEW YORK..
THE FETE SET!
AND, I ALMOST HATE TO SAY THIS..
THEIR FAVORITE SPORT IS TENNIS.
THE SET SET!
4-21
THAVES
© 1985 by NEA, Inc.

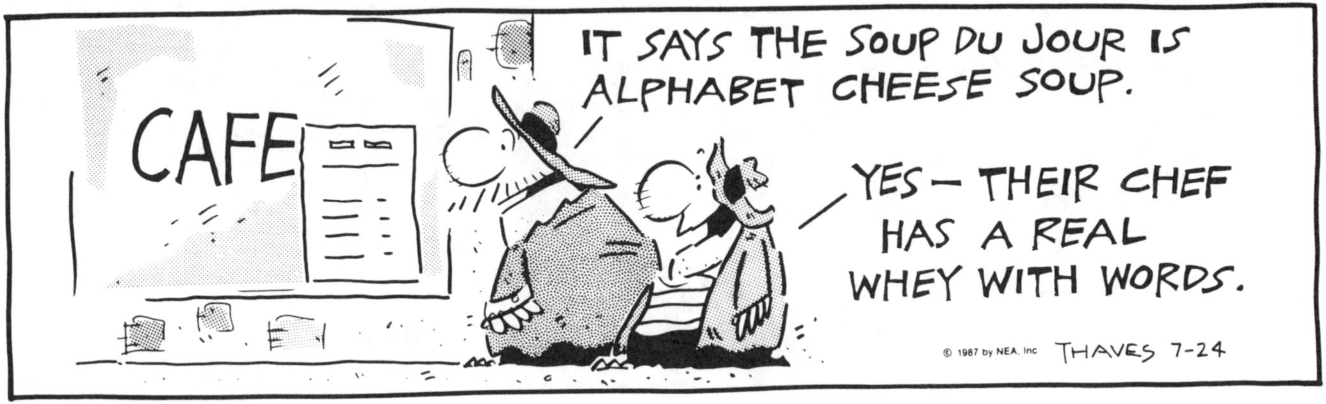
CAFE
IT SAYS THE SOUP DU JOUR IS ALPHABET CHEESE SOUP.
YES — THEIR CHEF HAS A REAL WHEY WITH WORDS.
© 1987 by NEA, Inc
THAVES 7-24

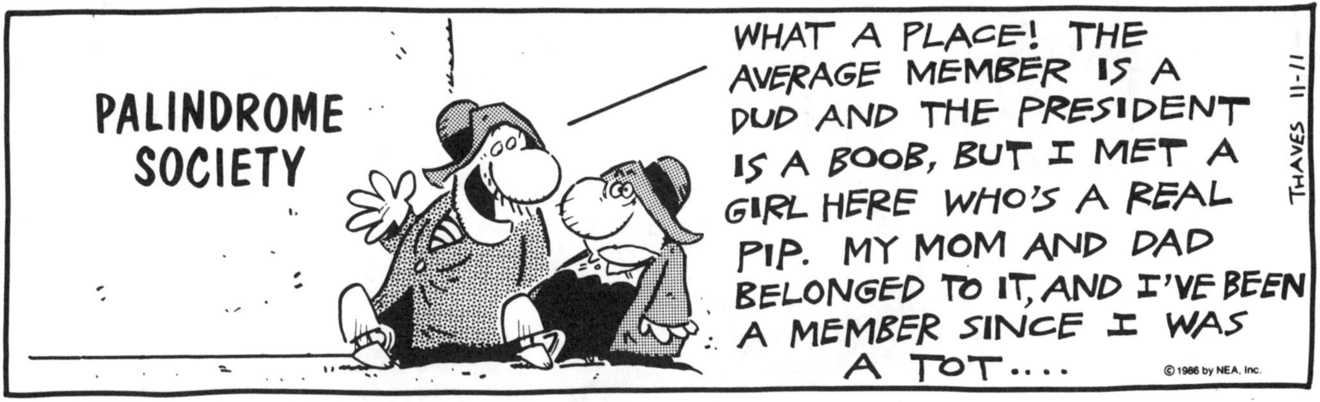
PALINDROME SOCIETY
WHAT A PLACE! THE AVERAGE MEMBER IS A DUD AND THE PRESIDENT IS A BOOB, BUT I MET A GIRL HERE WHO'S A REAL PIP. MY MOM AND DAD BELONGED TO IT, AND I'VE BEEN A MEMBER SINCE I WAS A TOT....
THAVES 11-11
©1986 by NEA, Inc.

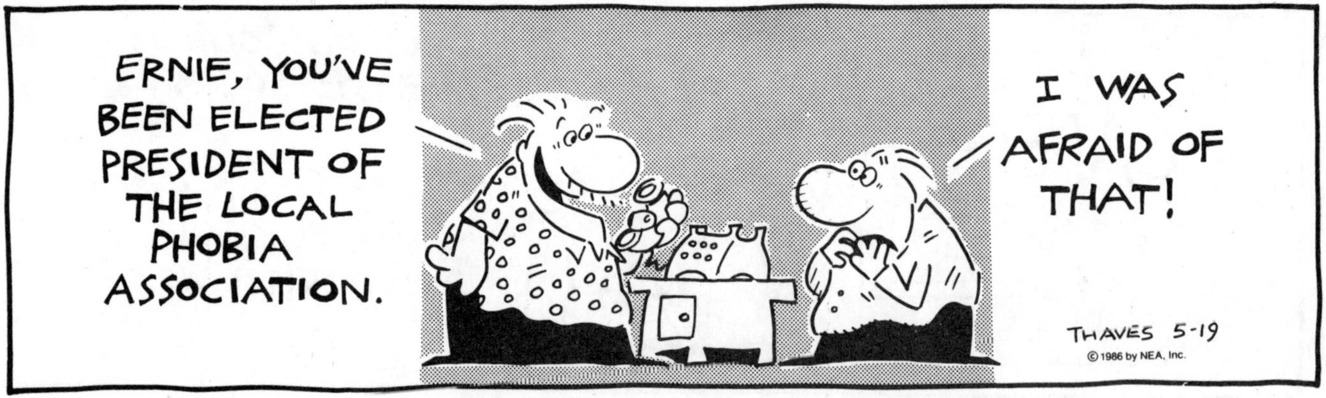
ERNIE, YOU'VE BEEN ELECTED PRESIDENT OF THE LOCAL PHOBIA ASSOCIATION.
I WAS AFRAID OF THAT!
THAVES 5-19
© 1986 by NEA, Inc.

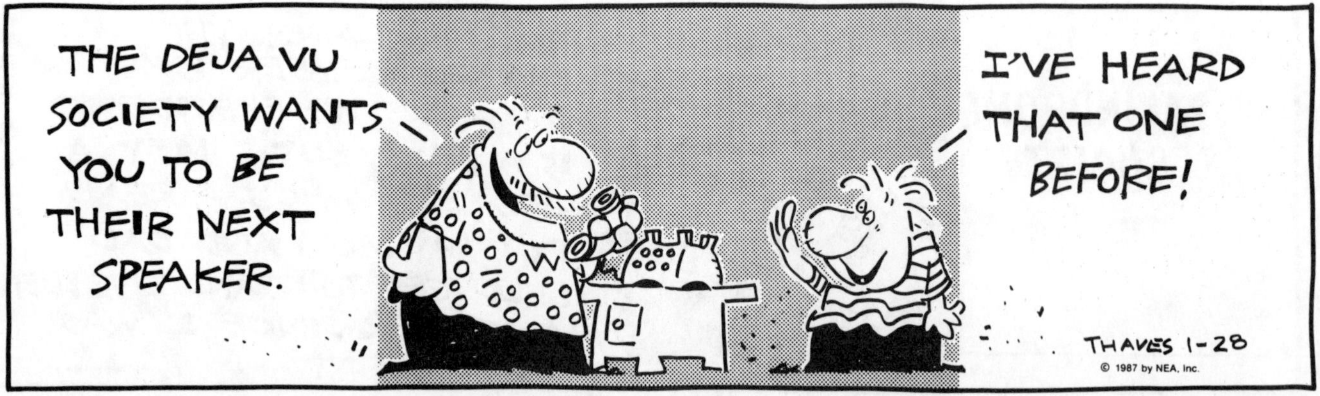
THE DEJA VU SOCIETY WANTS YOU TO BE THEIR NEXT SPEAKER.
I'VE HEARD THAT ONE BEFORE!
THAVES 1-28
© 1987 by NEA, Inc.

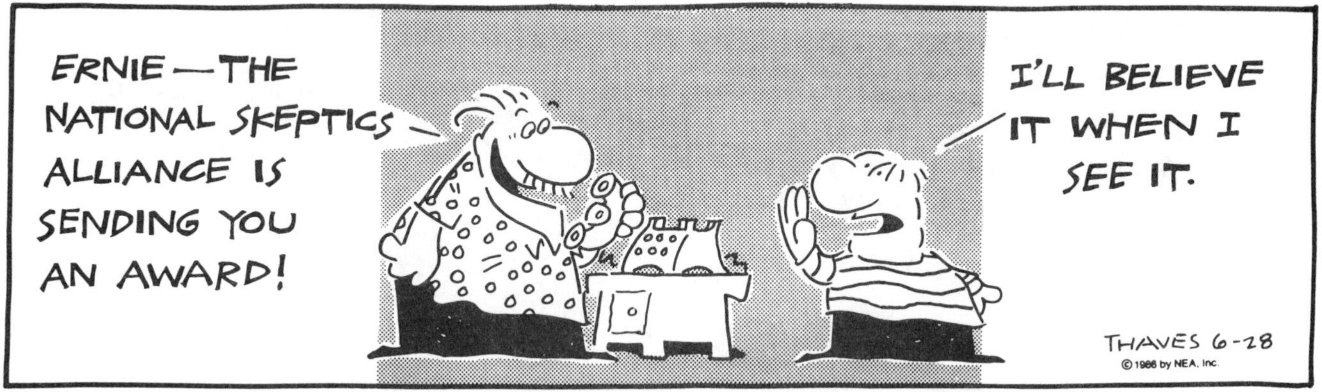
ERNIE—THE NATIONAL SKEPTICS ALLIANCE IS SENDING YOU AN AWARD!
I'LL BELIEVE IT WHEN I SEE IT.
THAVES 6-28

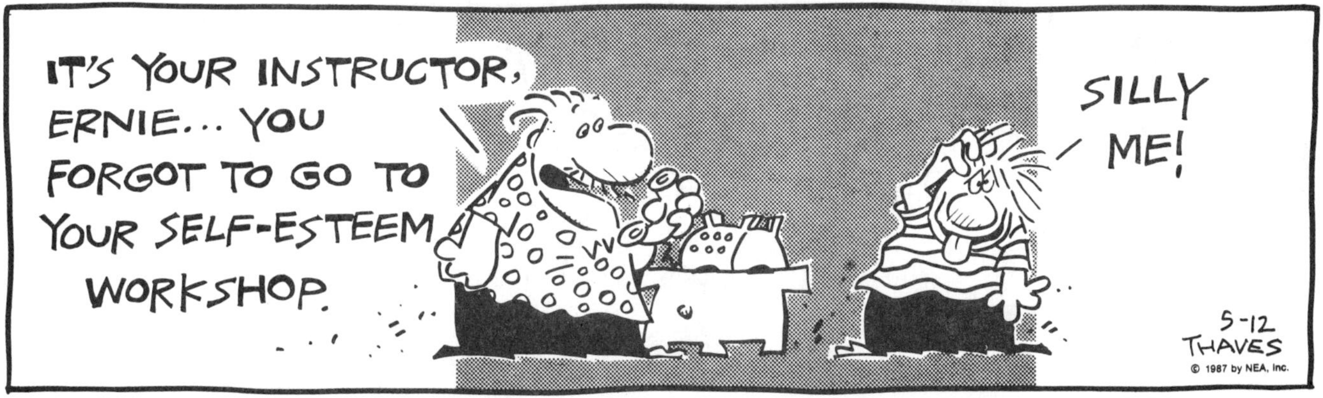
IT'S YOUR INSTRUCTOR, ERNIE... YOU FORGOT TO GO TO YOUR SELF-ESTEEM WORKSHOP.
SILLY ME!
5-12 THAVES
© 1987 by NEA, Inc.

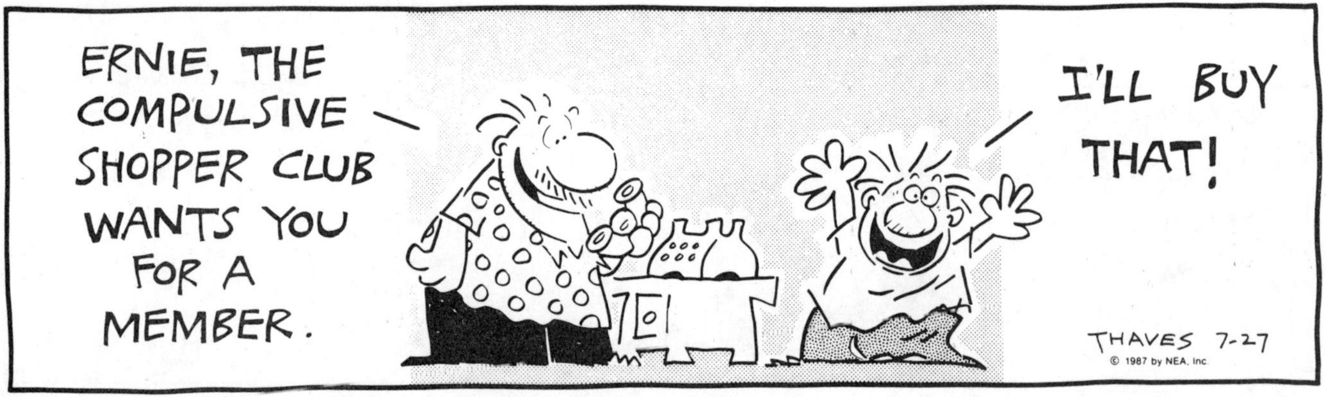

ERNIE, THE COMPULSIVE SHOPPER CLUB WANTS YOU FOR A MEMBER.
I'LL BUY THAT!
THAVES 7-27
© 1987 by NEA, Inc

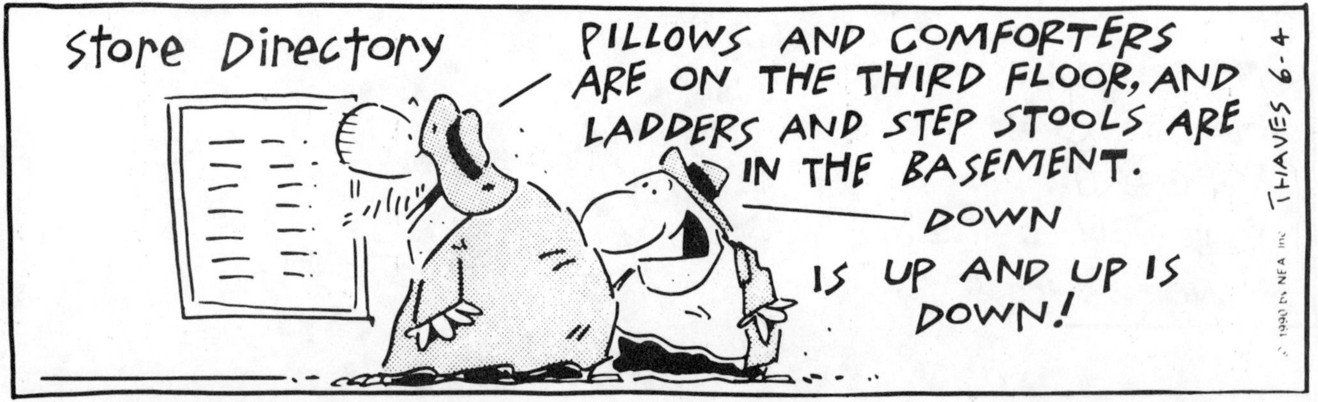

Store Directory
PILLOWS AND COMFORTERS ARE ON THE THIRD FLOOR, AND LADDERS AND STEP STOOLS ARE IN THE BASEMENT.
DOWN IS UP AND UP IS DOWN!
THAVES 6-4
© 1990 by NEA, Inc

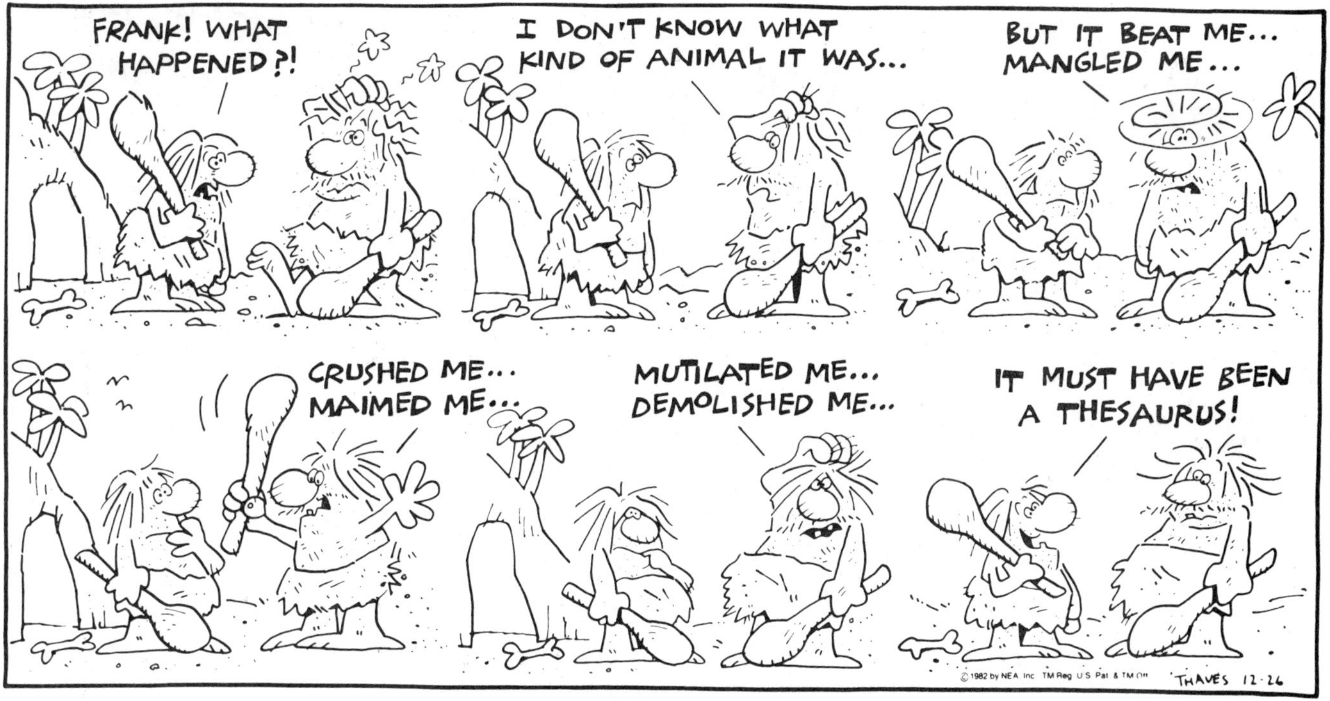
FRANK! WHAT HAPPENED?!
I DON'T KNOW WHAT KIND OF ANIMAL IT WAS...
BUT IT BEAT ME... MANGLED ME...
CRUSHED ME... MAIMED ME...
MUTILATED ME... DEMOLISHED ME...
IT MUST HAVE BEEN A THESAURUS!
© 1982 by NEA Inc TM Reg U.S. Pat & TM Off
THAVES 12·26

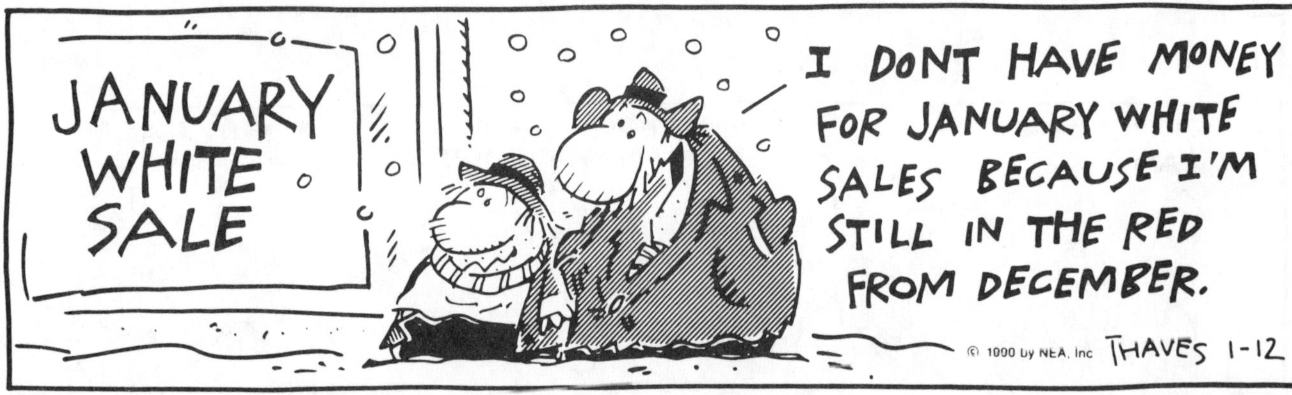
JANUARY WHITE SALE
I DONT HAVE MONEY FOR JANUARY WHITE SALES BECAUSE I'M STILL IN THE RED FROM DECEMBER.
© 1990 by NEA, Inc
THAVES 1-12

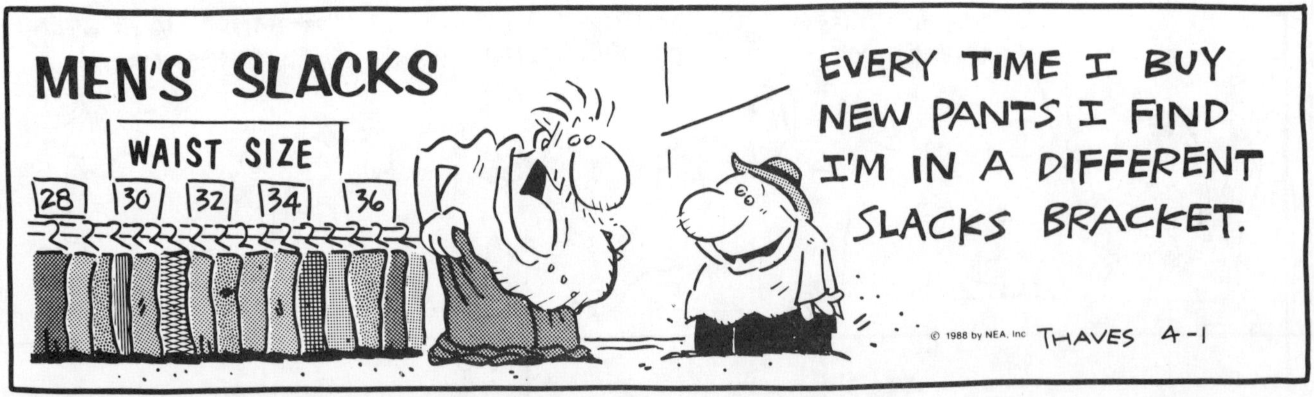
MEN'S SLACKS
WAIST SIZE
28
30
32
34
36
EVERY TIME I BUY NEW PANTS I FIND I'M IN A DIFFERENT SLACKS BRACKET.
© 1988 by NEA, Inc
THAVES 4-1

FRANK AND ERNEST ® by Bob Thaves

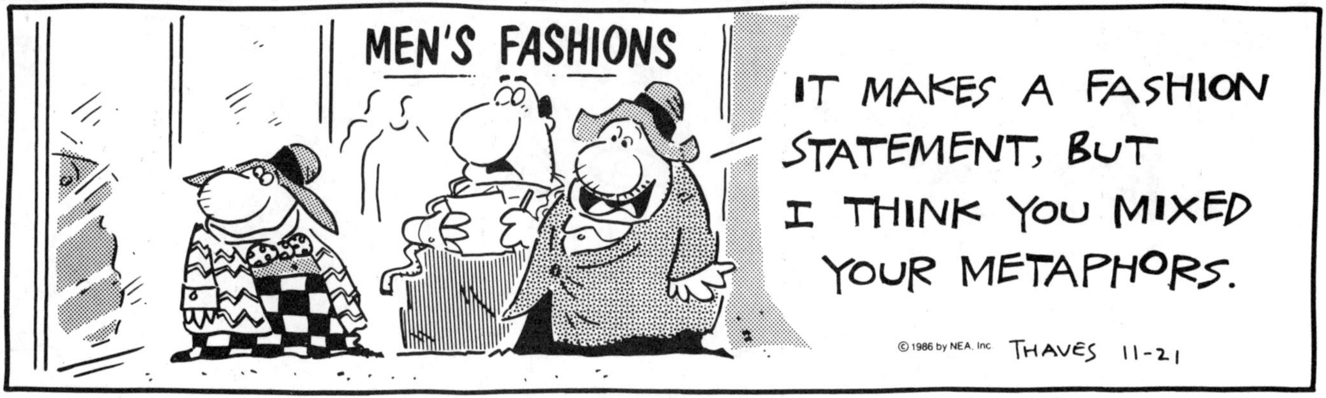
MEN'S FASHIONS
IT MAKES A FASHION STATEMENT, BUT I THINK YOU MIXED YOUR METAPHORS.
© 1986 by NEA, Inc
THAVES 11-21

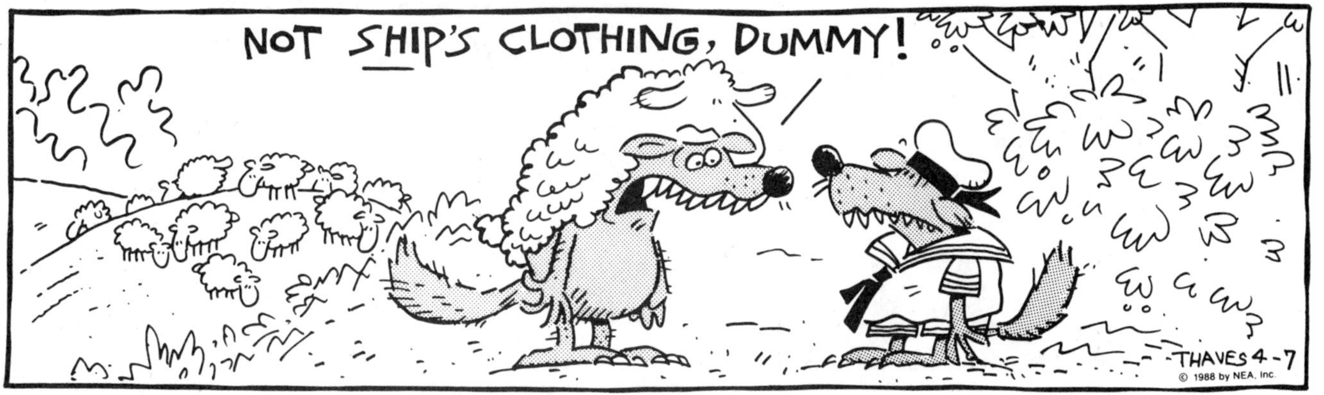
NOT SHIP'S CLOTHING, DUMMY!
THAVES 4-7
© 1988 by NEA, Inc.

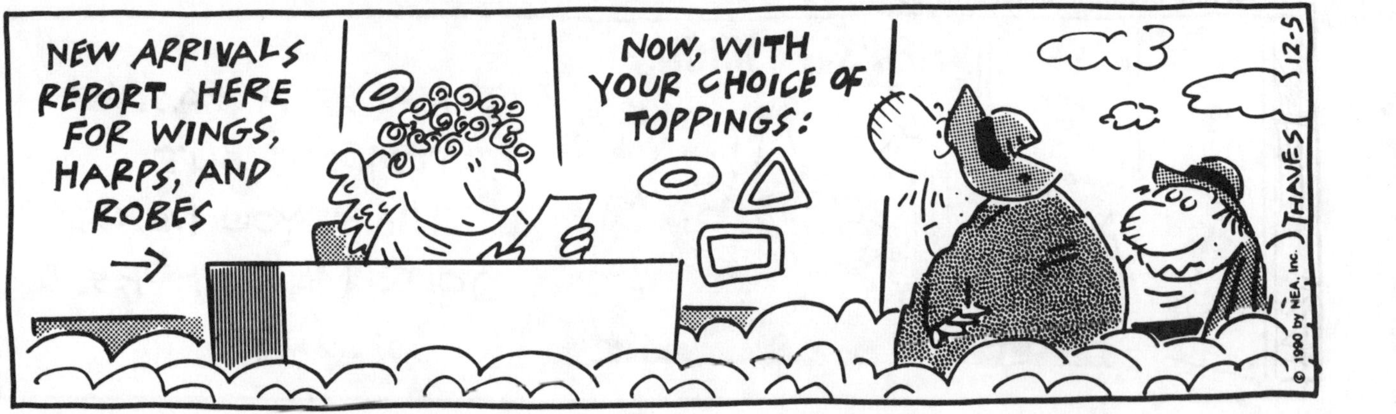
NEW ARRIVALS REPORT HERE FOR WINGS, HARPS, AND ROBES →
NOW, WITH YOUR CHOICE OF TOPPINGS:
12-5
THAVES
© 1990 by NEA, Inc.

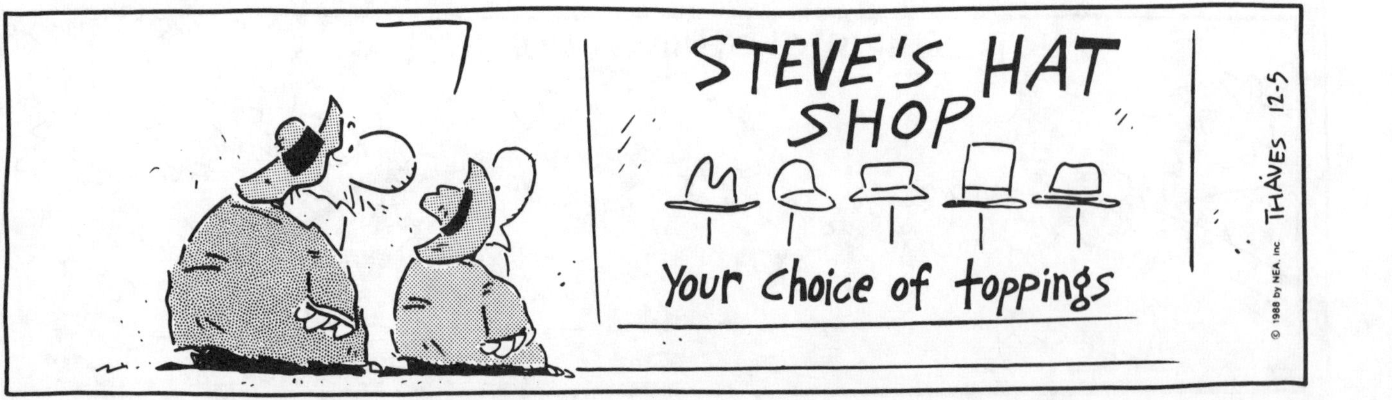
STEVE'S HAT SHOP
Your choice of toppings
12-5
THAVES
© 1988 by NEA, Inc.

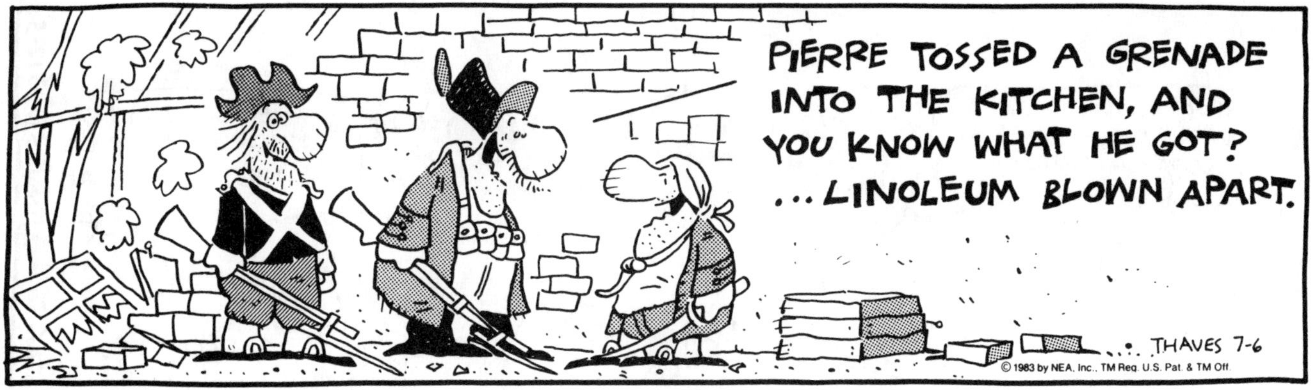
PIERRE TOSSED A GRENADE INTO THE KITCHEN, AND YOU KNOW WHAT HE GOT? ...LINOLEUM BLOWN APART.
THAVES 7-6
© 1983 by NEA, Inc., TM Reg. U.S. Pat. & TM Off.

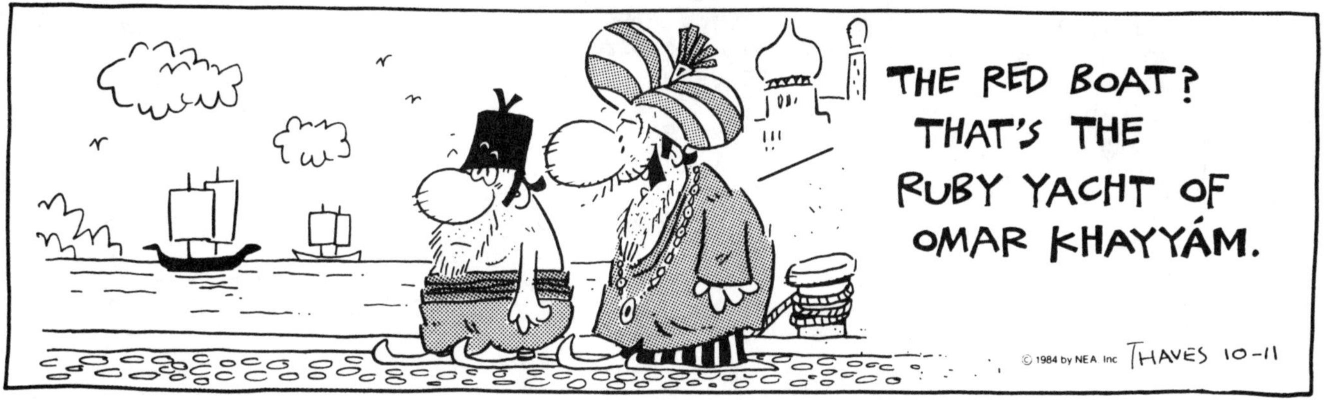
THE RED BOAT? THAT'S THE RUBY YACHT OF OMAR KHAYYÁM.
© 1984 by NEA, Inc
THAVES 10-11

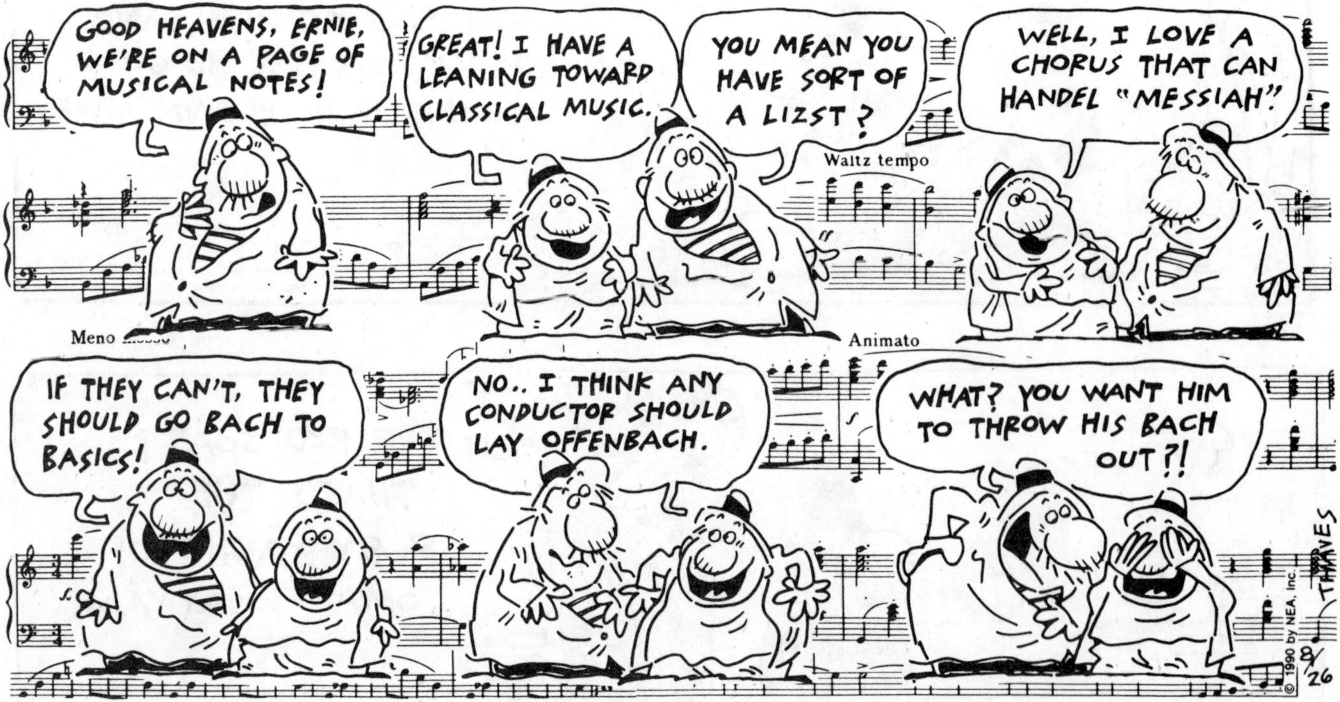
GOOD HEAVENS, ERNIE, WE'RE ON A PAGE OF MUSICAL NOTES!
GREAT! I HAVE A LEANING TOWARD CLASSICAL MUSIC.
YOU MEAN YOU HAVE SORT OF A LIZST?
Waltz tempo
WELL, I LOVE A CHORUS THAT CAN HANDEL "MESSIAH".
Meno
IF THEY CAN'T, THEY SHOULD GO BACH TO BASICS!
NO.. I THINK ANY CONDUCTOR SHOULD LAY OFFENBACH.
Animato
WHAT? YOU WANT HIM TO THROW HIS BACH OUT?!
THAVES
© 1990 by NEA, Inc.
8/26

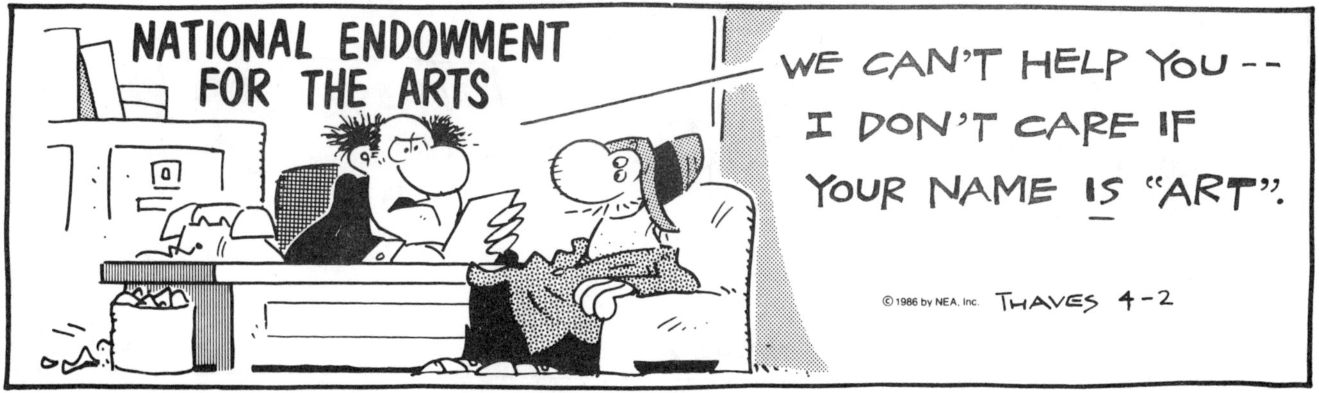
NATIONAL ENDOWMENT FOR THE ARTS
WE CAN'T HELP YOU -- I DON'T CARE IF YOUR NAME IS "ART".
© 1986 by NEA, Inc. THAVES 4-2

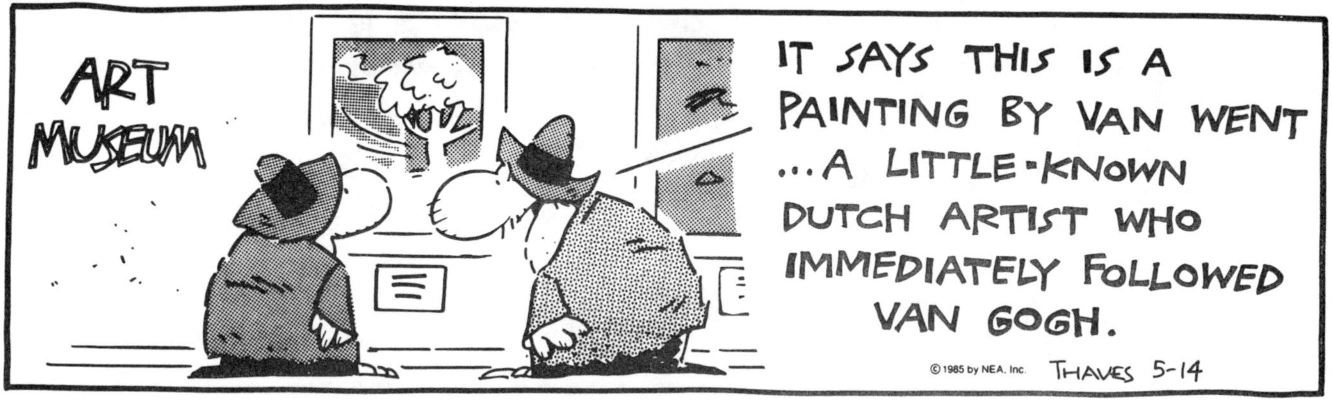
ART MUSEUM
IT SAYS THIS IS A PAINTING BY VAN WENT ...A LITTLE-KNOWN DUTCH ARTIST WHO IMMEDIATELY FOLLOWED VAN GOGH.
© 1985 by NEA, Inc. THAVES 5-14

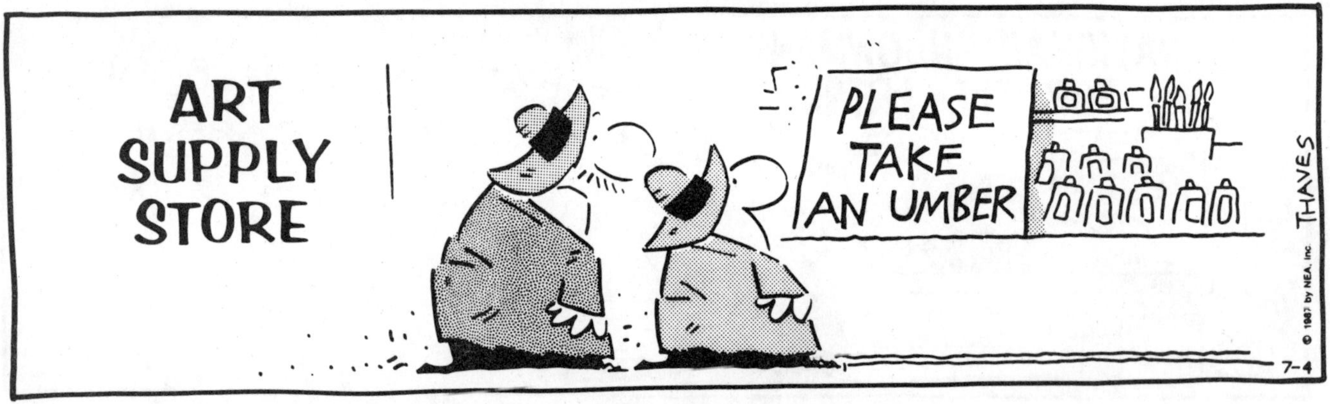
ART
SUPPLY
STORE
PLEASE
TAKE
AN UMBER
THAVES
© 1987 by NEA, Inc.
7-4

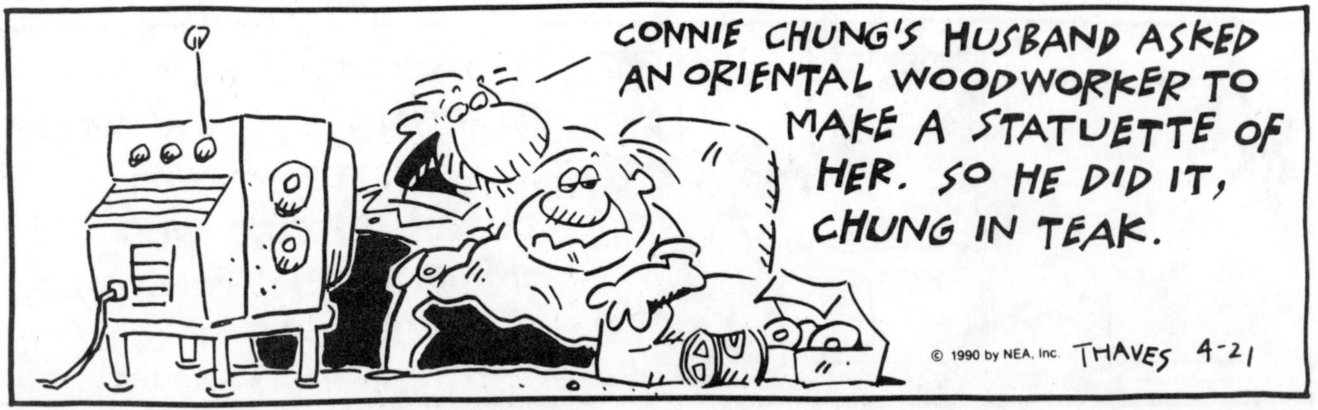
CONNIE CHUNG'S HUSBAND ASKED AN ORIENTAL WOODWORKER TO MAKE A STATUETTE OF HER. SO HE DID IT, CHUNG IN TEAK.
© 1990 by NEA, Inc.
THAVES 4-21

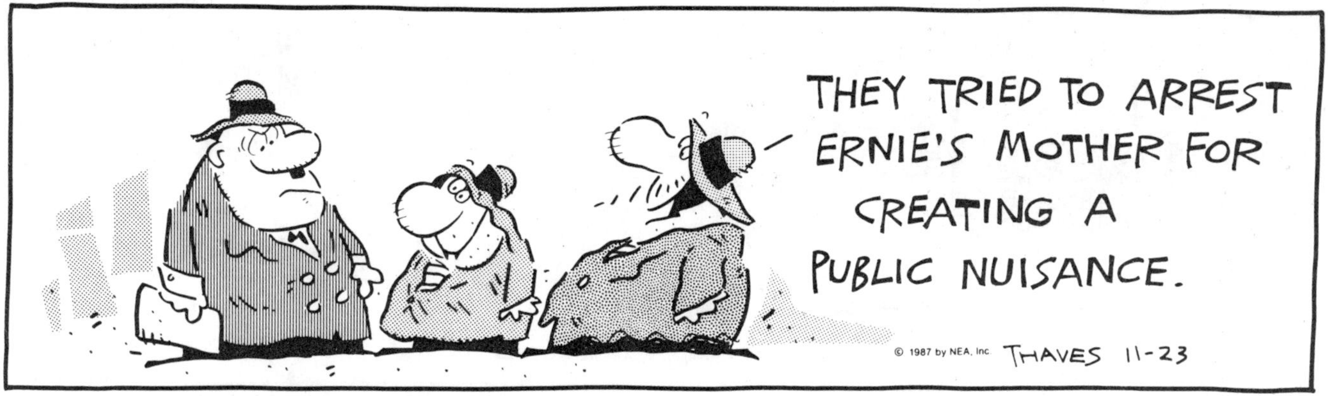
THEY TRIED TO ARREST ERNIE'S MOTHER FOR CREATING A PUBLIC NUISANCE.
© 1987 by NEA, Inc.
THAVES 11-23

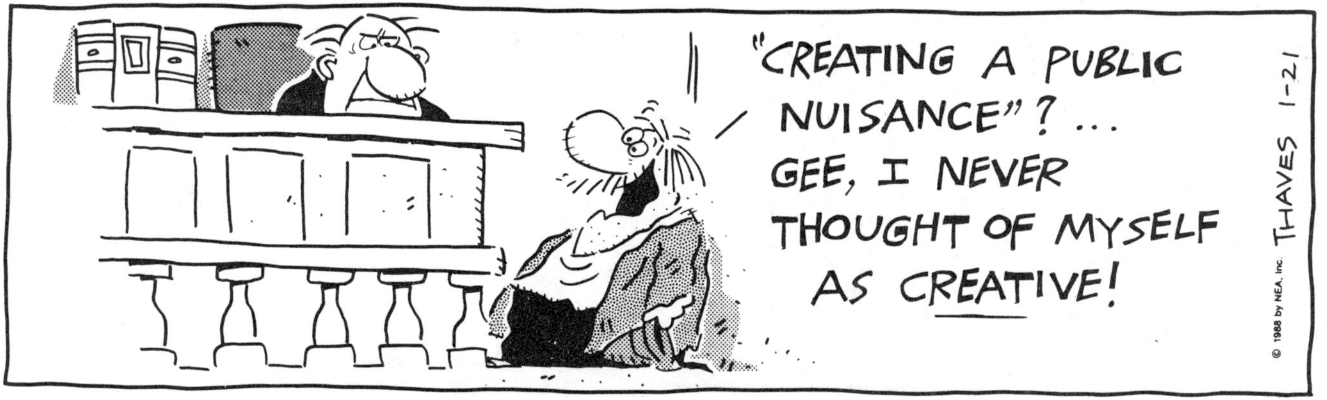
"CREATING A PUBLIC NUISANCE"? ... GEE, I NEVER THOUGHT OF MYSELF AS CREATIVE!
© 1988 by NEA, Inc.
THAVES 1-21

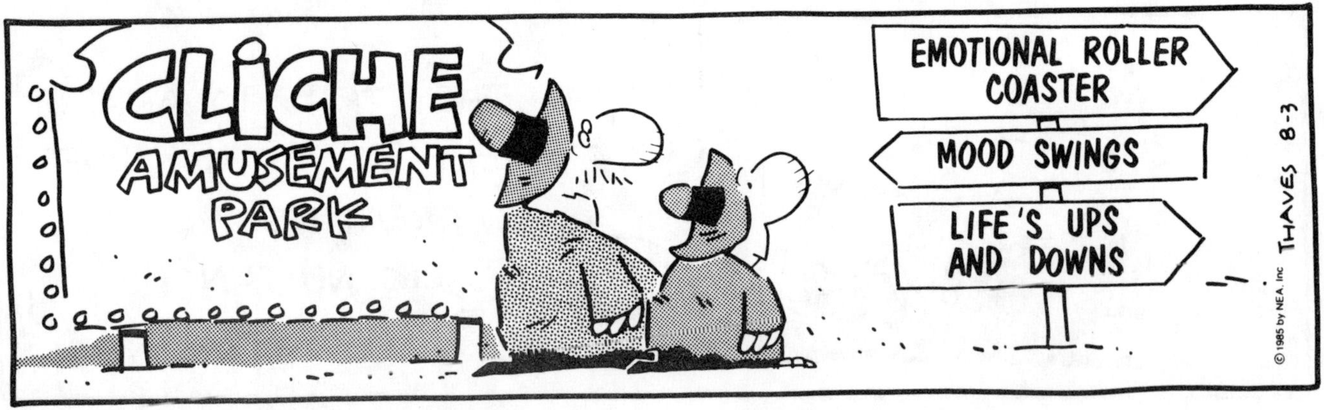
CLICHE
AMUSEMENT
PARK
EMOTIONAL ROLLER COASTER
MOOD SWINGS
LIFE'S UPS AND DOWNS
THAVES 8-3
© 1985 by NEA, Inc

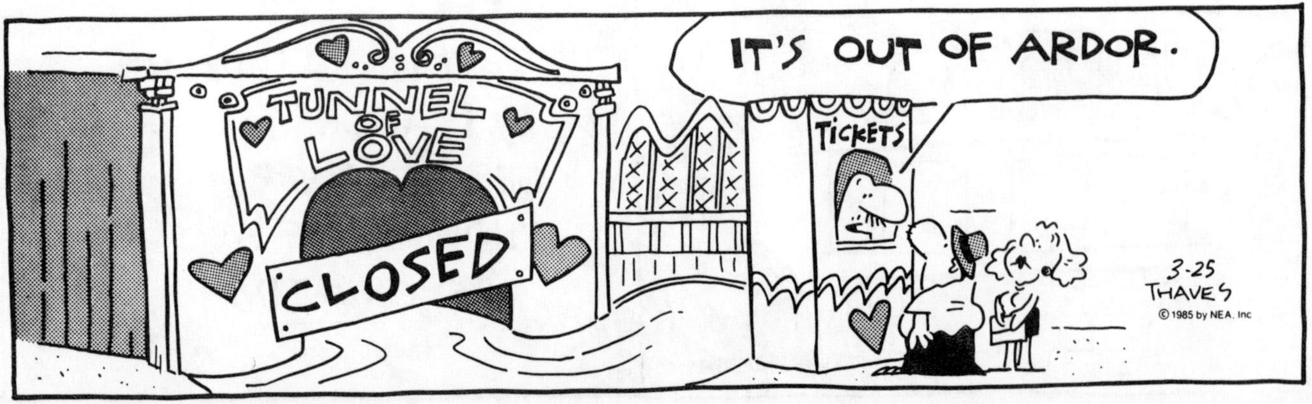
IT'S OUT OF ARDOR.
TUNNEL OF LOVE
CLOSED
TICKETS
3-25
THAVES
© 1985 by NEA, Inc

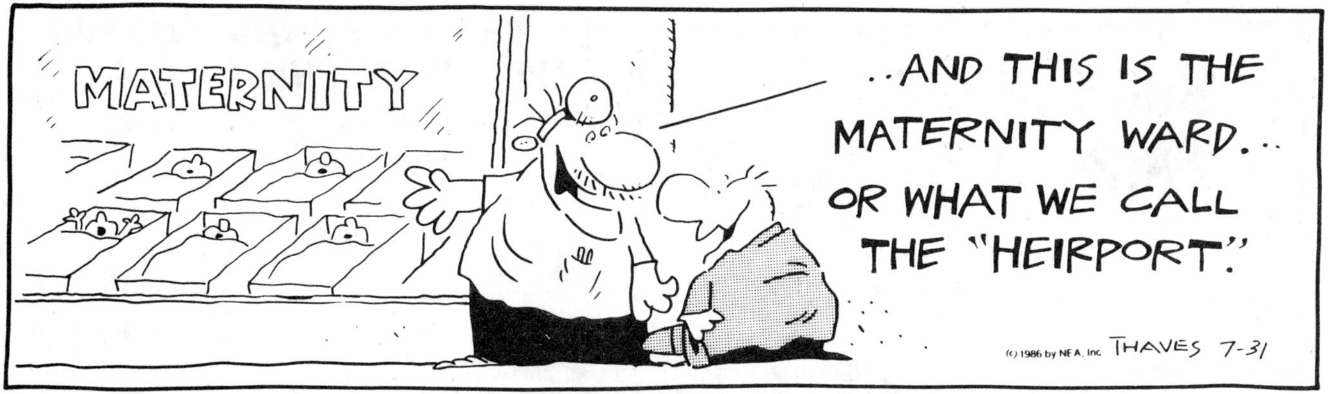
MATERNITY
..AND THIS IS THE MATERNITY WARD... OR WHAT WE CALL THE "HEIRPORT."
(c) 1986 by NEA, Inc
THAVES 7-31

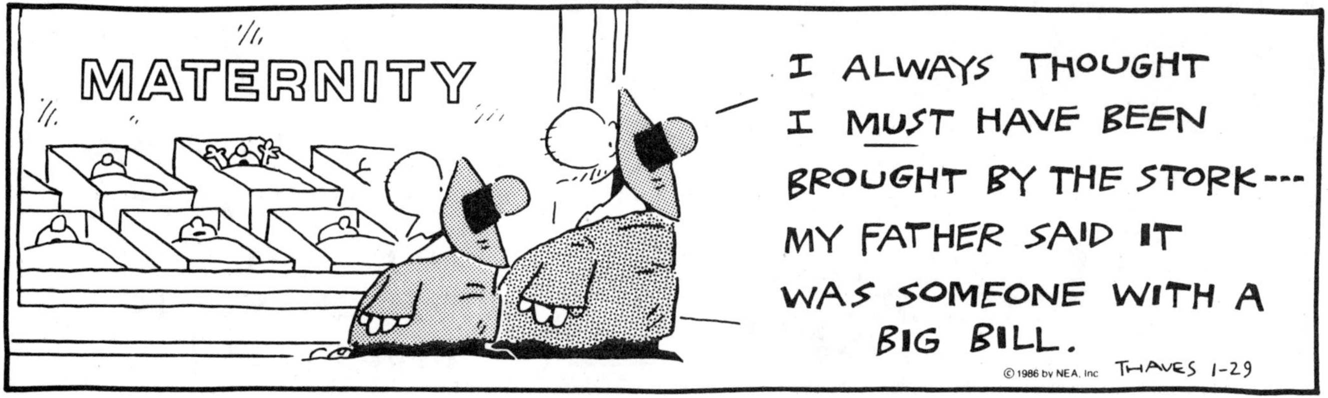
MATERNITY
I ALWAYS THOUGHT I MUST HAVE BEEN BROUGHT BY THE STORK--- MY FATHER SAID IT WAS SOMEONE WITH A BIG BILL.
© 1986 by NEA, Inc
THAVES 1-29

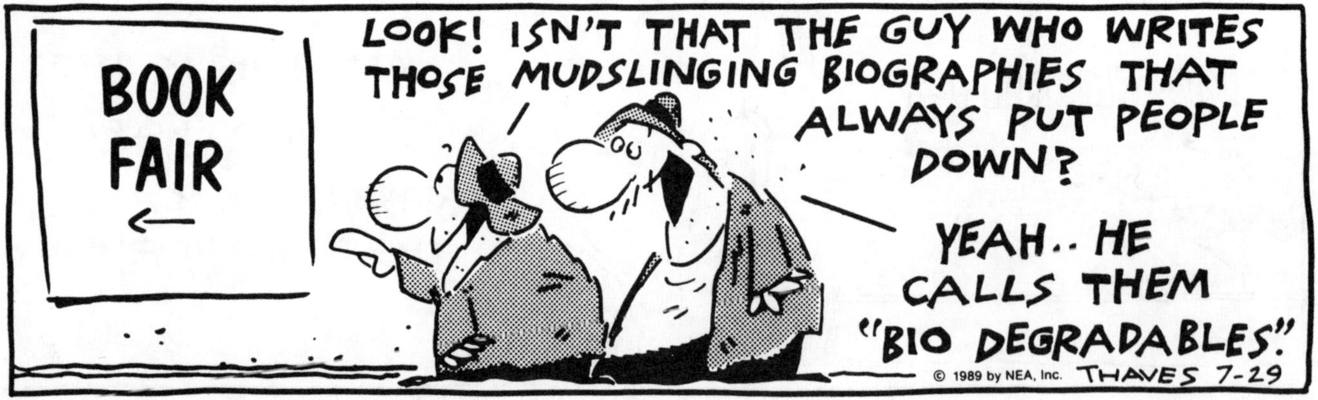
BOOK FAIR
LOOK! ISN'T THAT THE GUY WHO WRITES THOSE MUDSLINGING BIOGRAPHIES THAT ALWAYS PUT PEOPLE DOWN?
YEAH.. HE CALLS THEM "BIO DEGRADABLES."
© 1989 by NEA, Inc. THAVES 7-29

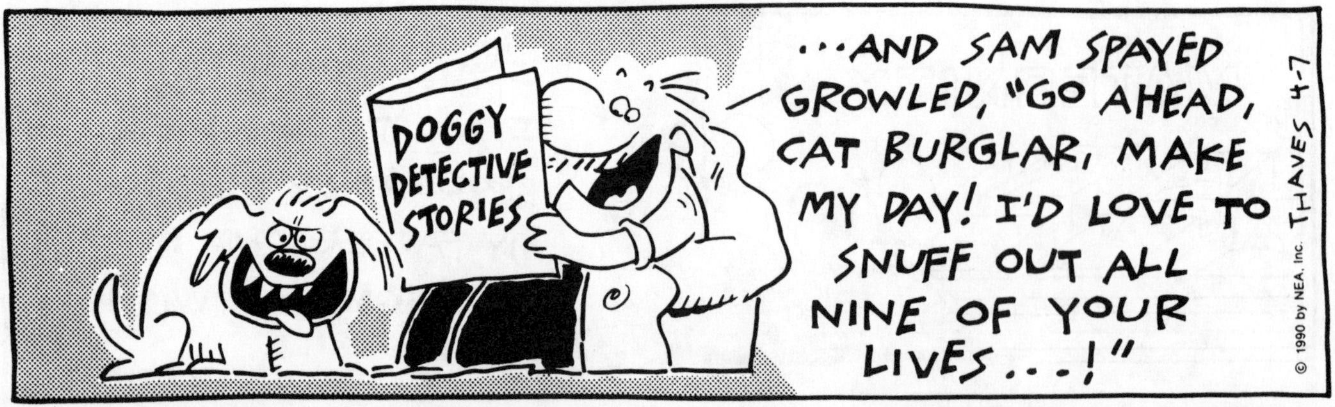
DOGGY DETECTIVE STORIES
...AND SAM SPAYED GROWLED, "GO AHEAD, CAT BURGLAR, MAKE MY DAY! I'D LOVE TO SNUFF OUT ALL NINE OF YOUR LIVES...!"
THAVES 4-7
© 1990 by NEA, Inc.

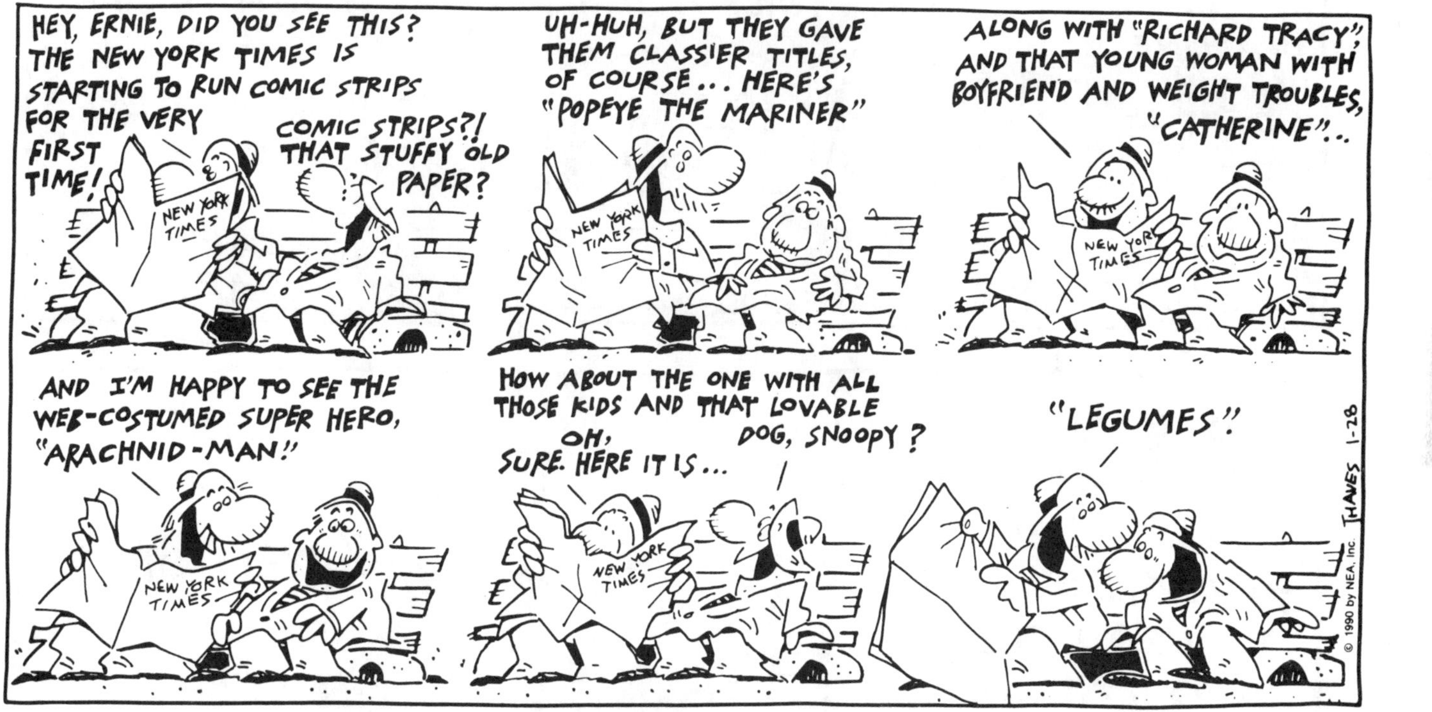
HEY, ERNIE, DID YOU SEE THIS? THE NEW YORK TIMES IS STARTING TO RUN COMIC STRIPS FOR THE VERY FIRST TIME!
COMIC STRIPS?! THAT STUFFY OLD PAPER?
NEW YORK TIMES
UH-HUH, BUT THEY GAVE THEM CLASSIER TITLES, OF COURSE... HERE'S "POPEYE THE MARINER"
NEW YORK TIMES
ALONG WITH "RICHARD TRACY", AND THAT YOUNG WOMAN WITH BOYFRIEND AND WEIGHT TROUBLES, "CATHERINE"...
NEW YORK TIMES
AND I'M HAPPY TO SEE THE WEB-COSTUMED SUPER HERO, "ARACHNID-MAN!"
NEW YORK TIMES
HOW ABOUT THE ONE WITH ALL THOSE KIDS AND THAT LOVABLE DOG, SNOOPY?
OH, SURE. HERE IT IS...
NEW YORK TIMES
"LEGUMES"!
THAVES 1-28
© 1990 by NEA, Inc.

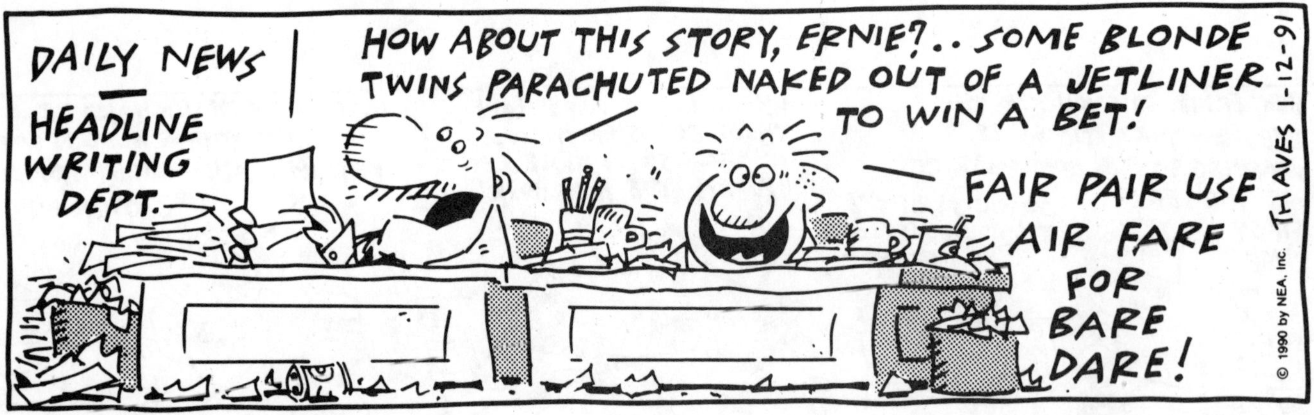
DAILY NEWS — HEADLINE WRITING DEPT.
HOW ABOUT THIS STORY, ERNIE?.. SOME BLONDE TWINS PARACHUTED NAKED OUT OF A JETLINER TO WIN A BET!
FAIR PAIR USE AIR FARE FOR BARE DARE!
THAVES 1-12-91
© 1990 by NEA, Inc.

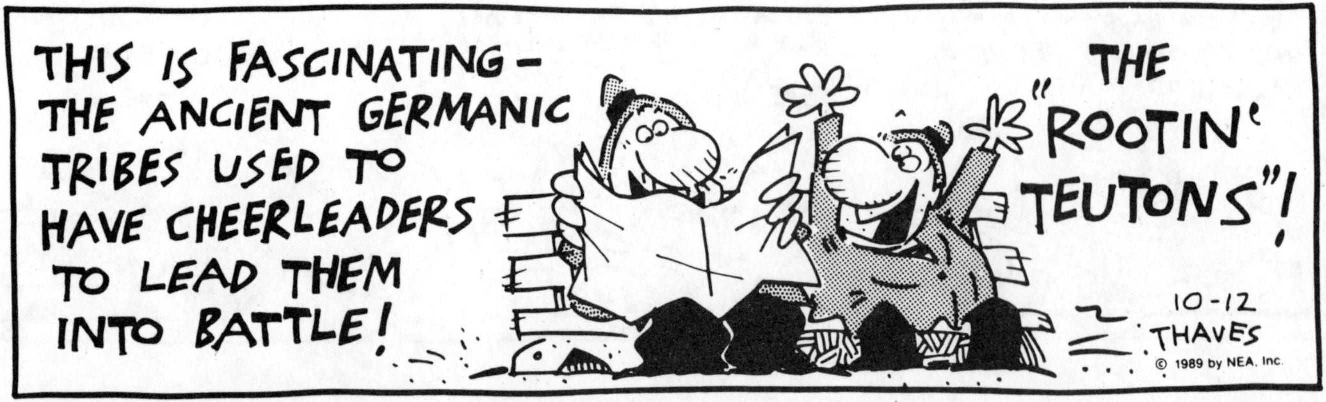
THIS IS FASCINATING — THE ANCIENT GERMANIC TRIBES USED TO HAVE CHEERLEADERS TO LEAD THEM INTO BATTLE!
THE "ROOTIN' TEUTONS"!
10-12 THAVES
© 1989 by NEA, Inc.

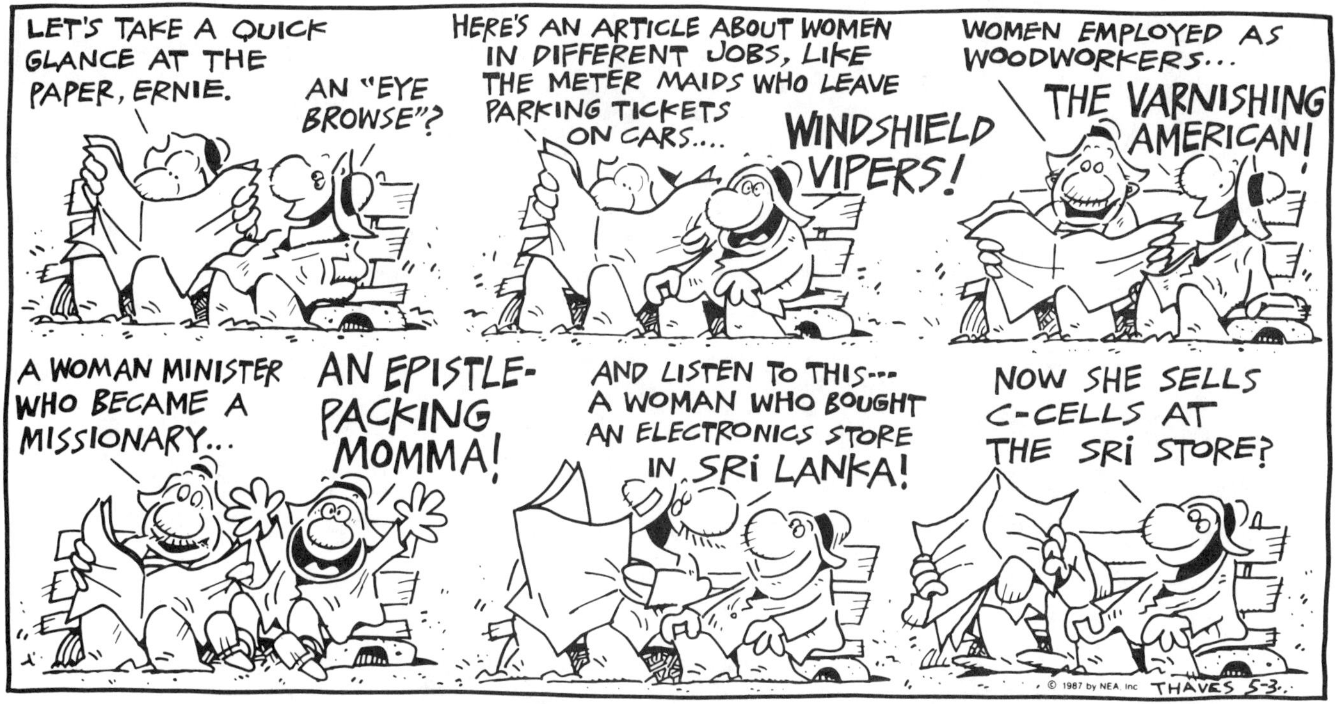
LET'S TAKE A QUICK GLANCE AT THE PAPER, ERNIE.
AN "EYE BROWSE"?
HERE'S AN ARTICLE ABOUT WOMEN IN DIFFERENT JOBS, LIKE THE METER MAIDS WHO LEAVE PARKING TICKETS ON CARS....
WINDSHIELD VIPERS!
WOMEN EMPLOYED AS WOODWORKERS...
THE VARNISHING AMERICAN!
A WOMAN MINISTER WHO BECAME A MISSIONARY...
AN EPISTLE-PACKING MOMMA!
AND LISTEN TO THIS--- A WOMAN WHO BOUGHT AN ELECTRONICS STORE IN SRI LANKA!
NOW SHE SELLS C-CELLS AT THE SRI STORE?
© 1987 by NEA, Inc
THAVES 5-3

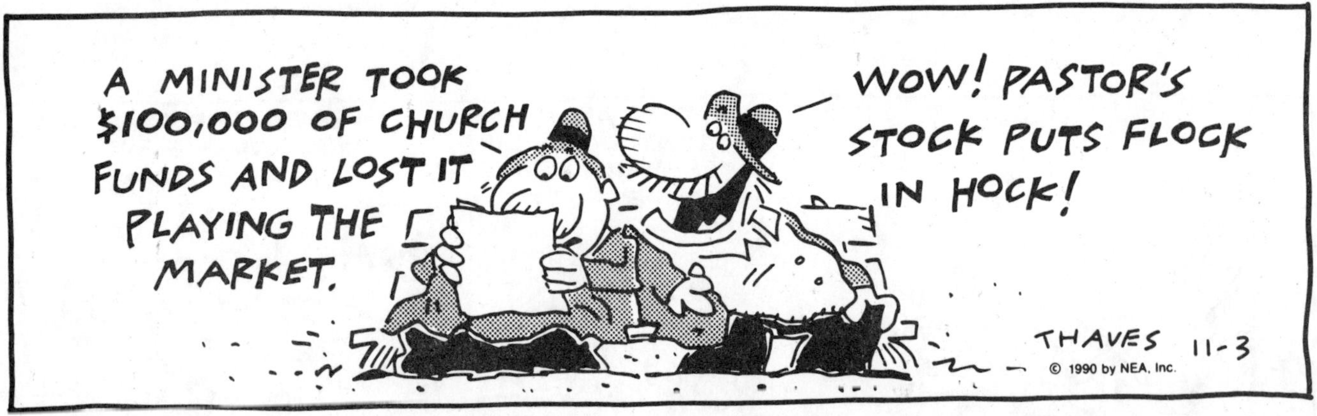
A MINISTER TOOK $100,000 OF CHURCH FUNDS AND LOST IT PLAYING THE MARKET.
WOW! PASTOR'S STOCK PUTS FLOCK IN HOCK!
THAVES 11-3
© 1990 by NEA, Inc.

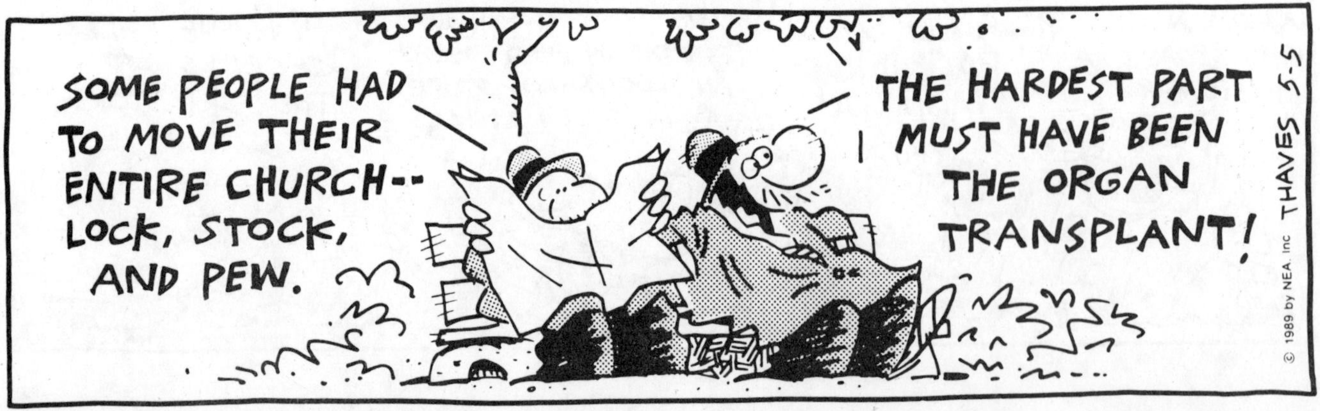
SOME PEOPLE HAD TO MOVE THEIR ENTIRE CHURCH-- LOCK, STOCK, AND PEW.
THE HARDEST PART MUST HAVE BEEN THE ORGAN TRANSPLANT!
THAVES 5-5
© 1989 by NEA, Inc

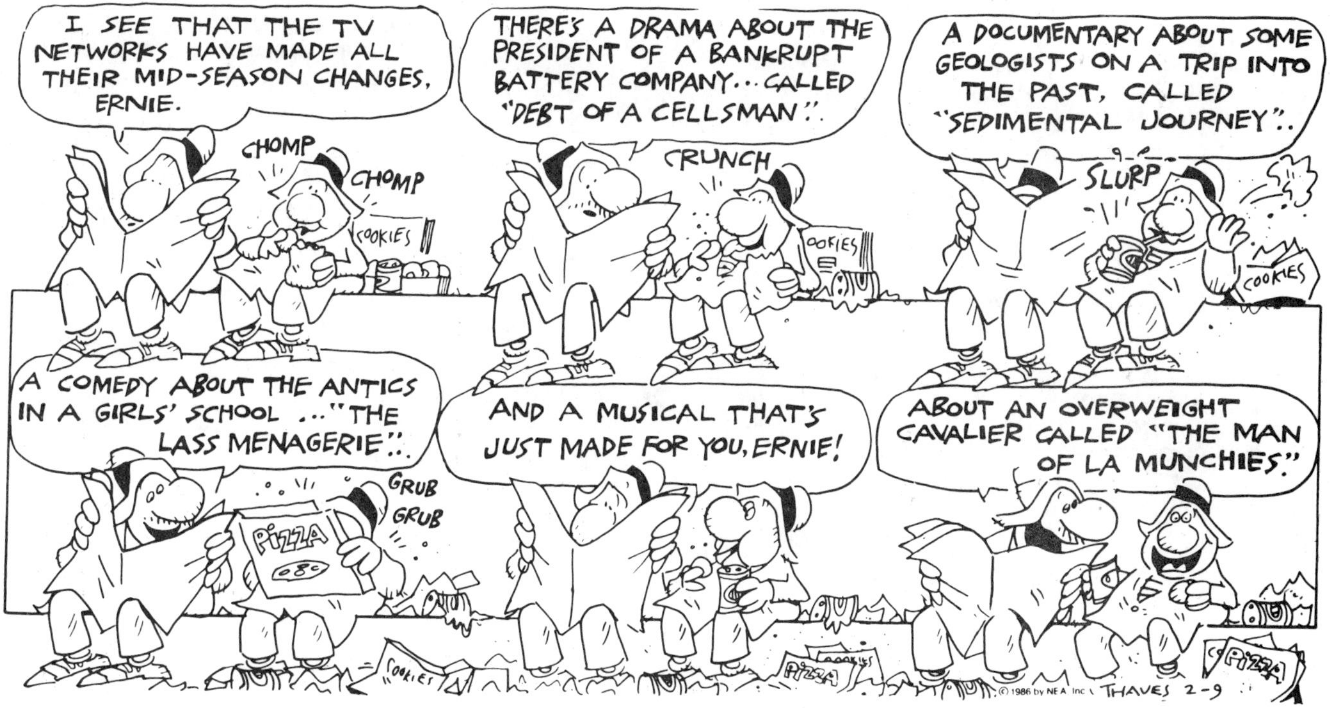
I SEE THAT THE TV NETWORKS HAVE MADE ALL THEIR MID-SEASON CHANGES, ERNIE.
CHOMP
CHOMP
COOKIES
THERE'S A DRAMA ABOUT THE PRESIDENT OF A BANKRUPT BATTERY COMPANY... CALLED "DEBT OF A CELLSMAN".
CRUNCH
COOKIES
A DOCUMENTARY ABOUT SOME GEOLOGISTS ON A TRIP INTO THE PAST, CALLED "SEDIMENTAL JOURNEY".
SLURP
COOKIES
A COMEDY ABOUT THE ANTICS IN A GIRLS' SCHOOL ... "THE LASS MENAGERIE".
GRUB
GRUB
PIZZA
AND A MUSICAL THAT'S JUST MADE FOR YOU, ERNIE!
ABOUT AN OVERWEIGHT CAVALIER CALLED "THE MAN OF LA MUNCHIES."
COOKIES
PIZZA
PIZZA
© 1986 by NEA, Inc.
THAVES 2-9

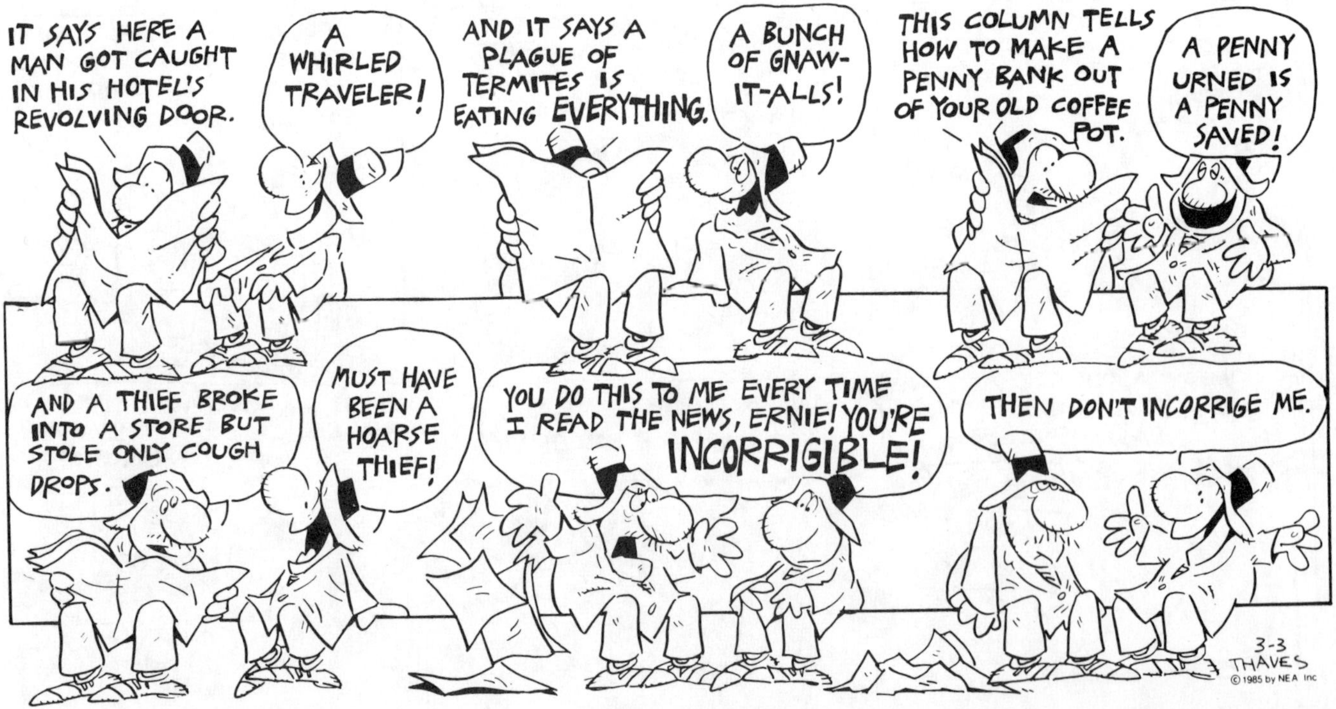
IT SAYS HERE A MAN GOT CAUGHT IN HIS HOTEL'S REVOLVING DOOR.
A WHIRLED TRAVELER!
AND IT SAYS A PLAGUE OF TERMITES IS EATING EVERYTHING.
A BUNCH OF GNAW-IT-ALLS!
THIS COLUMN TELLS HOW TO MAKE A PENNY BANK OUT OF YOUR OLD COFFEE POT.
A PENNY URNED IS A PENNY SAVED!
AND A THIEF BROKE INTO A STORE BUT STOLE ONLY COUGH DROPS.
MUST HAVE BEEN A HOARSE THIEF!
YOU DO THIS TO ME EVERY TIME I READ THE NEWS, ERNIE! YOU'RE INCORRIGIBLE!
THEN DON'T INCORRIGE ME.
3-3
THAVES
© 1985 by NEA Inc

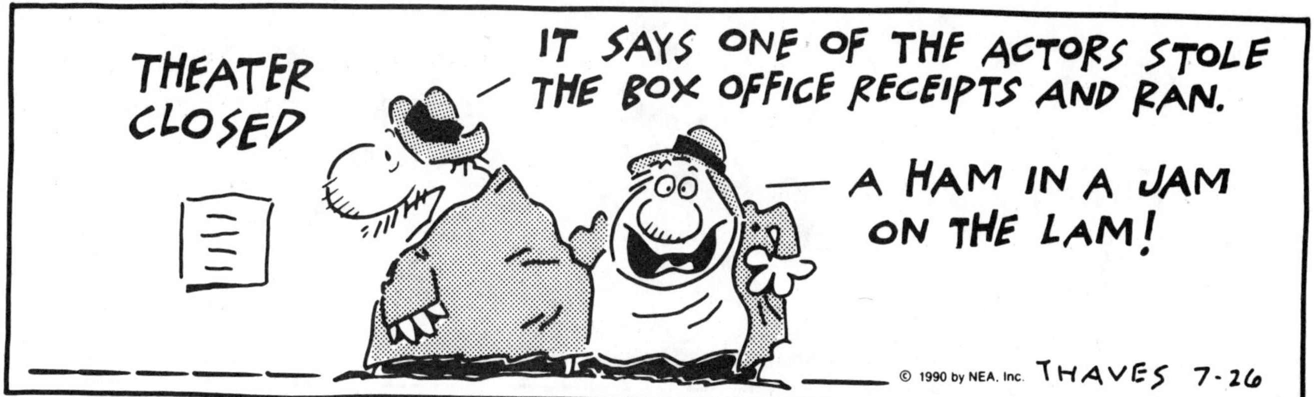
THEATER CLOSED
IT SAYS ONE OF THE ACTORS STOLE THE BOX OFFICE RECEIPTS AND RAN.
A HAM IN A JAM ON THE LAM!
© 1990 by NEA, Inc.
THAVES 7-26

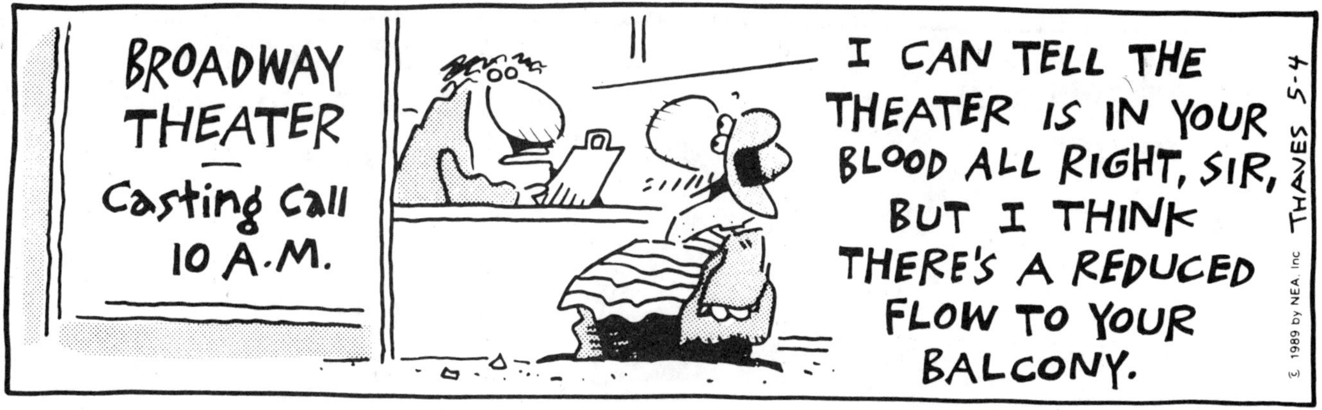
BROADWAY THEATER
—
Casting Call 10 A.M.
I CAN TELL THE THEATER IS IN YOUR BLOOD ALL RIGHT, SIR, BUT I THINK THERE'S A REDUCED FLOW TO YOUR BALCONY.
© 1989 by NEA, Inc
THAVES 5-4

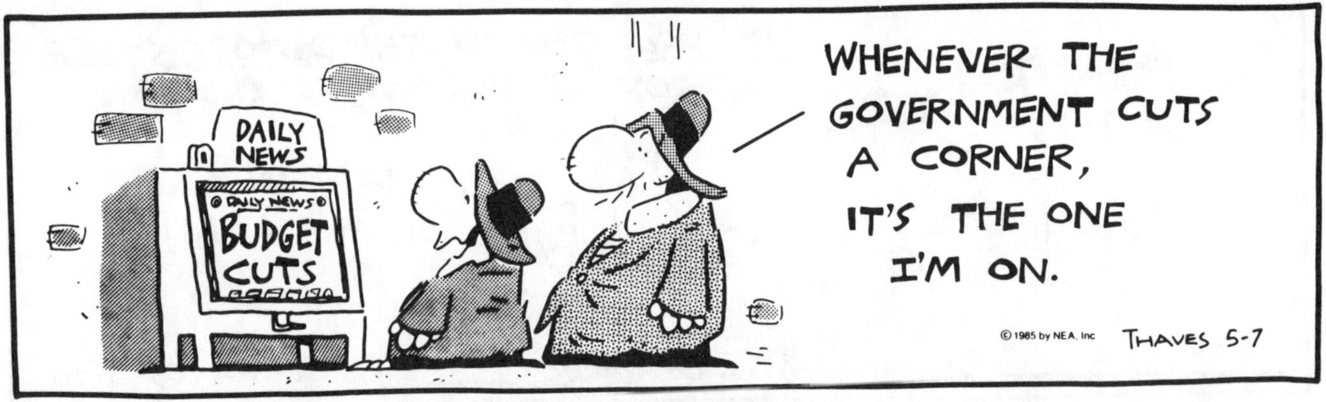
DAILY NEWS
DAILY NEWS
BUDGET CUTS
WHENEVER THE GOVERNMENT CUTS A CORNER, IT'S THE ONE I'M ON.
© 1985 by NEA, Inc
THAVES 5-7

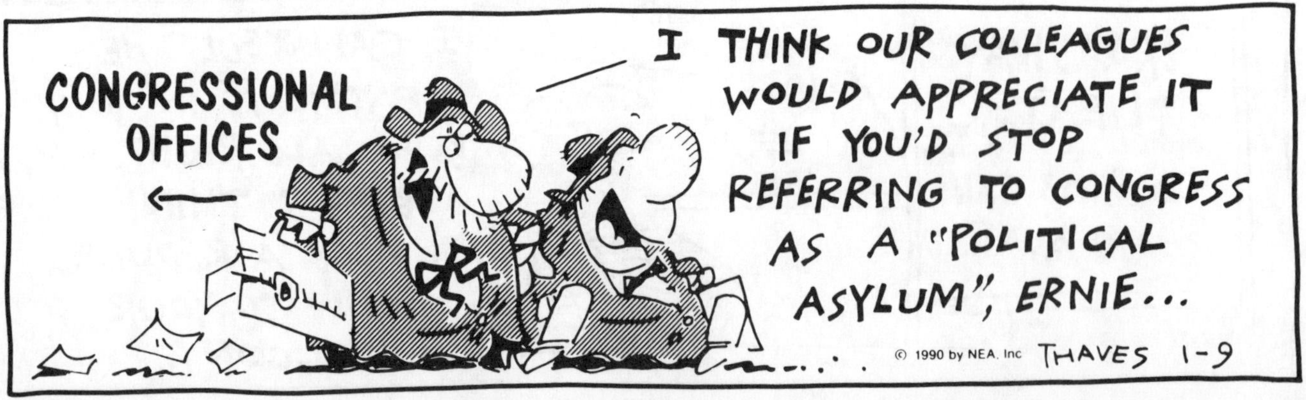
CONGRESSIONAL OFFICES
I THINK OUR COLLEAGUES WOULD APPRECIATE IT IF YOU'D STOP REFERRING TO CONGRESS AS A "POLITICAL ASYLUM", ERNIE...
© 1990 by NEA, Inc
THAVES 1-9

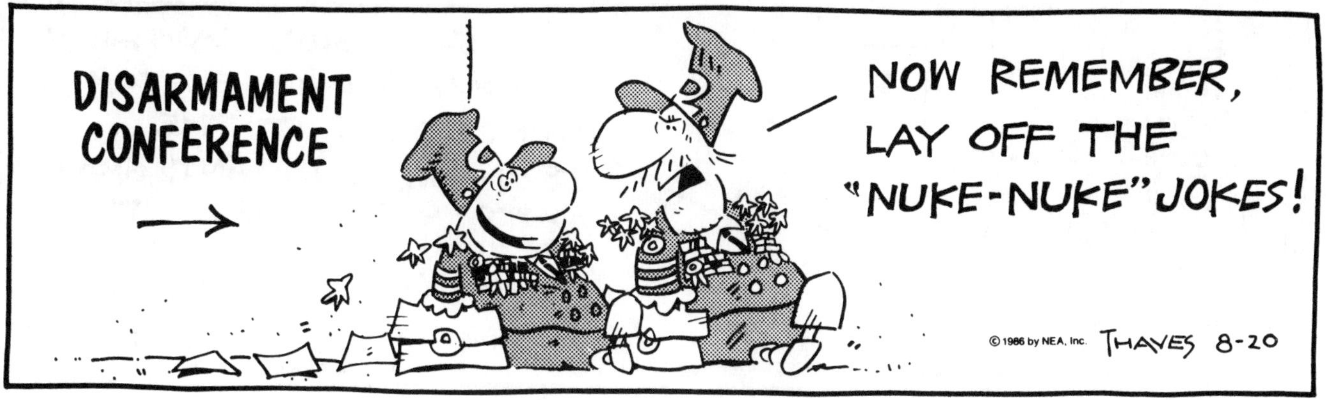
DISARMAMENT CONFERENCE
NOW REMEMBER, LAY OFF THE "NUKE-NUKE" JOKES!
© 1986 by NEA, Inc.
THAVES 8-20

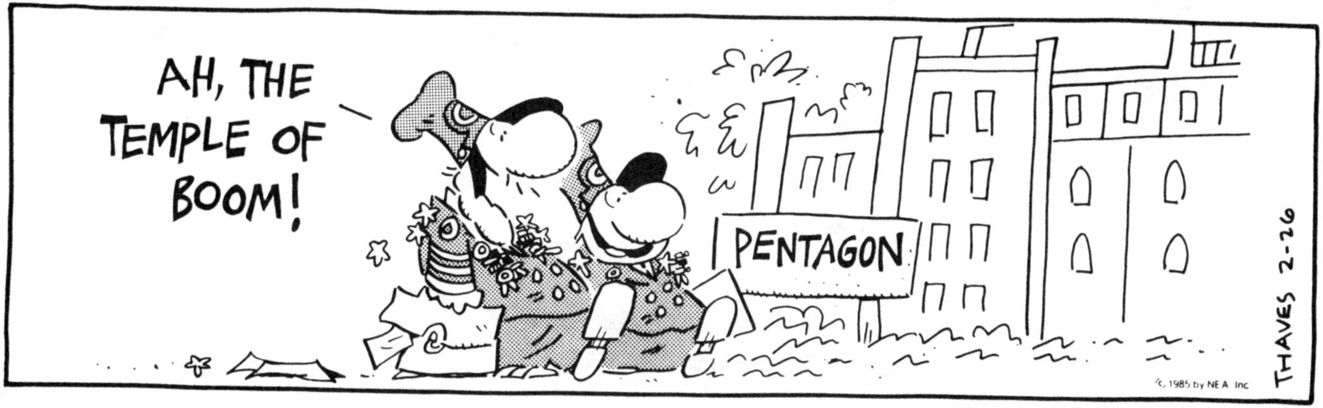
AH, THE TEMPLE OF BOOM!
PENTAGON
THAVES 2-26
© 1985 by NEA Inc

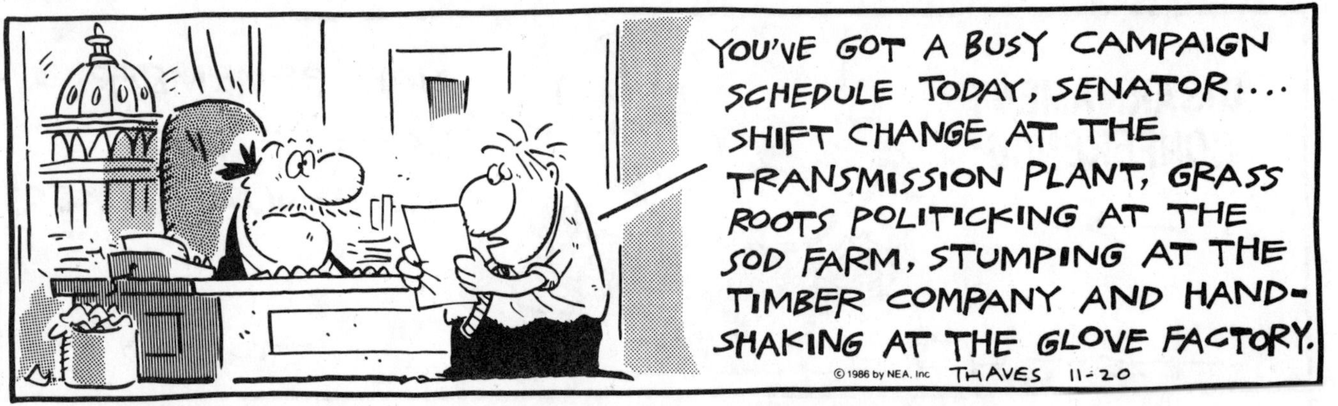
YOU'VE GOT A BUSY CAMPAIGN SCHEDULE TODAY, SENATOR.... SHIFT CHANGE AT THE TRANSMISSION PLANT, GRASS ROOTS POLITICKING AT THE SOD FARM, STUMPING AT THE TIMBER COMPANY AND HAND-SHAKING AT THE GLOVE FACTORY.
© 1986 by NEA, Inc
THAVES 11-20

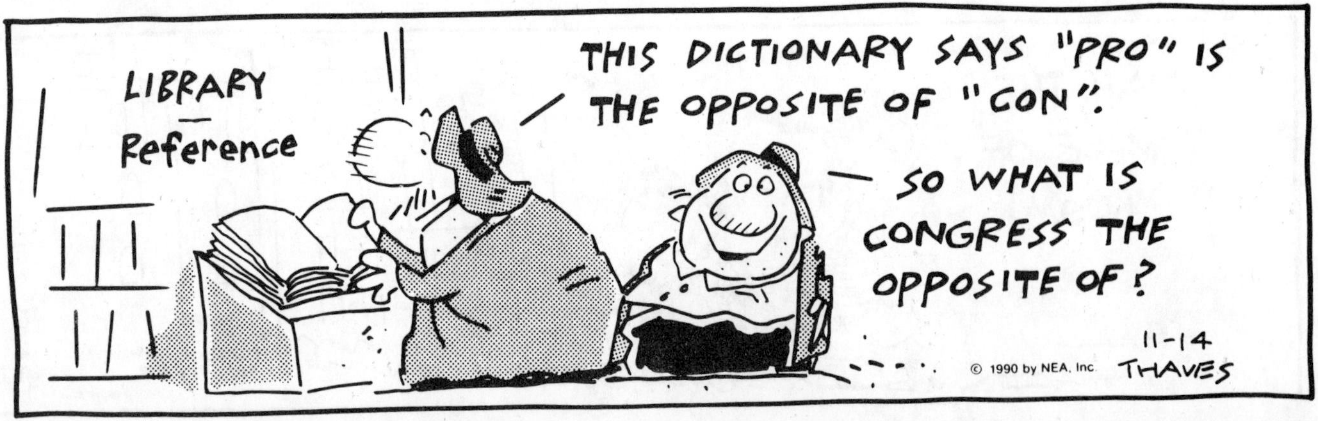
LIBRARY
Reference
THIS DICTIONARY SAYS "PRO" IS THE OPPOSITE OF "CON".
SO WHAT IS CONGRESS THE OPPOSITE OF?
11-14
© 1990 by NEA, Inc
THAVES

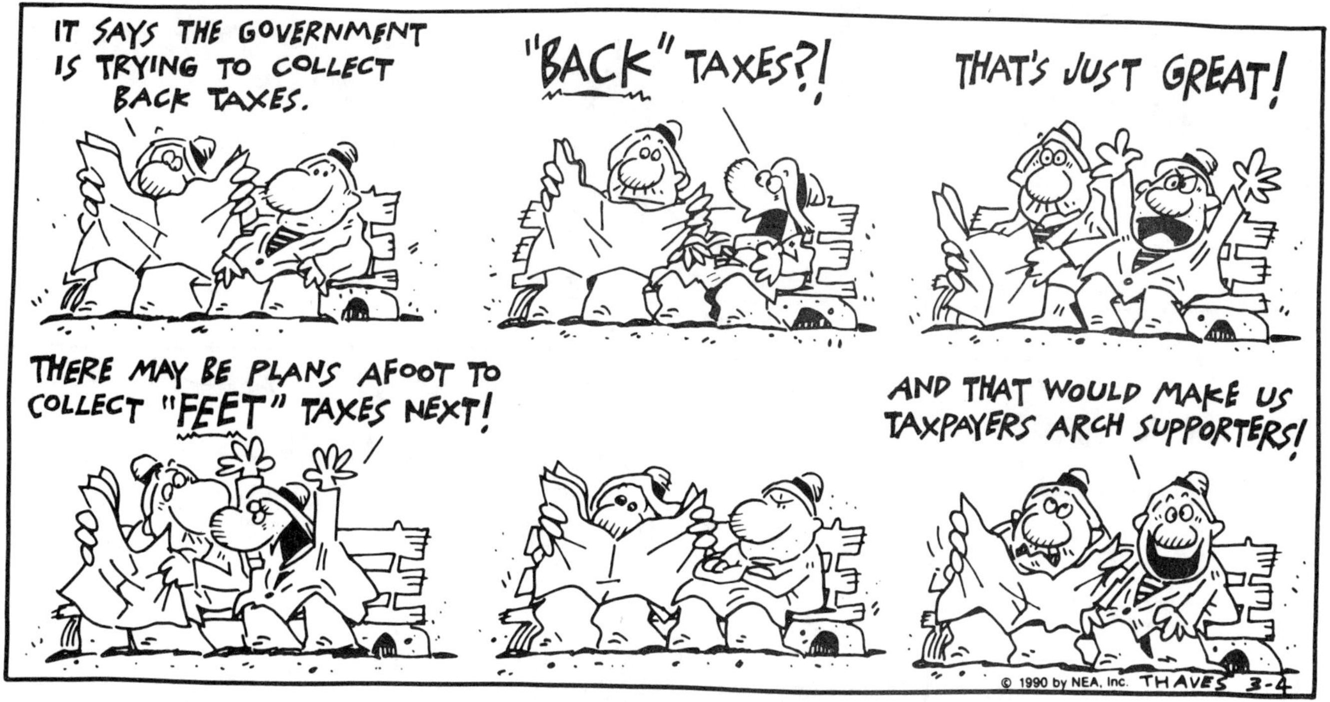
IT SAYS THE GOVERNMENT IS TRYING TO COLLECT BACK TAXES.
"BACK" TAXES?!
THAT'S JUST GREAT!
THERE MAY BE PLANS AFOOT TO COLLECT "FEET" TAXES NEXT!
AND THAT WOULD MAKE US TAXPAYERS ARCH SUPPORTERS!
© 1990 by NEA, Inc. THAVES 3-4

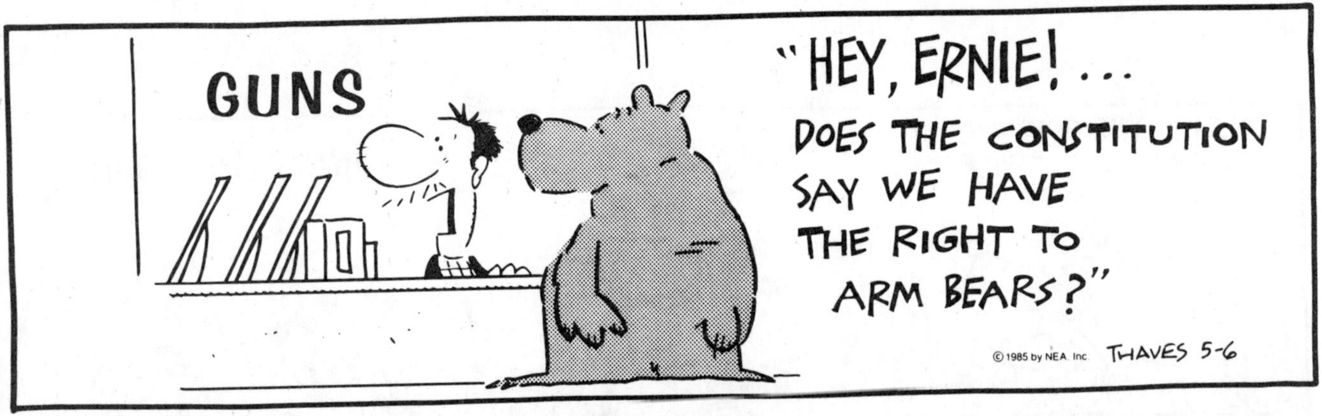
GUNS
"HEY, ERNIE! ...
DOES THE CONSTITUTION
SAY WE HAVE
THE RIGHT TO
ARM BEARS?"
© 1985 by NEA. Inc.
THAVES 5-6

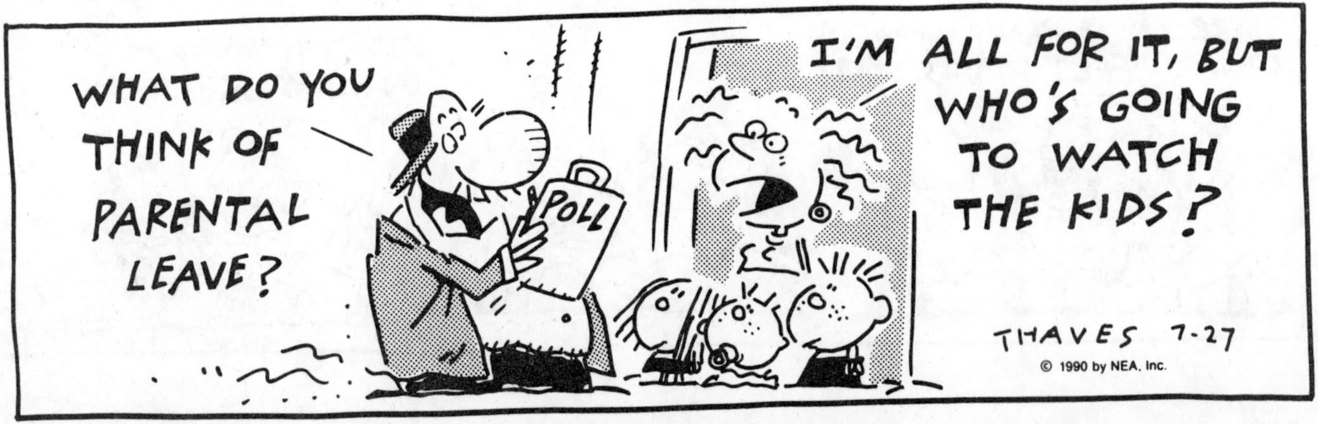
WHAT DO YOU
THINK OF
PARENTAL
LEAVE?
POLL
I'M ALL FOR IT, BUT
WHO'S GOING
TO WATCH
THE KIDS?
THAVES 7-27
© 1990 by NEA, Inc.

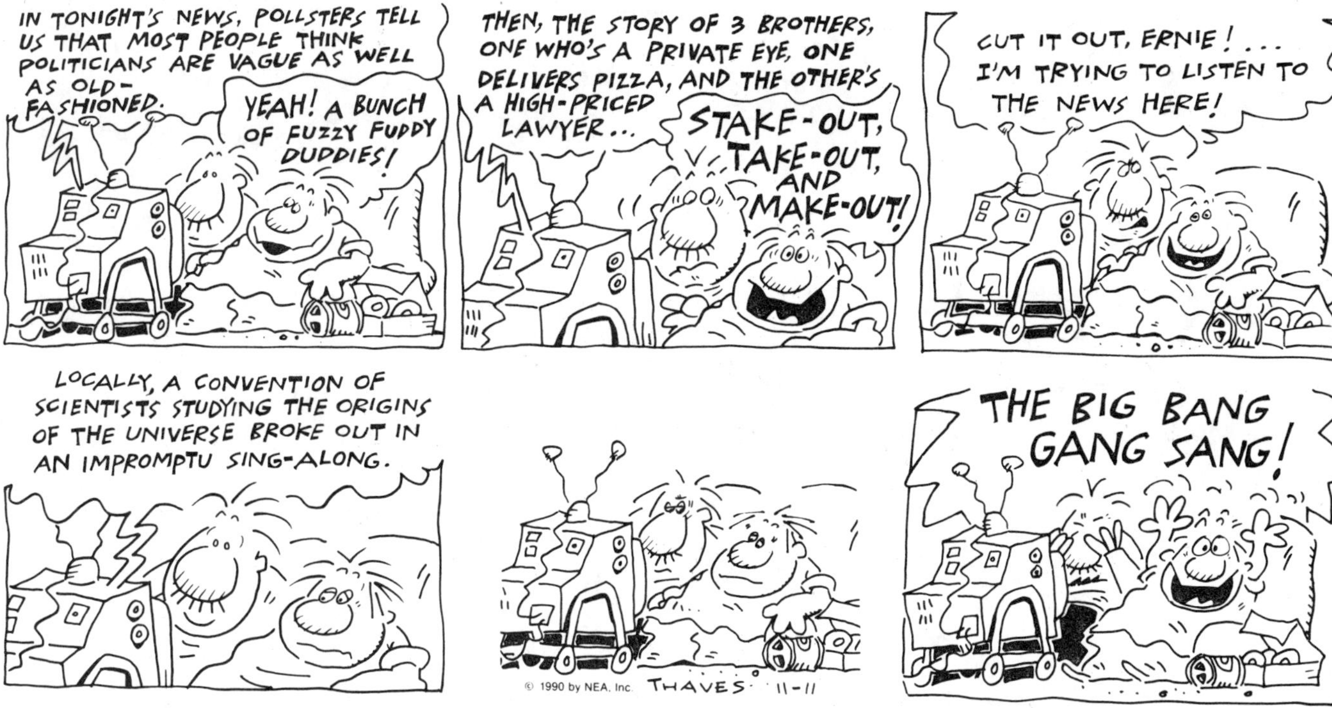

IN TONIGHT'S NEWS, POLLSTERS TELL US THAT MOST PEOPLE THINK POLITICIANS ARE VAGUE AS WELL AS OLD-FASHIONED.
YEAH! A BUNCH OF FUZZY FUDDY DUDDIES!
THEN, THE STORY OF 3 BROTHERS, ONE WHO'S A PRIVATE EYE, ONE DELIVERS PIZZA, AND THE OTHER'S A HIGH-PRICED LAWYER...
STAKE-OUT, TAKE-OUT, AND MAKE-OUT!
CUT IT OUT, ERNIE! ... I'M TRYING TO LISTEN TO THE NEWS HERE!
LOCALLY, A CONVENTION OF SCIENTISTS STUDYING THE ORIGINS OF THE UNIVERSE BROKE OUT IN AN IMPROMPTU SING-ALONG.
THE BIG BANG GANG SANG!

 THAVES 11-11

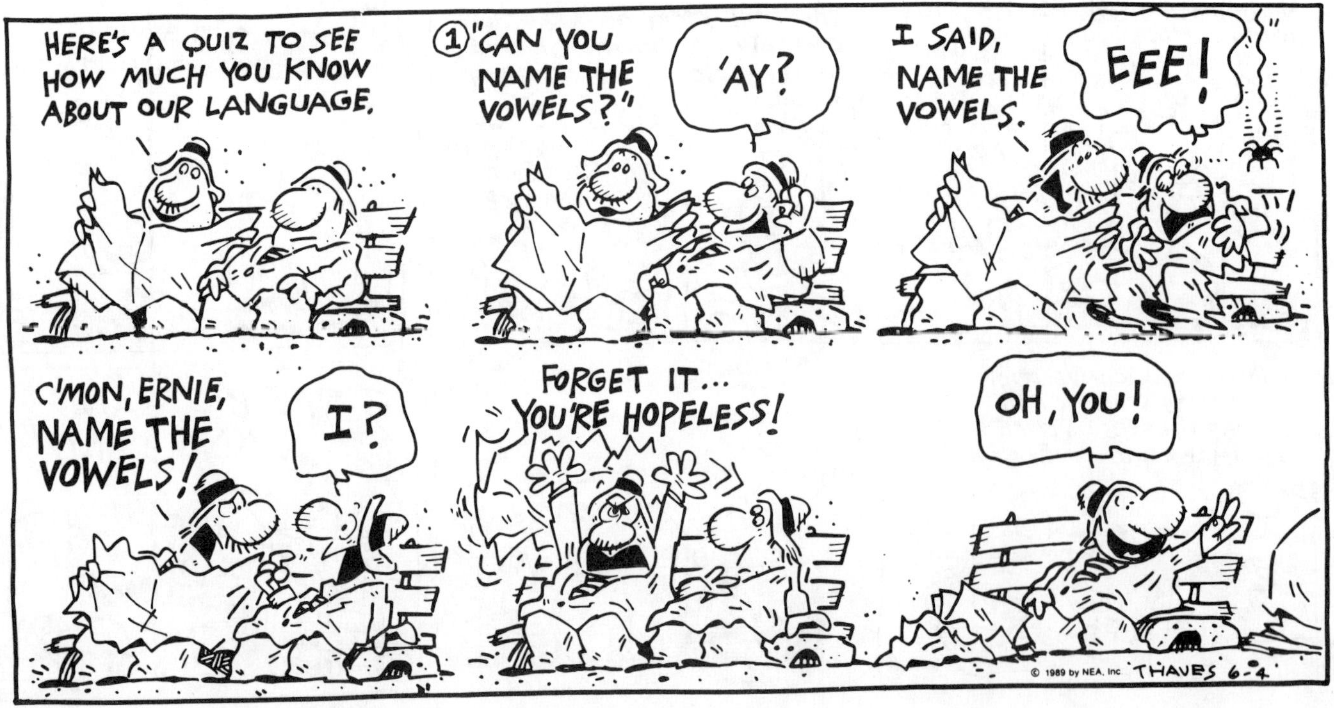
HERE'S A QUIZ TO SEE HOW MUCH YOU KNOW ABOUT OUR LANGUAGE.
①"CAN YOU NAME THE VOWELS?"
'AY?
I SAID, NAME THE VOWELS.
EEE!
C'MON, ERNIE, NAME THE VOWELS!
I?
FORGET IT... YOU'RE HOPELESS!
OH, YOU!
© 1989 by NEA, Inc
THAVES 6-4

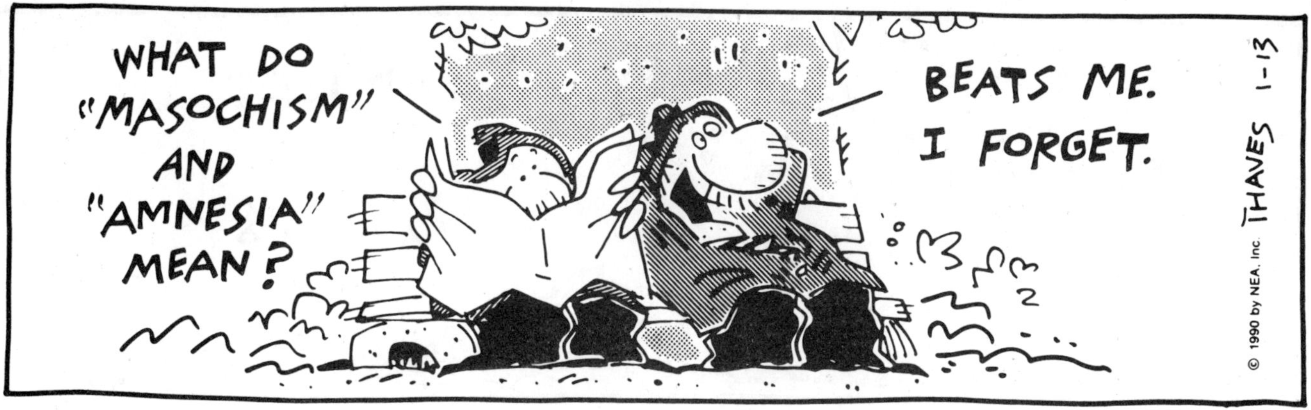
WHAT DO "MASOCHISM" AND "AMNESIA" MEAN?
BEATS ME. I FORGET.
THAVES 1-13
© 1990 by NEA, Inc.

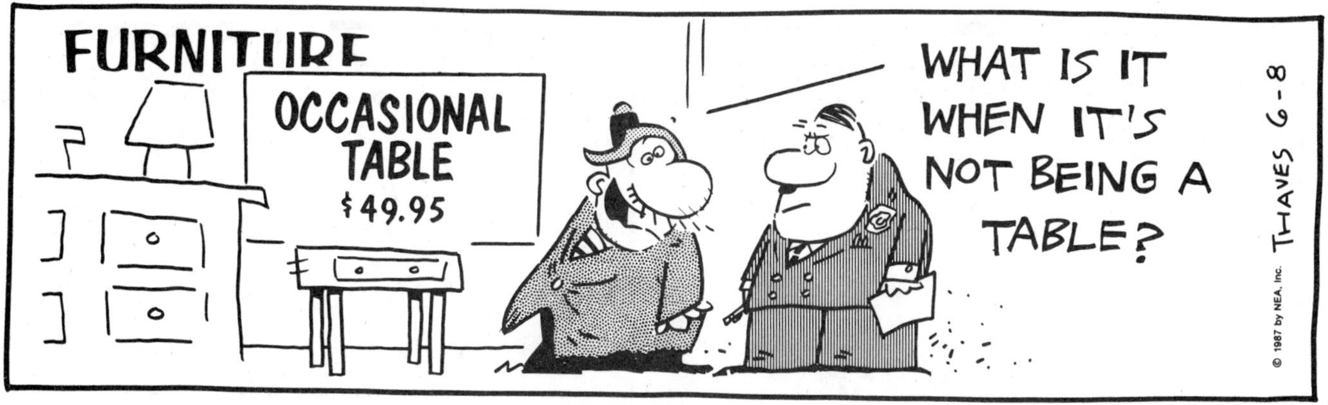
FURNITURE
OCCASIONAL TABLE $49.95
WHAT IS IT WHEN IT'S NOT BEING A TABLE?
THAVES 6-8
© 1987 by NEA, Inc.

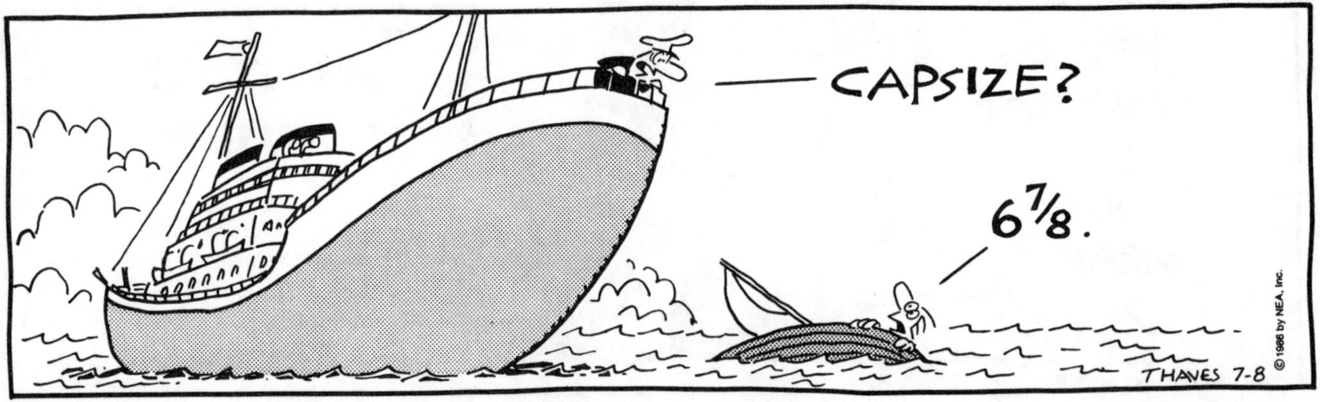
CAPSIZE?
6 7/8.
THAVES 7-8
© 1986 by NEA, Inc.

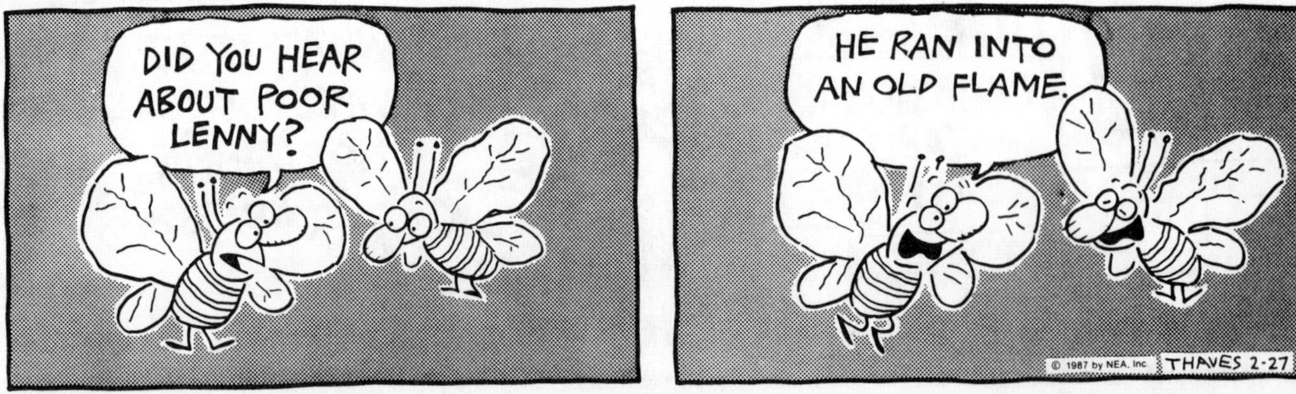
DID YOU HEAR ABOUT POOR LENNY?
HE RAN INTO AN OLD FLAME.
© 1987 by NEA, Inc.
THAVES 2-27

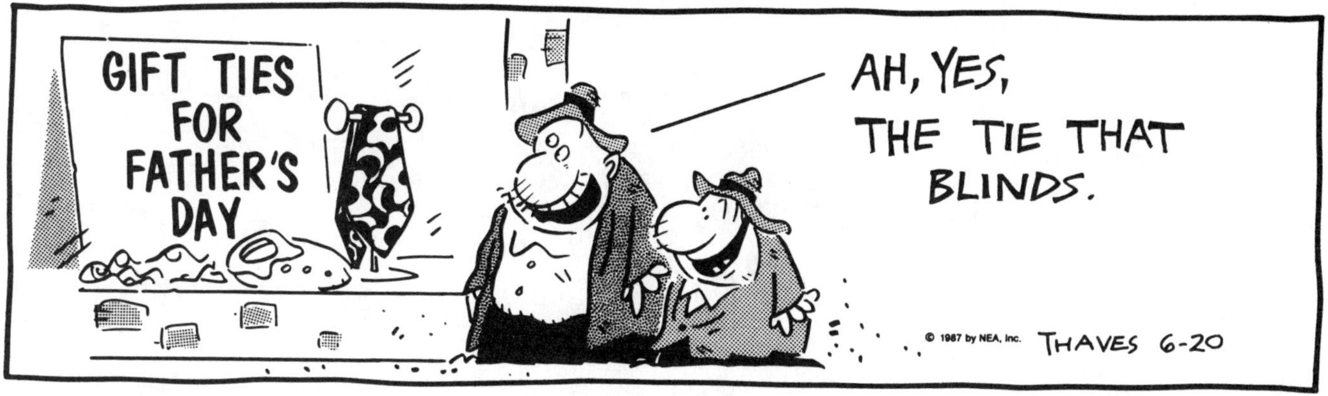
GIFT TIES FOR FATHER'S DAY
AH, YES, THE TIE THAT BLINDS.
© 1987 by NEA, Inc.
THAVES 6-20

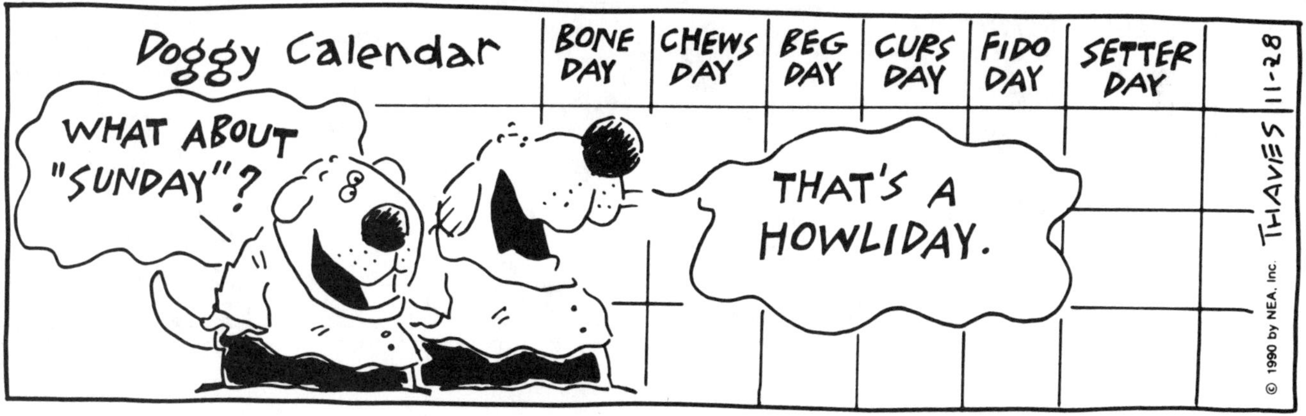
Doggy Calendar
BONE DAY
CHEWS DAY
BEG DAY
CURS DAY
FIDO DAY
SETTER DAY
WHAT ABOUT "SUNDAY"?
THAT'S A HOWLIDAY.
THAVES 11-28
© 1990 by NEA, Inc.

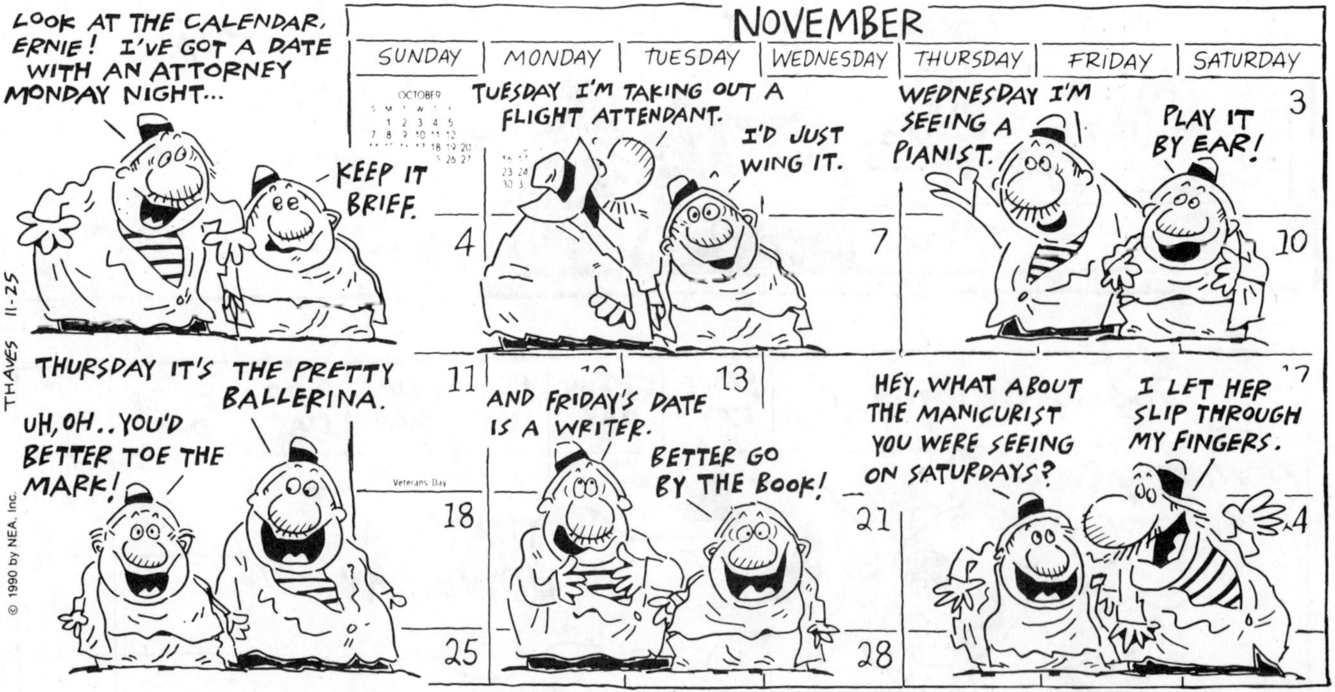
LOOK AT THE CALENDAR, ERNIE! I'VE GOT A DATE WITH AN ATTORNEY MONDAY NIGHT...
KEEP IT BRIEF.
NOVEMBER
SUNDAY
MONDAY
TUESDAY
WEDNESDAY
THURSDAY
FRIDAY
SATURDAY
TUESDAY I'M TAKING OUT A FLIGHT ATTENDANT.
I'D JUST WING IT.
WEDNESDAY I'M SEEING A PIANIST.
PLAY IT BY EAR!
THURSDAY IT'S THE PRETTY BALLERINA.
UH, OH.. YOU'D BETTER TOE THE MARK!
AND FRIDAY'S DATE IS A WRITER.
BETTER GO BY THE BOOK!
HEY, WHAT ABOUT THE MANICURIST YOU WERE SEEING ON SATURDAYS?
I LET HER SLIP THROUGH MY FINGERS.
Veterans Day
THAVES 11-25
© 1990 by NEA, Inc.

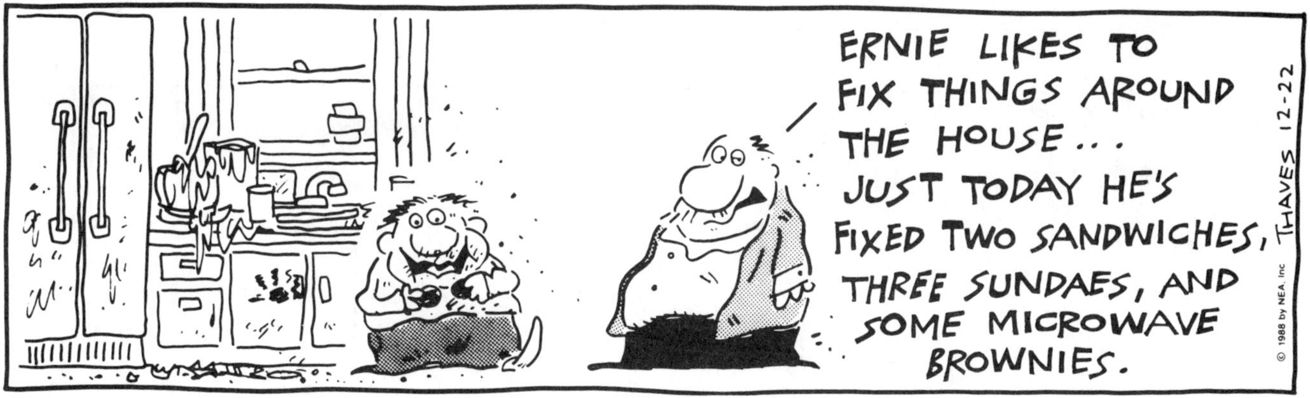
ERNIE LIKES TO FIX THINGS AROUND THE HOUSE... JUST TODAY HE'S FIXED TWO SANDWICHES, THREE SUNDAES, AND SOME MICROWAVE BROWNIES.
THAVES 12-22
© 1988 by NEA, Inc

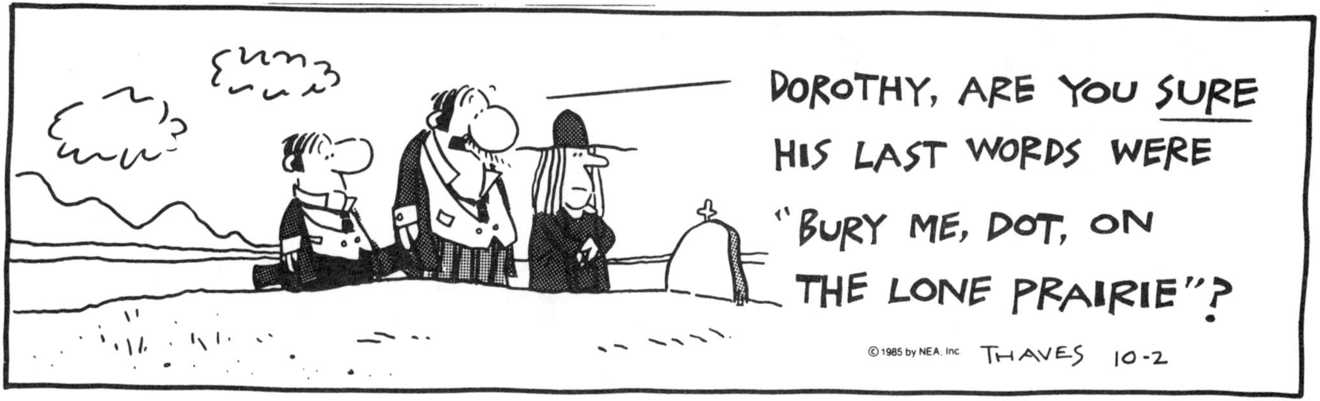
DOROTHY, ARE YOU SURE HIS LAST WORDS WERE "BURY ME, DOT, ON THE LONE PRAIRIE"?
© 1985 by NEA, Inc
THAVES 10-2

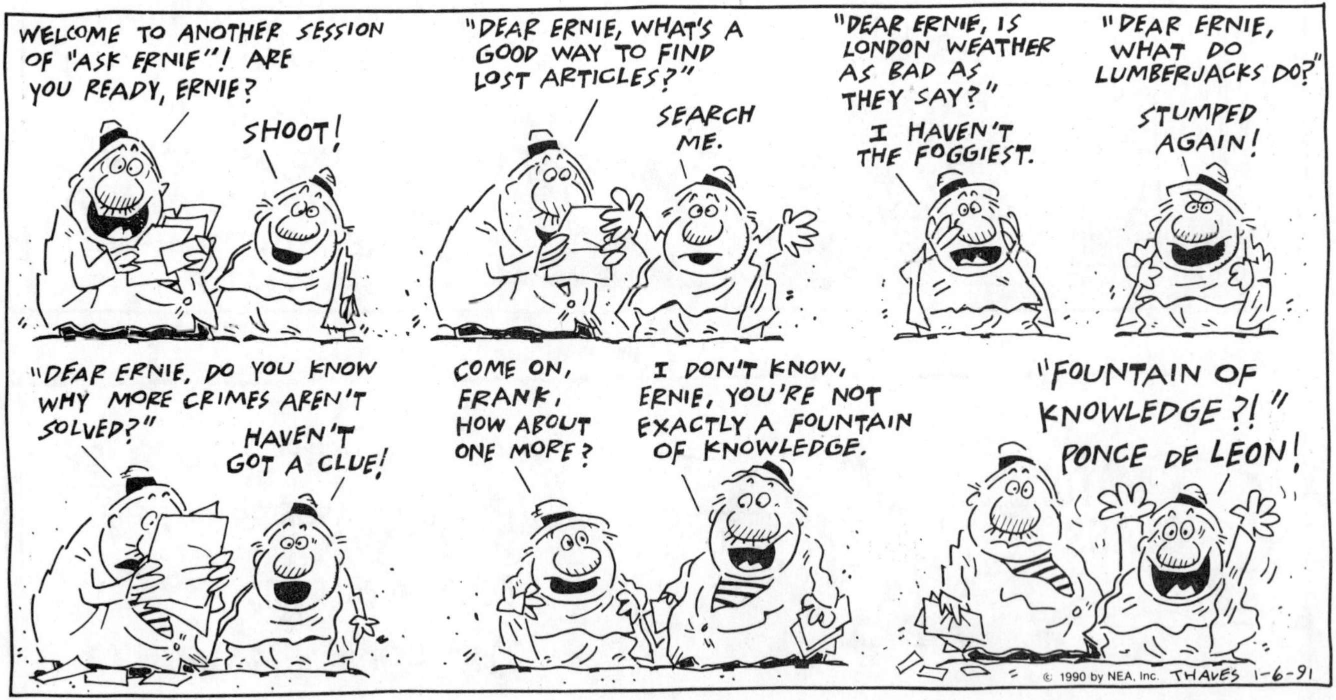

WELCOME TO ANOTHER SESSION OF "ASK ERNIE"! ARE YOU READY, ERNIE?
SHOOT!
"DEAR ERNIE, WHAT'S A GOOD WAY TO FIND LOST ARTICLES?"
SEARCH ME.
"DEAR ERNIE, IS LONDON WEATHER AS BAD AS THEY SAY?"
I HAVEN'T THE FOGGIEST.
"DEAR ERNIE, WHAT DO LUMBERJACKS DO?"
STUMPED AGAIN!
"DEAR ERNIE, DO YOU KNOW WHY MORE CRIMES AREN'T SOLVED?"
HAVEN'T GOT A CLUE!
COME ON, FRANK, HOW ABOUT ONE MORE?
I DON'T KNOW, ERNIE, YOU'RE NOT EXACTLY A FOUNTAIN OF KNOWLEDGE.
"FOUNTAIN OF KNOWLEDGE?!" PONCE DE LEON!
© 1990 by NEA, Inc.
THAVES 1-6-91

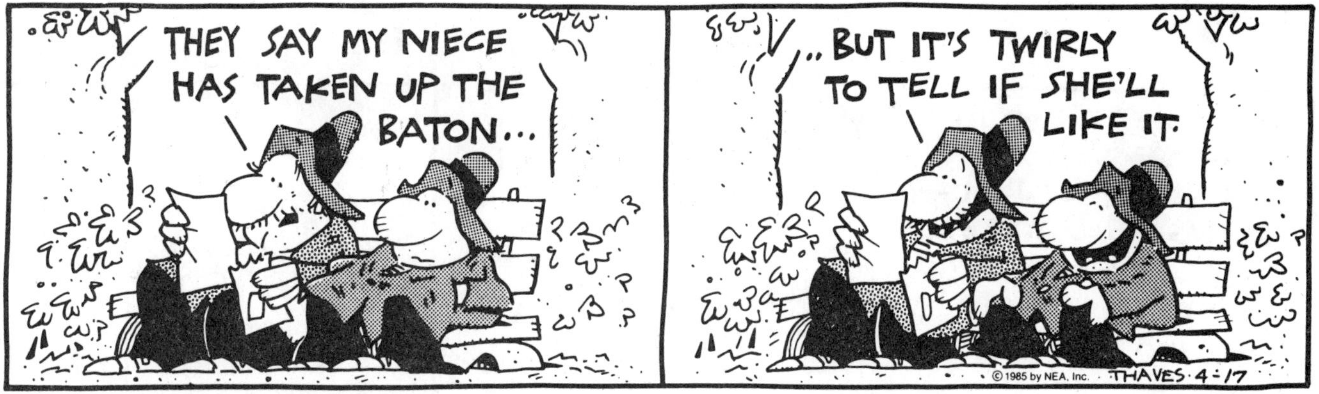
THEY SAY MY NIECE HAS TAKEN UP THE BATON...
..BUT IT'S TWIRLY TO TELL IF SHE'LL LIKE IT.
© 1985 by NEA, Inc.
THAVES 4-17

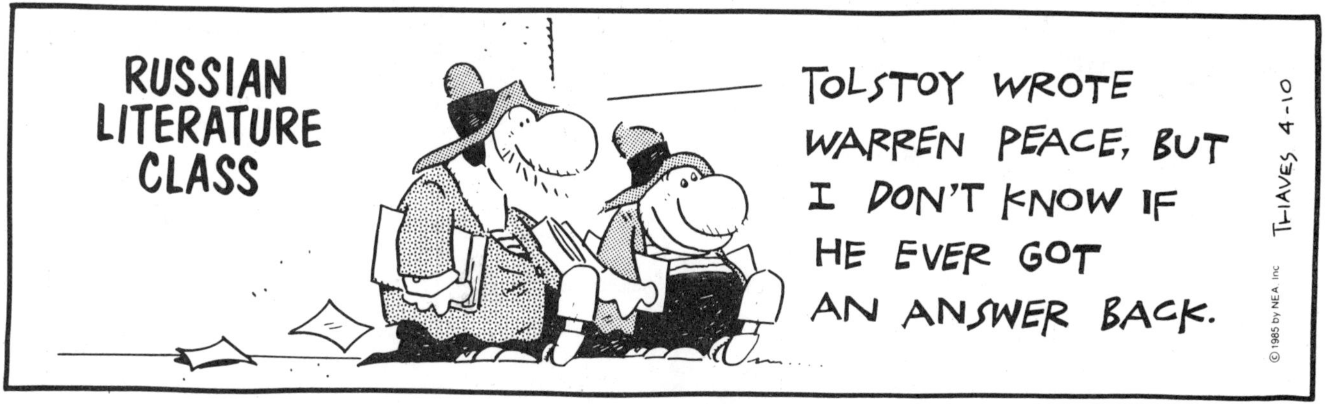
RUSSIAN LITERATURE CLASS
TOLSTOY WROTE WARREN PEACE, BUT I DON'T KNOW IF HE EVER GOT AN ANSWER BACK.
THAVES 4-10
© 1985 by NEA, Inc

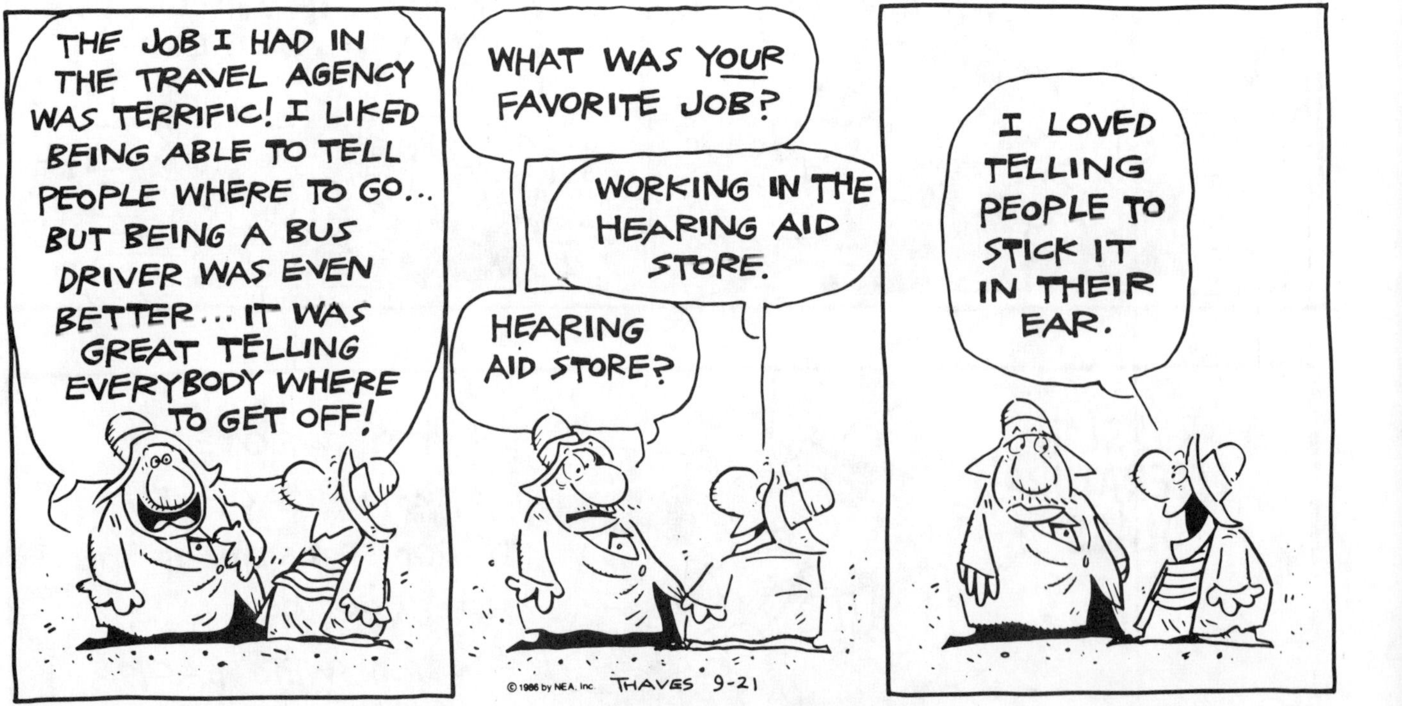
THE JOB I HAD IN THE TRAVEL AGENCY WAS TERRIFIC! I LIKED BEING ABLE TO TELL PEOPLE WHERE TO GO... BUT BEING A BUS DRIVER WAS EVEN BETTER... IT WAS GREAT TELLING EVERYBODY WHERE TO GET OFF!
WHAT WAS YOUR FAVORITE JOB?
WORKING IN THE HEARING AID STORE.
HEARING AID STORE?
I LOVED TELLING PEOPLE TO STICK IT IN THEIR EAR.
© 1986 by NEA, Inc.
THAVES 9-21

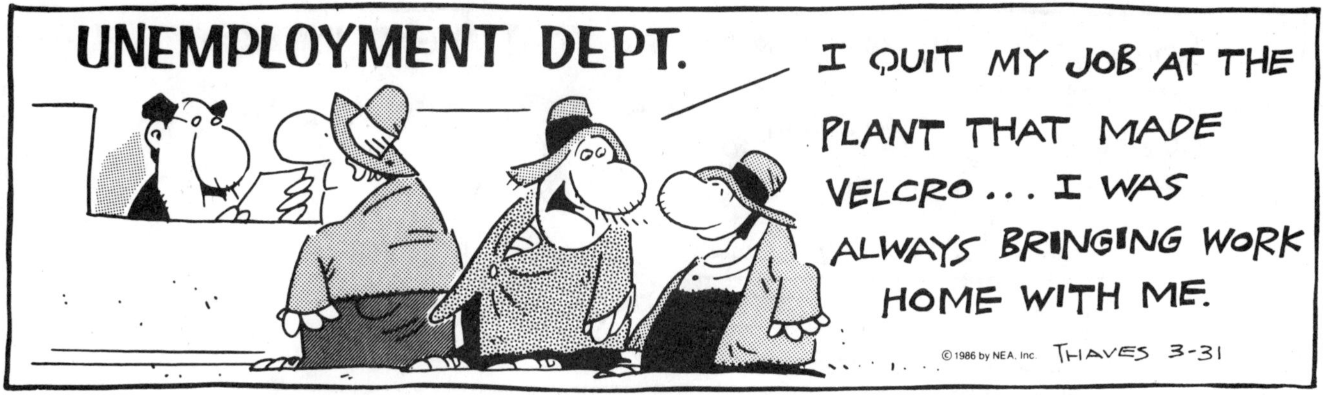
UNEMPLOYMENT DEPT.
I QUIT MY JOB AT THE PLANT THAT MADE VELCRO . . . I WAS ALWAYS BRINGING WORK HOME WITH ME.
© 1986 by NEA, Inc.
THAVES 3-31

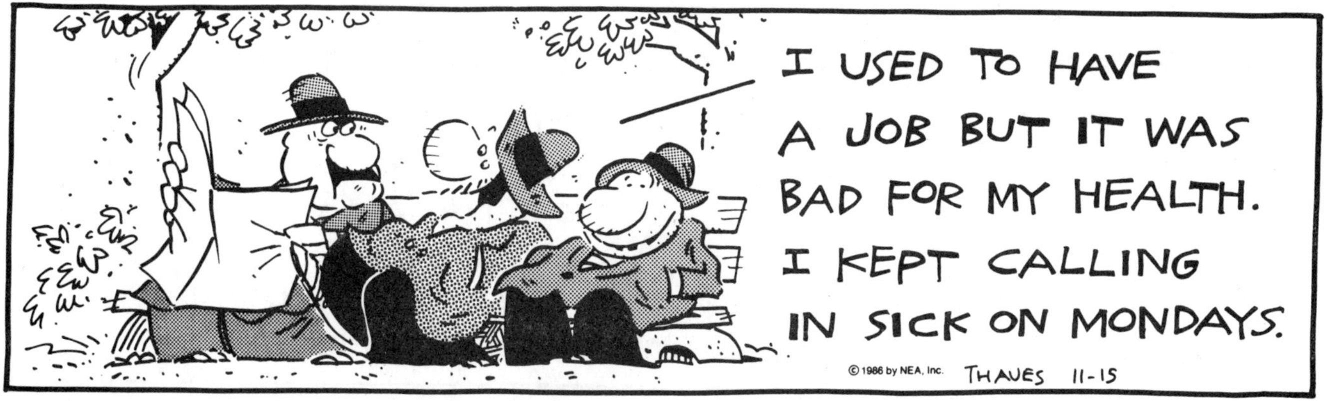
I USED TO HAVE A JOB BUT IT WAS BAD FOR MY HEALTH. I KEPT CALLING IN SICK ON MONDAYS.
© 1986 by NEA, Inc.
THAVES 11-15

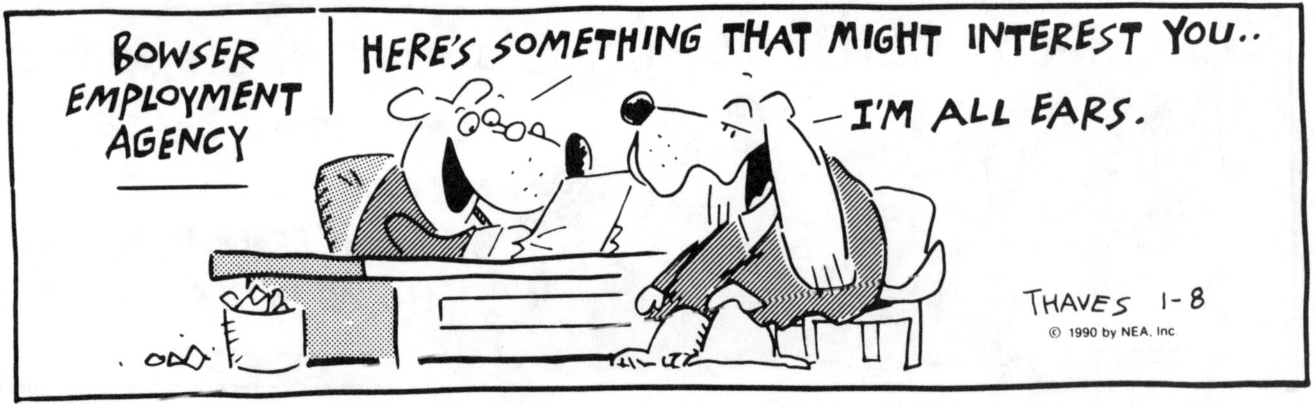

BOWSER EMPLOYMENT AGENCY
HERE'S SOMETHING THAT MIGHT INTEREST YOU..
I'M ALL EARS.
THAVES 1-8
© 1990 by NEA, Inc.

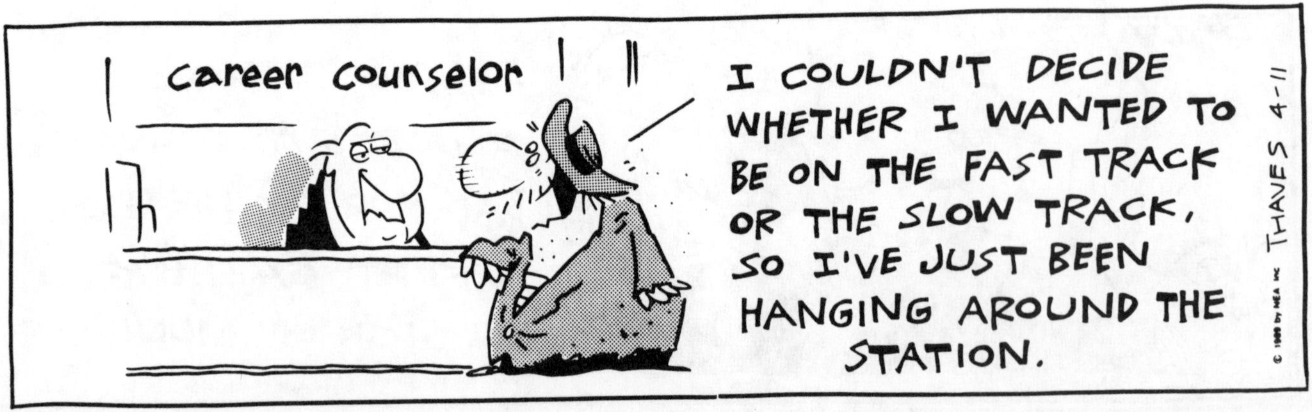

career counselor
I COULDN'T DECIDE WHETHER I WANTED TO BE ON THE FAST TRACK OR THE SLOW TRACK, SO I'VE JUST BEEN HANGING AROUND THE STATION.
THAVES 4-11

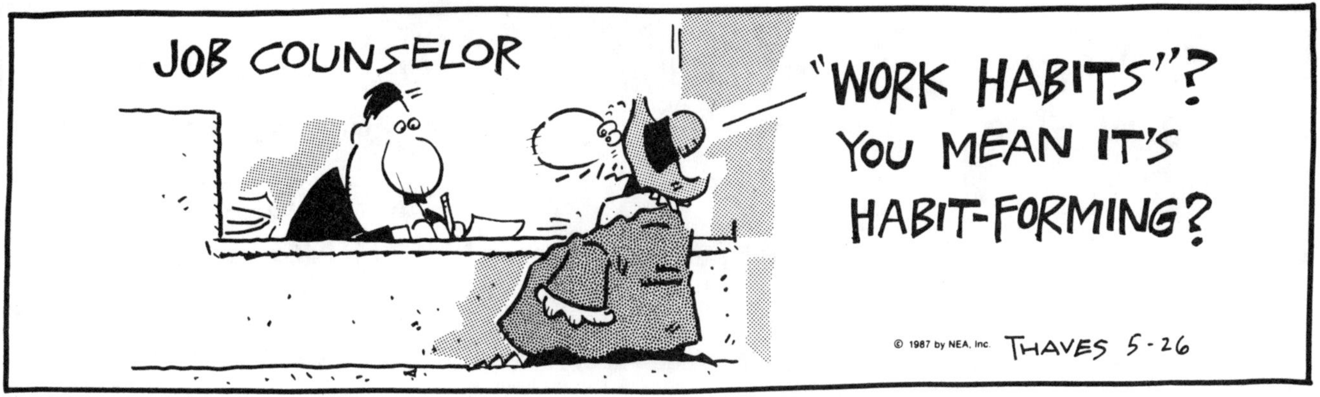
JOB COUNSELOR
"WORK HABITS"? YOU MEAN IT'S HABIT-FORMING?
© 1987 by NEA, Inc.
THAVES 5-26

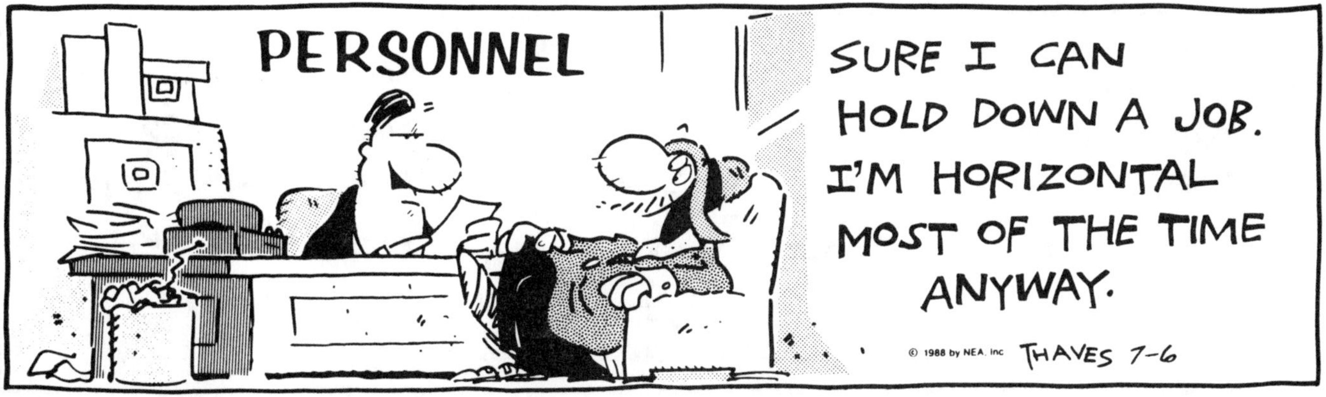
PERSONNEL
SURE I CAN HOLD DOWN A JOB. I'M HORIZONTAL MOST OF THE TIME ANYWAY.
© 1988 by NEA, Inc
THAVES 7-6

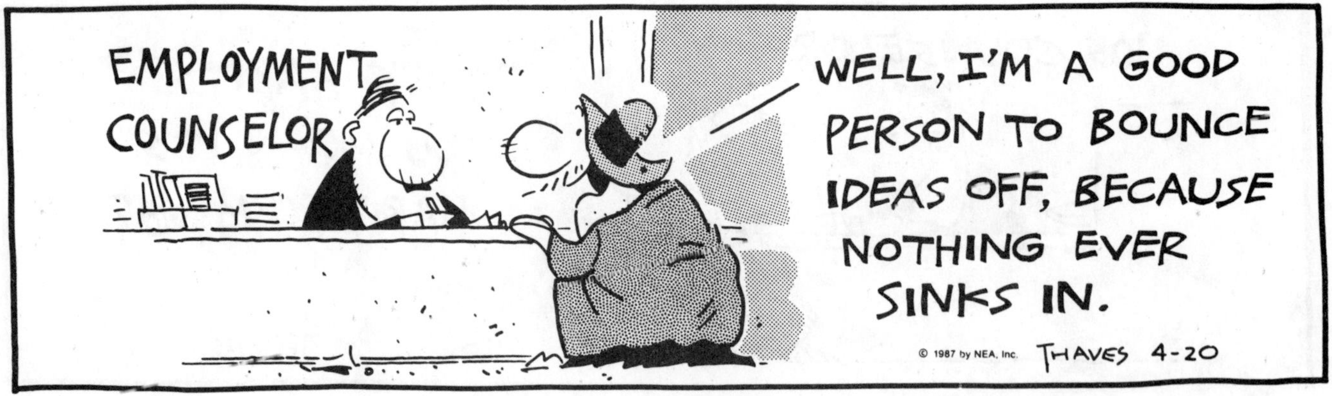
EMPLOYMENT COUNSELOR
WELL, I'M A GOOD PERSON TO BOUNCE IDEAS OFF, BECAUSE NOTHING EVER SINKS IN.
© 1987 by NEA, Inc. THAVES 4-20

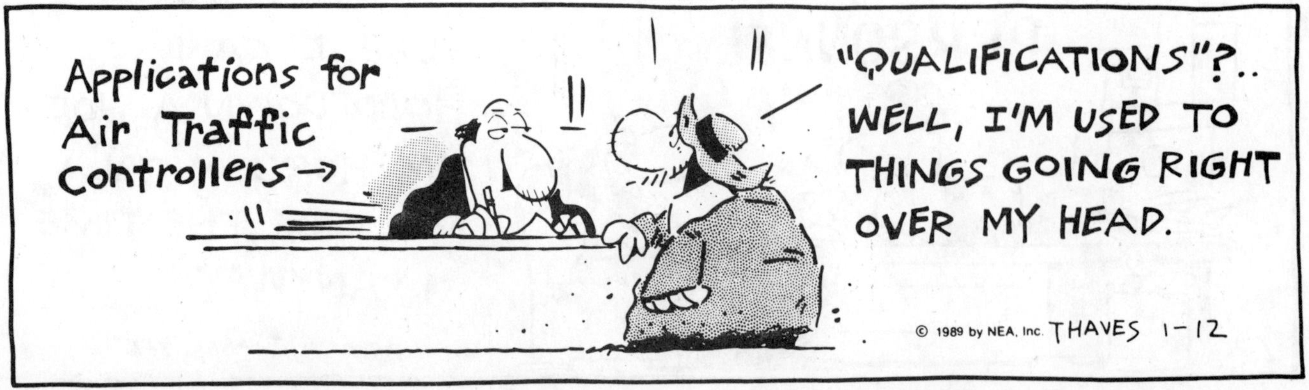
Applications for Air Traffic Controllers →
"QUALIFICATIONS"?.. WELL, I'M USED TO THINGS GOING RIGHT OVER MY HEAD.
© 1989 by NEA, Inc. THAVES 1-12

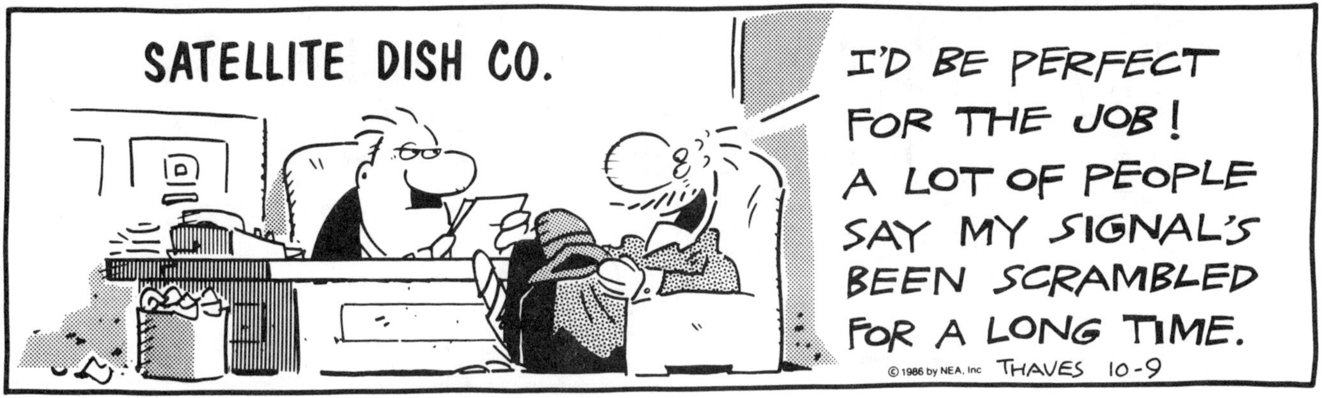
SATELLITE DISH CO.
I'D BE PERFECT FOR THE JOB! A LOT OF PEOPLE SAY MY SIGNAL'S BEEN SCRAMBLED FOR A LONG TIME.
© 1986 by NEA, Inc THAVES 10-9

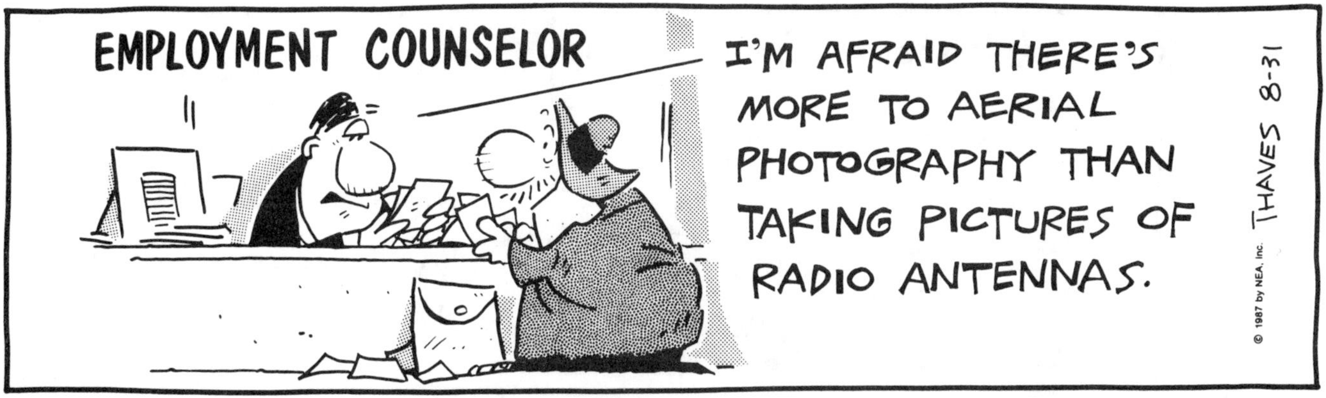
EMPLOYMENT COUNSELOR
I'M AFRAID THERE'S MORE TO AERIAL PHOTOGRAPHY THAN TAKING PICTURES OF RADIO ANTENNAS.
THAVES 8-31
© 1987 by NEA, Inc.

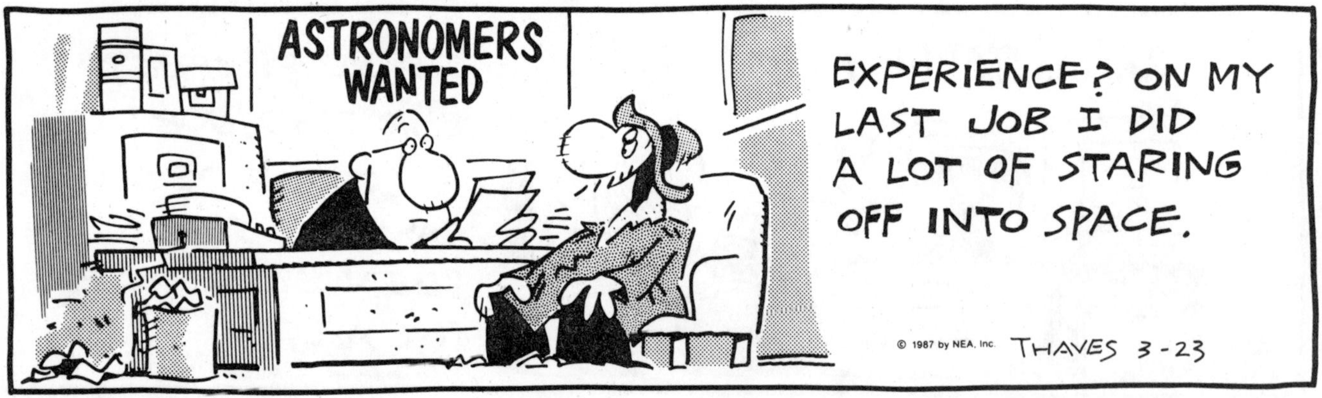
ASTRONOMERS WANTED
EXPERIENCE? ON MY LAST JOB I DID A LOT OF STARING OFF INTO SPACE.
© 1987 by NEA, Inc.
THAVES 3-23

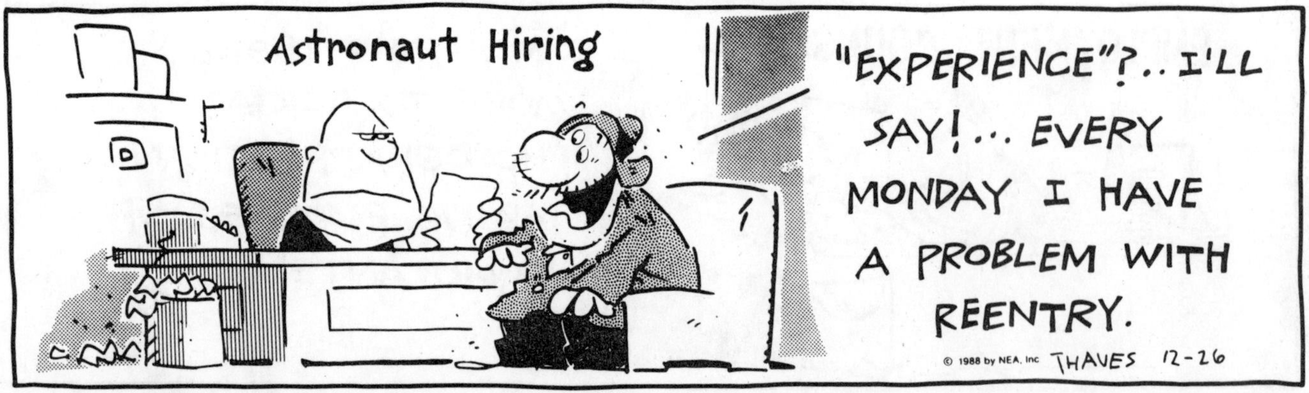
Astronaut Hiring
"EXPERIENCE"?.. I'LL SAY!... EVERY MONDAY I HAVE A PROBLEM WITH REENTRY.
© 1988 by NEA, Inc
THAVES 12-26

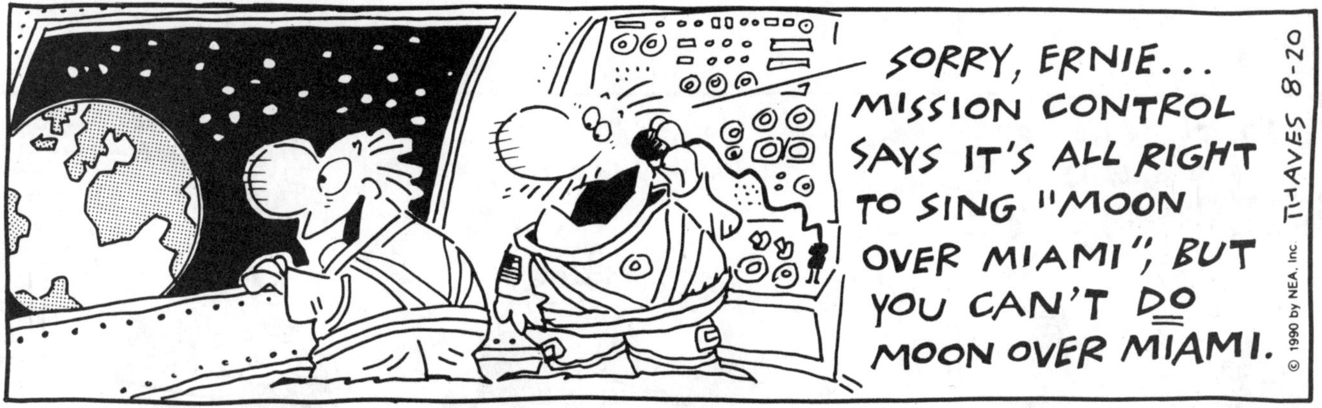
SORRY, ERNIE... MISSION CONTROL SAYS IT'S ALL RIGHT TO SING "MOON OVER MIAMI", BUT YOU CAN'T DO MOON OVER MIAMI.
THAVES 8-20
© 1990 by NEA, Inc.

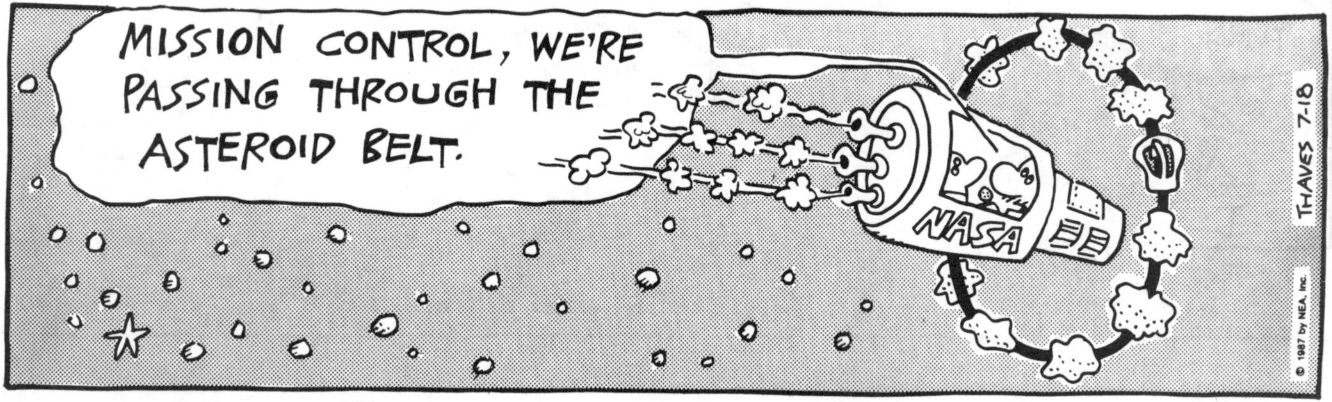
MISSION CONTROL, WE'RE PASSING THROUGH THE ASTEROID BELT.
NASA
THAVES 7-18
© 1987 by NEA, Inc.

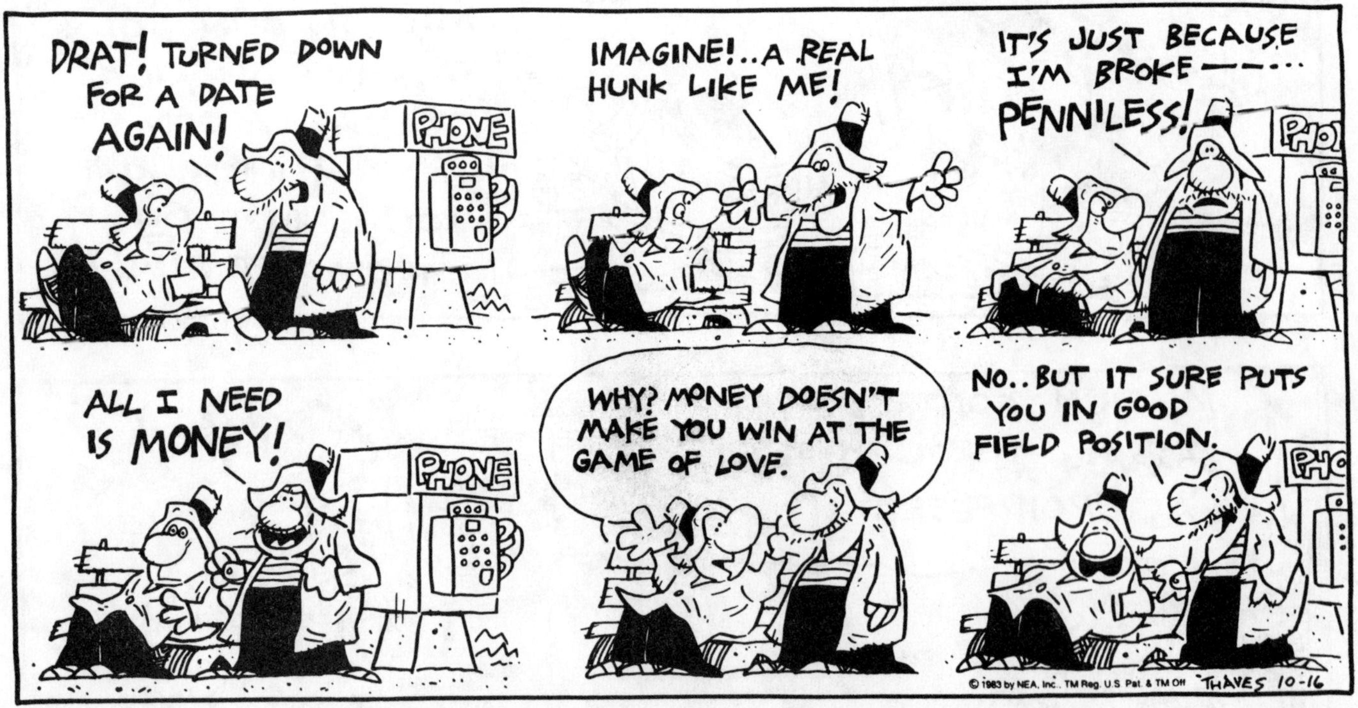
DRAT! TURNED DOWN FOR A DATE AGAIN!
PHONE
IMAGINE!..A REAL HUNK LIKE ME!
IT'S JUST BECAUSE I'M BROKE ———... PENNILESS!
ALL I NEED IS MONEY!
PHONE
WHY? MONEY DOESN'T MAKE YOU WIN AT THE GAME OF LOVE.
NO..BUT IT SURE PUTS YOU IN GOOD FIELD POSITION.
© 1983 by NEA, Inc., TM Reg. U.S. Pat. & TM Off
THAVES 10-16

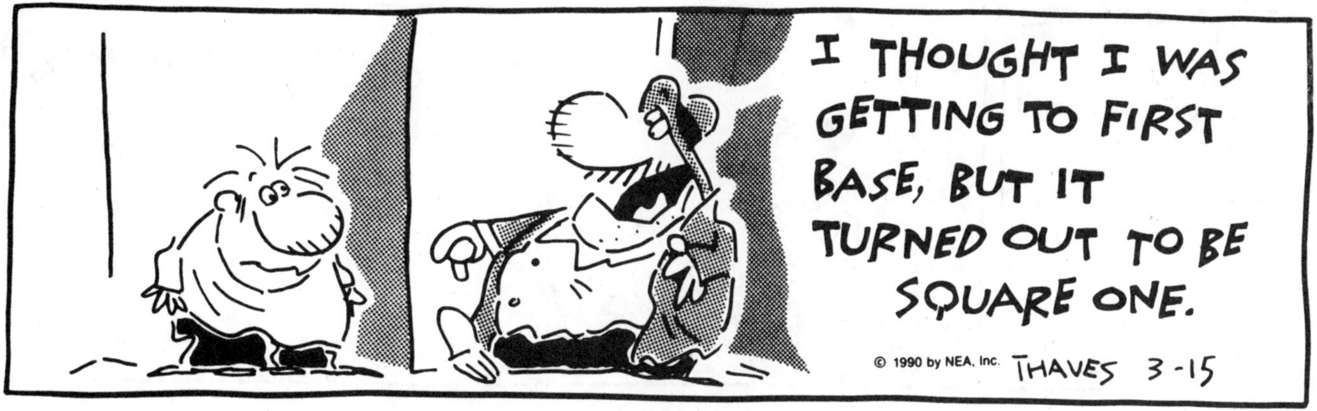
I THOUGHT I WAS GETTING TO FIRST BASE, BUT IT TURNED OUT TO BE SQUARE ONE.
© 1990 by NEA, Inc. THAVES 3-15

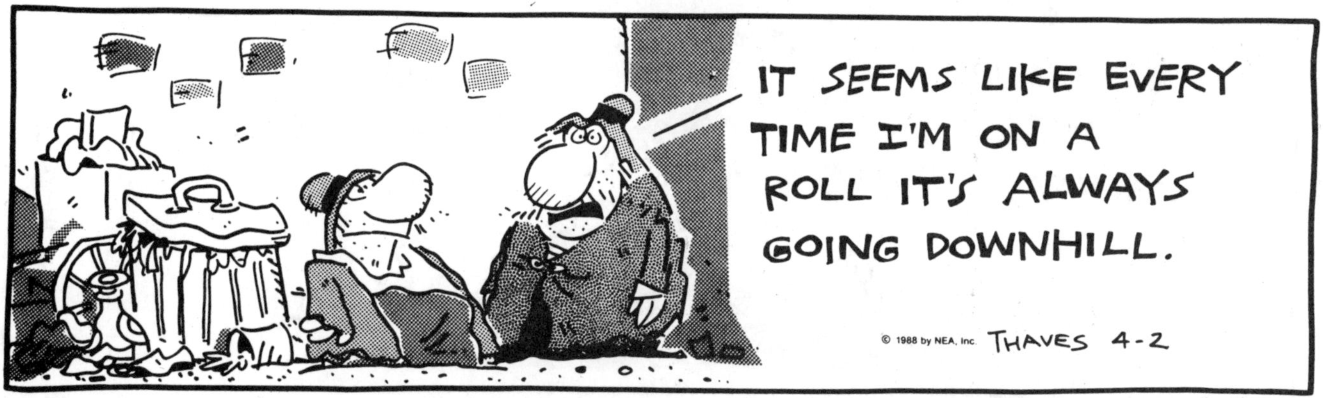
IT SEEMS LIKE EVERY TIME I'M ON A ROLL IT'S ALWAYS GOING DOWNHILL.
© 1988 by NEA, Inc. THAVES 4-2

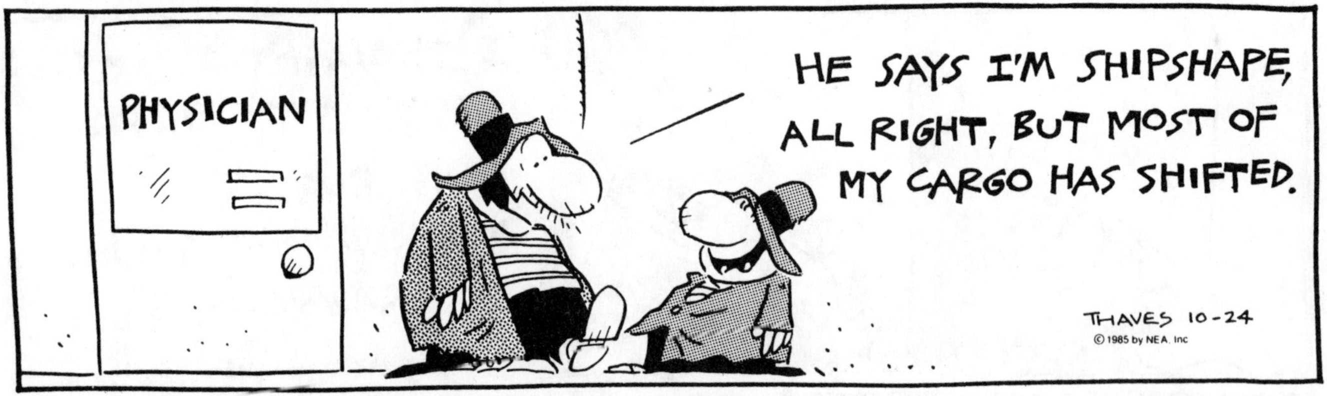
PHYSICIAN
HE SAYS I'M SHIPSHAPE, ALL RIGHT, BUT MOST OF MY CARGO HAS SHIFTED.
THAVES 10-24
© 1985 by NEA, Inc

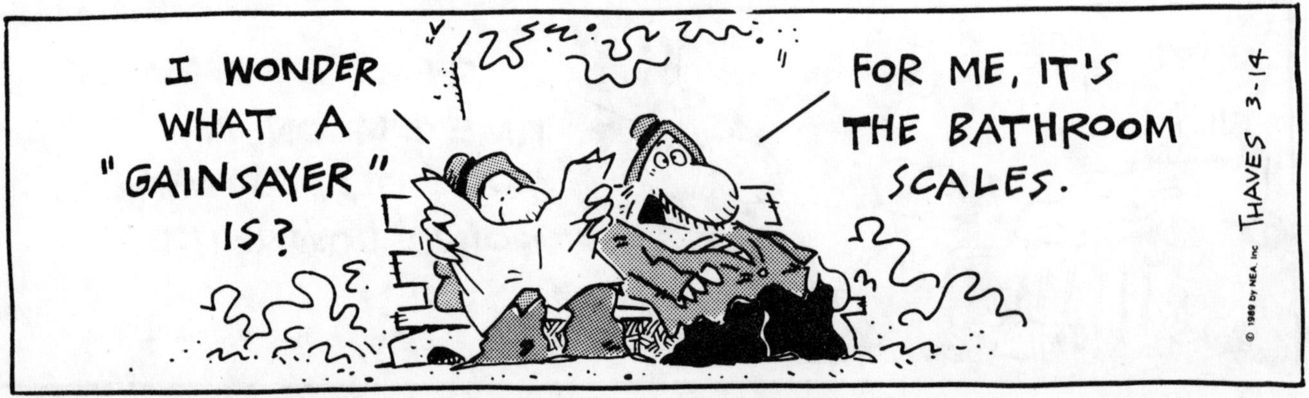
I WONDER WHAT A "GAINSAYER" IS?
FOR ME, IT'S THE BATHROOM SCALES.
THAVES 3-14
© 1989 by NEA, Inc

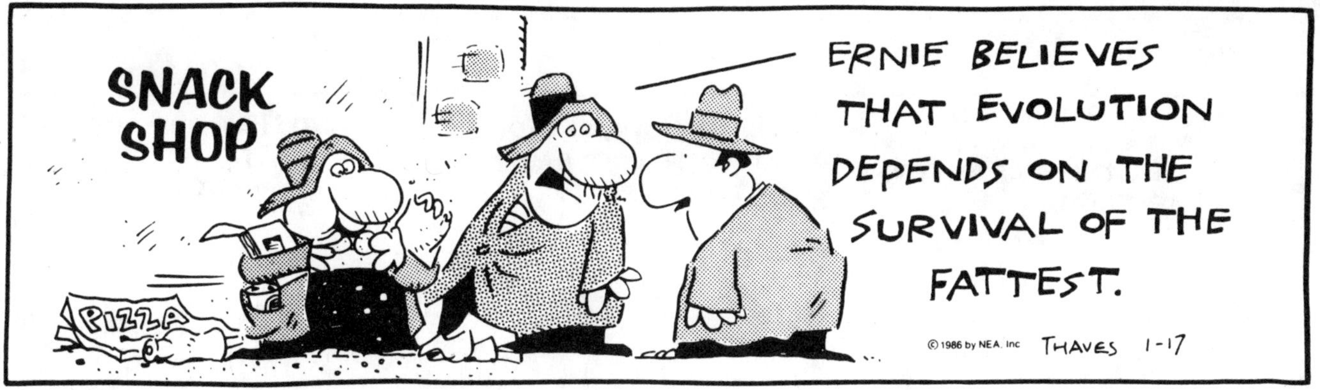
SNACK SHOP
PIZZA
ERNIE BELIEVES THAT EVOLUTION DEPENDS ON THE SURVIVAL OF THE FATTEST.
© 1986 by NEA, Inc
THAVES 1-17

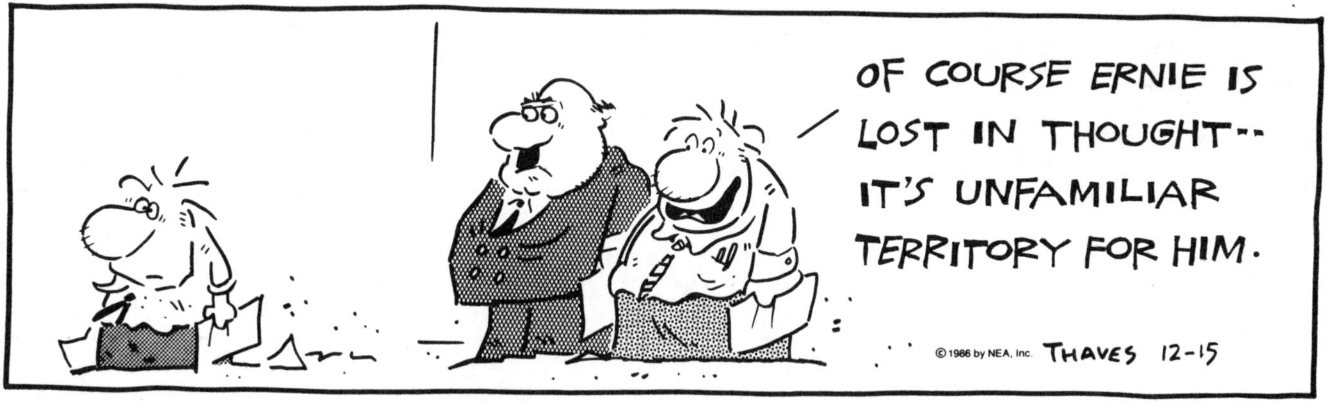
OF COURSE ERNIE IS LOST IN THOUGHT-- IT'S UNFAMILIAR TERRITORY FOR HIM.
© 1986 by NEA, Inc.
THAVES 12-15

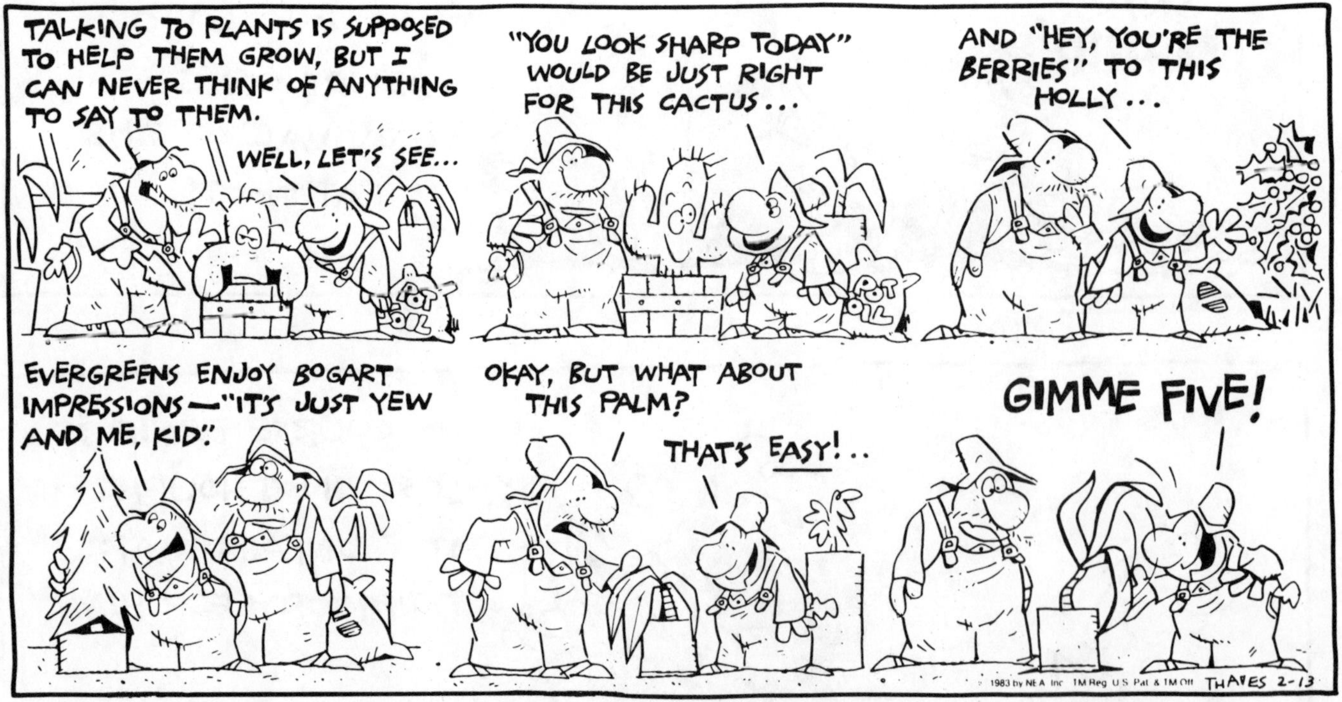
TALKING TO PLANTS IS SUPPOSED TO HELP THEM GROW, BUT I CAN NEVER THINK OF ANYTHING TO SAY TO THEM.
WELL, LET'S SEE...
POT SOIL
"YOU LOOK SHARP TODAY" WOULD BE JUST RIGHT FOR THIS CACTUS...
POT SOIL
AND "HEY, YOU'RE THE BERRIES" TO THIS HOLLY...
EVERGREENS ENJOY BOGART IMPRESSIONS—"IT'S JUST YEW AND ME, KID".
OKAY, BUT WHAT ABOUT THIS PALM?
THAT'S EASY!..
GIMME FIVE!
© 1983 by NEA, Inc. TM Reg. U.S. Pat. & TM Off. THAVES 2-13

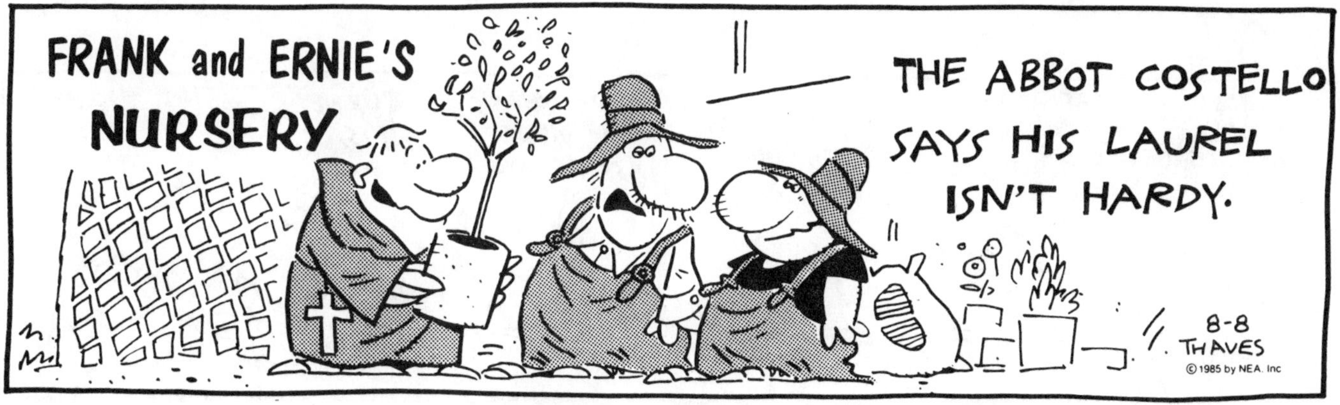
FRANK and ERNIE'S
NURSERY
THE ABBOT COSTELLO SAYS HIS LAUREL ISN'T HARDY.
8-8
THAVES
© 1985 by NEA. Inc

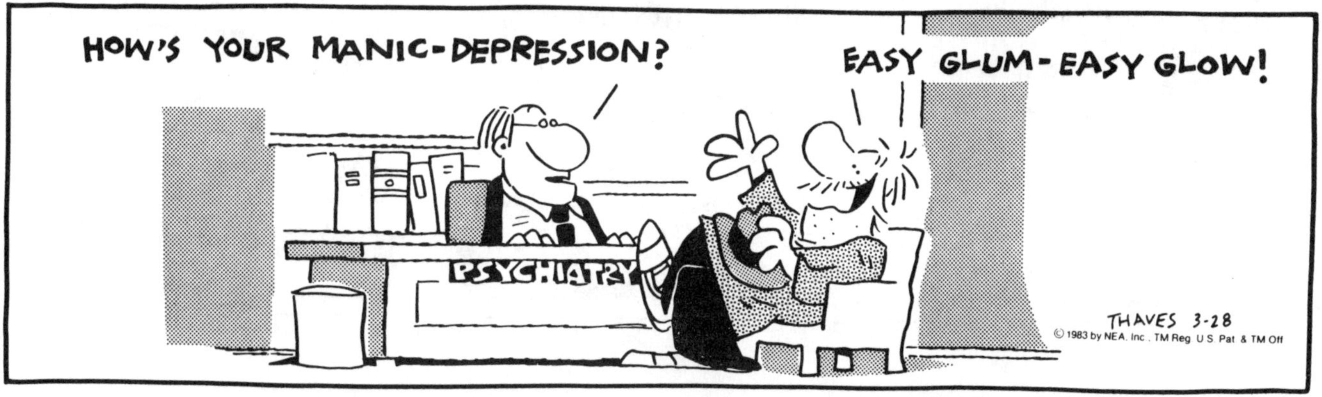
HOW'S YOUR MANIC-DEPRESSION?
EASY GLUM-EASY GLOW!
PSYCHIATRY
THAVES 3-28
© 1983 by NEA. Inc. TM Reg U.S. Pat & TM Off

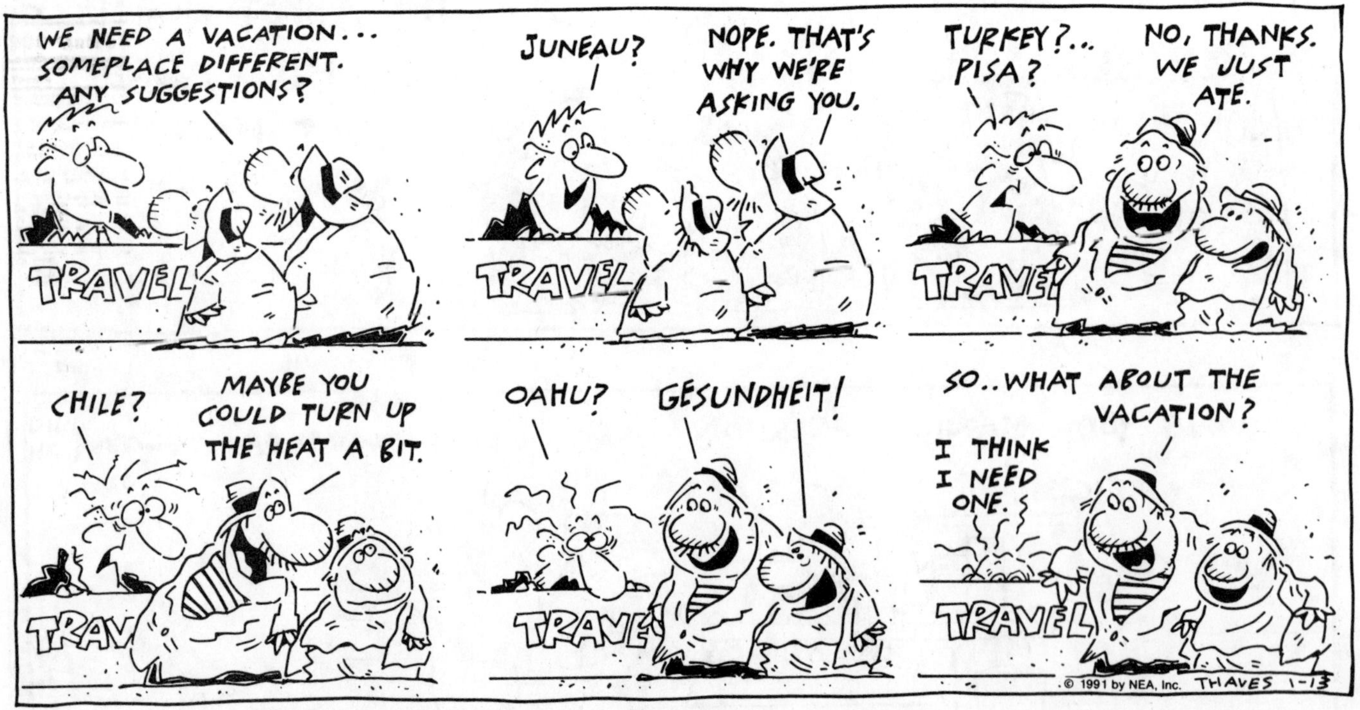
WE NEED A VACATION... SOMEPLACE DIFFERENT. ANY SUGGESTIONS?
TRAVEL
JUNEAU?
NOPE. THAT'S WHY WE'RE ASKING YOU.
TRAVEL
TURKEY?... PISA?
NO, THANKS. WE JUST ATE.
TRAVEL
CHILE?
MAYBE YOU COULD TURN UP THE HEAT A BIT.
TRAV
OAHU?
GESUNDHEIT!
TRAVE
SO.. WHAT ABOUT THE VACATION?
I THINK I NEED ONE.
TRAVEL
© 1991 by NEA, Inc.
THAVES 1-13

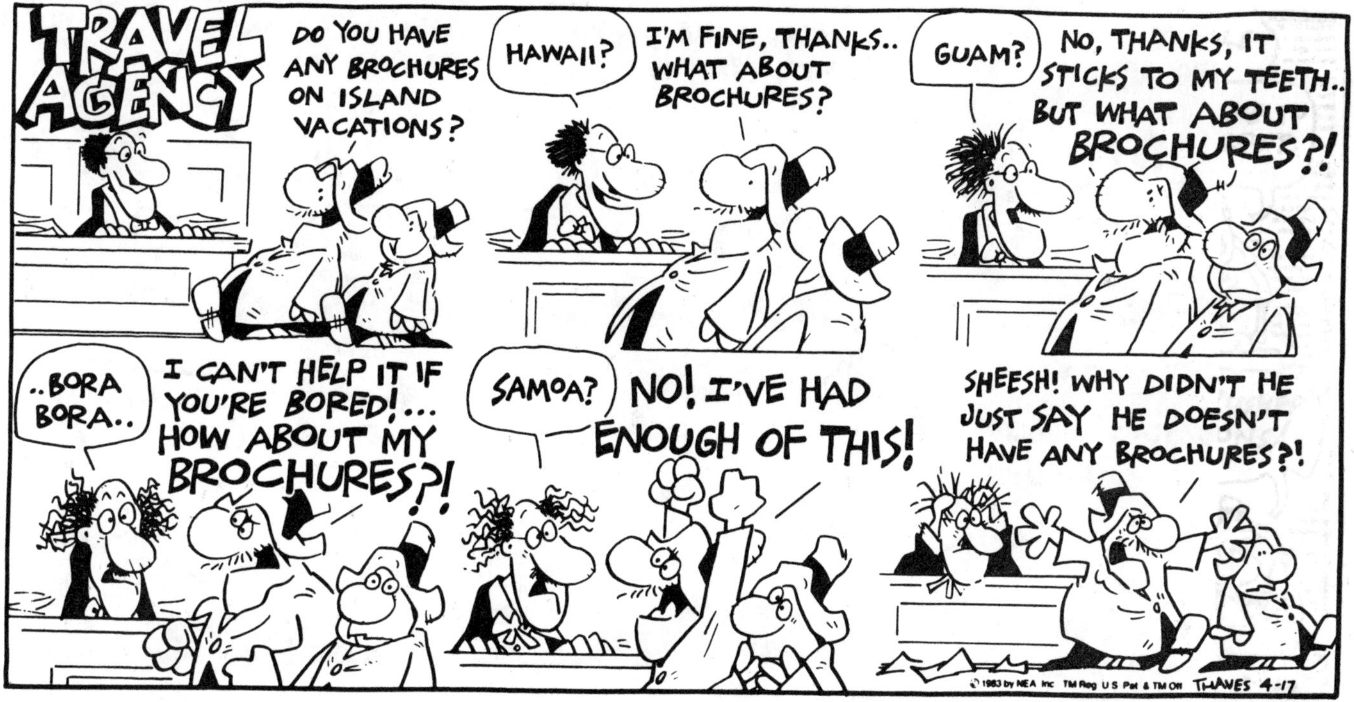
TRAVEL AGENCY
DO YOU HAVE ANY BROCHURES ON ISLAND VACATIONS?
HAWAII?
I'M FINE, THANKS.. WHAT ABOUT BROCHURES?
GUAM?
NO, THANKS, IT STICKS TO MY TEETH.. BUT WHAT ABOUT BROCHURES?!
..BORA BORA..
I CAN'T HELP IT IF YOU'RE BORED!... HOW ABOUT MY BROCHURES?!
SAMOA?
NO! I'VE HAD ENOUGH OF THIS!
SHEESH! WHY DIDN'T HE JUST SAY HE DOESN'T HAVE ANY BROCHURES?!
© 1983 by NEA Inc TM Reg U S Pat & TM Off THAVES 4-17

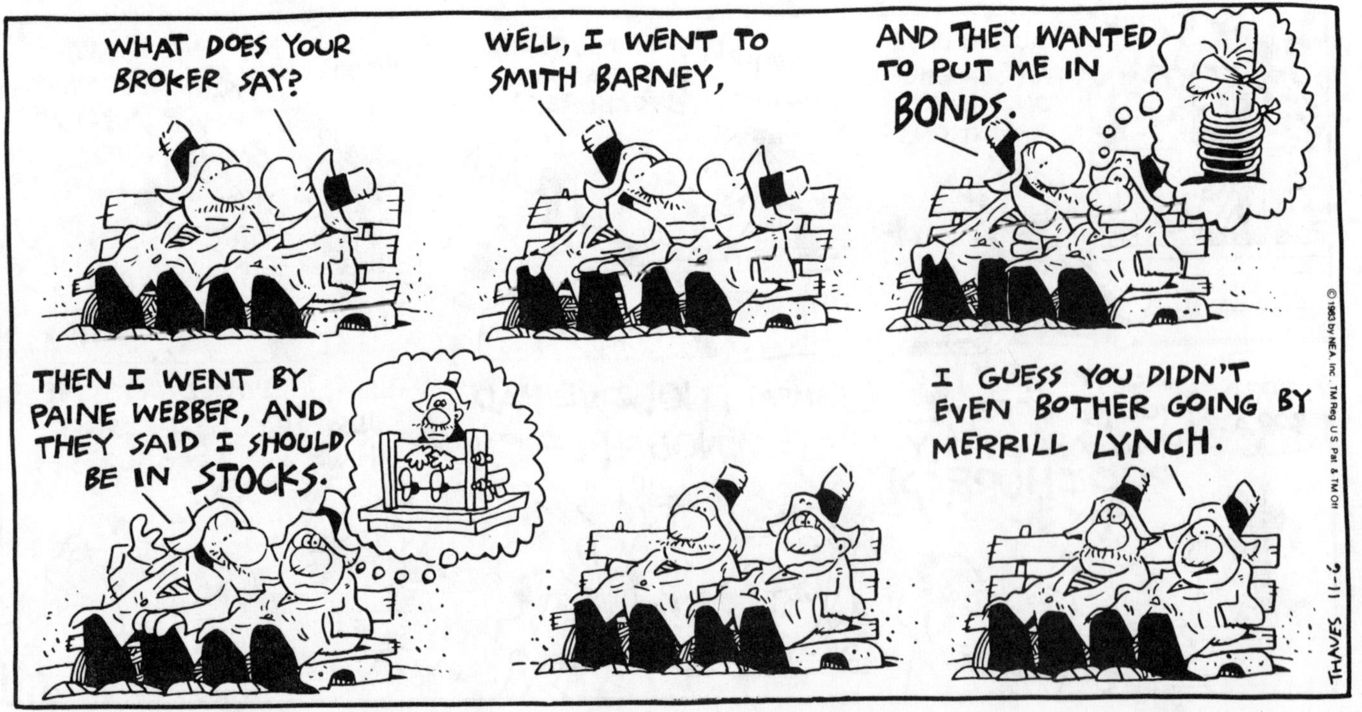
WHAT DOES YOUR BROKER SAY?
WELL, I WENT TO SMITH BARNEY,
AND THEY WANTED TO PUT ME IN BONDS.
THEN I WENT BY PAINE WEBBER, AND THEY SAID I SHOULD BE IN STOCKS.
I GUESS YOU DIDN'T EVEN BOTHER GOING BY MERRILL LYNCH.
© 1983 by NEA, Inc. TM Reg U S Pat & TM Off
THAVES 9-11

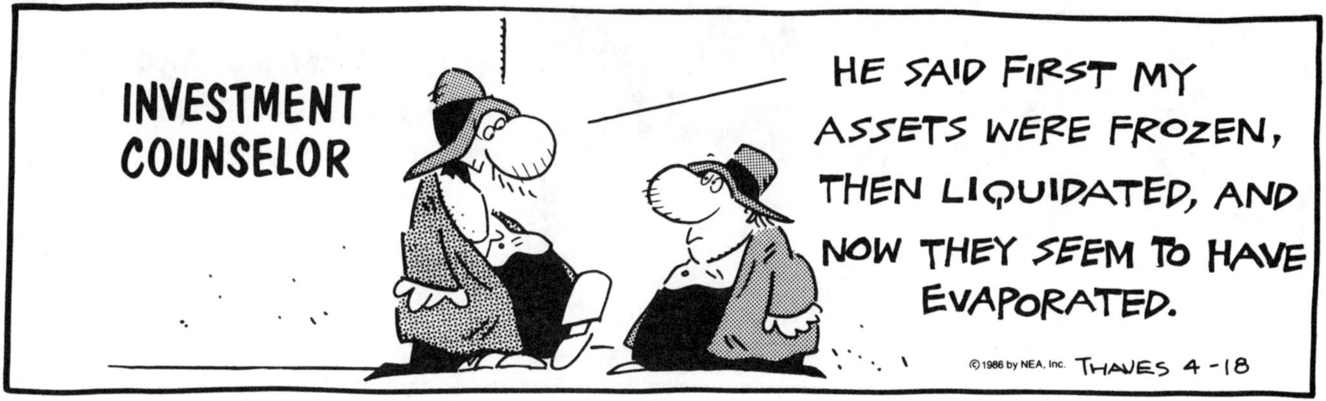
INVESTMENT COUNSELOR
HE SAID FIRST MY ASSETS WERE FROZEN, THEN LIQUIDATED, AND NOW THEY SEEM TO HAVE EVAPORATED.
© 1986 by NEA, Inc. THAVES 4-18

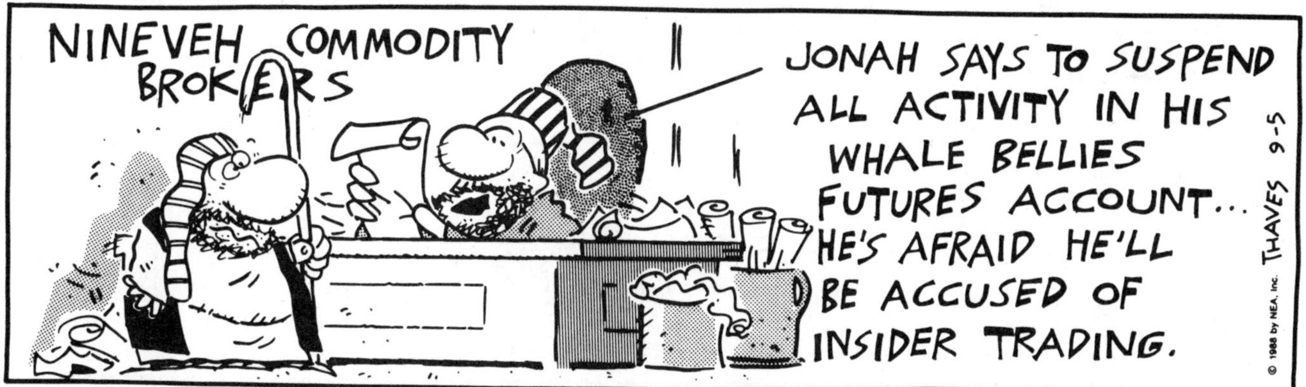
NINEVEH COMMODITY BROKERS
JONAH SAYS TO SUSPEND ALL ACTIVITY IN HIS WHALE BELLIES FUTURES ACCOUNT... HE'S AFRAID HE'LL BE ACCUSED OF INSIDER TRADING.
© 1988 by NEA, Inc. THAVES 9-5

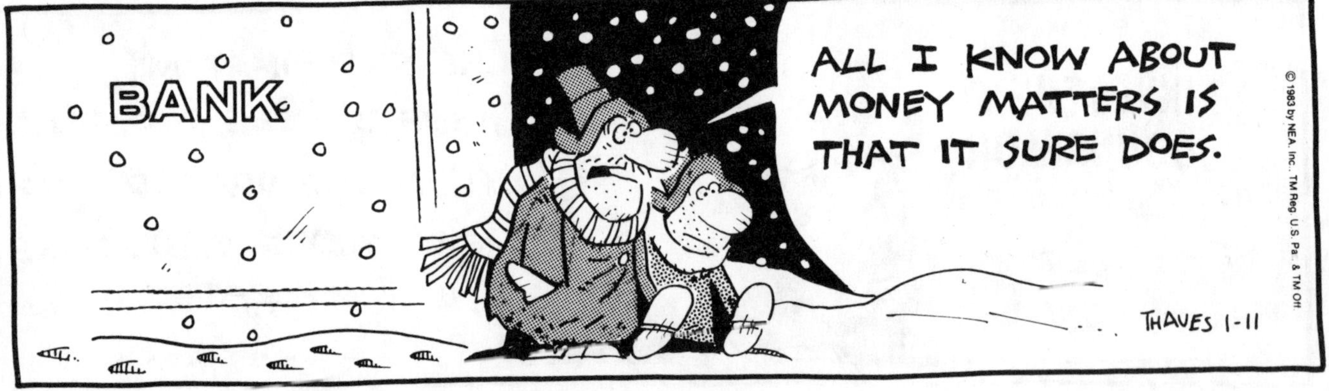
BANK
ALL I KNOW ABOUT MONEY MATTERS IS THAT IT SURE DOES.
THAVES 1-11
© 1983 by NEA, Inc.. TM Reg. U.S. Pa. & TM Off.

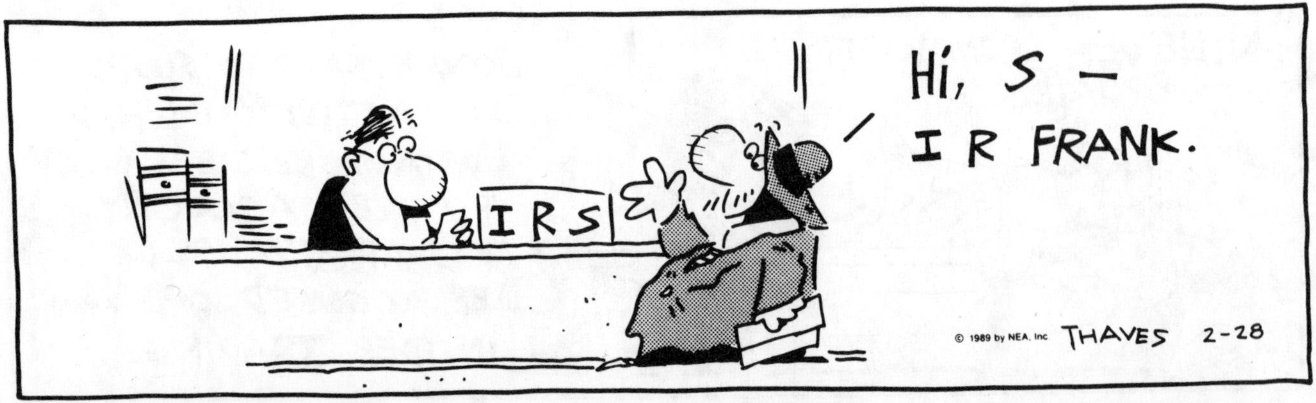
IRS
Hi, S — I R FRANK.
© 1989 by NEA, Inc
THAVES 2-28

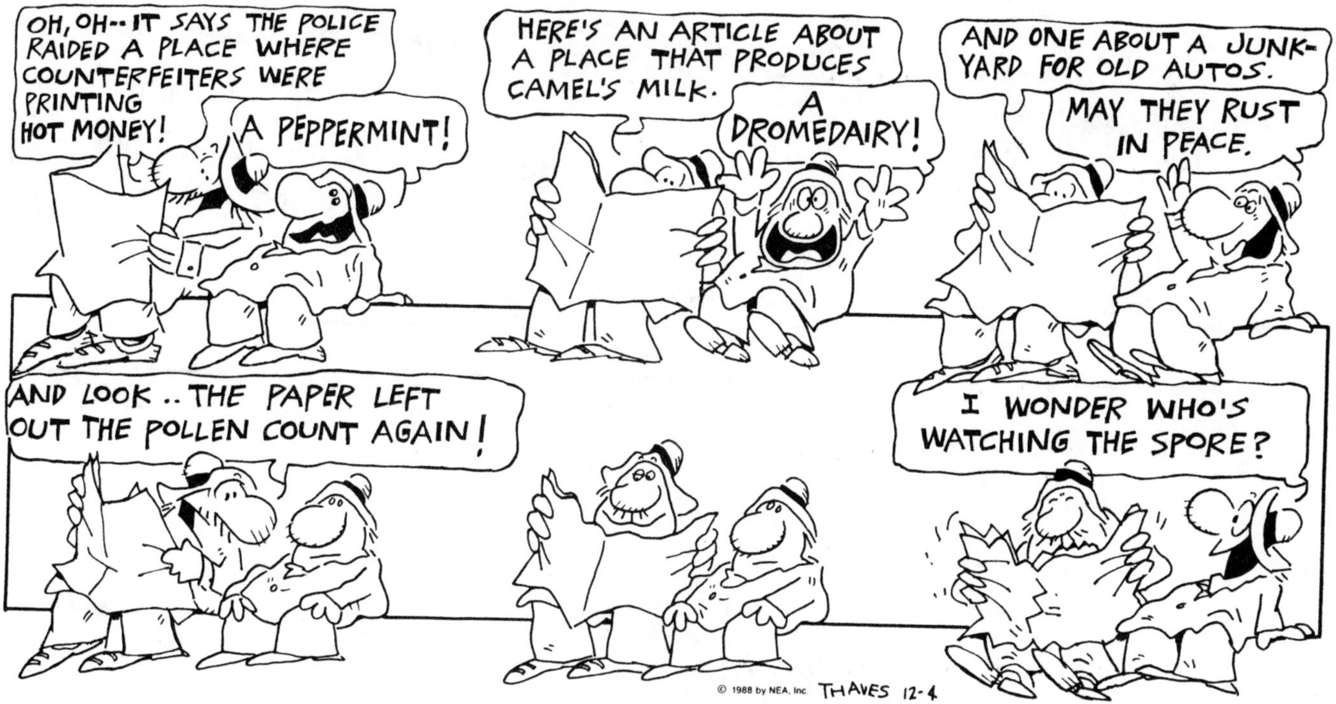
OH, OH-- IT SAYS THE POLICE RAIDED A PLACE WHERE COUNTERFEITERS WERE PRINTING HOT MONEY!
A PEPPERMINT!
HERE'S AN ARTICLE ABOUT A PLACE THAT PRODUCES CAMEL'S MILK.
A DROMEDAIRY!
AND ONE ABOUT A JUNK-YARD FOR OLD AUTOS.
MAY THEY RUST IN PEACE.
AND LOOK .. THE PAPER LEFT OUT THE POLLEN COUNT AGAIN!
I WONDER WHO'S WATCHING THE SPORE?
© 1988 by NEA, Inc.
THAVES 12-4

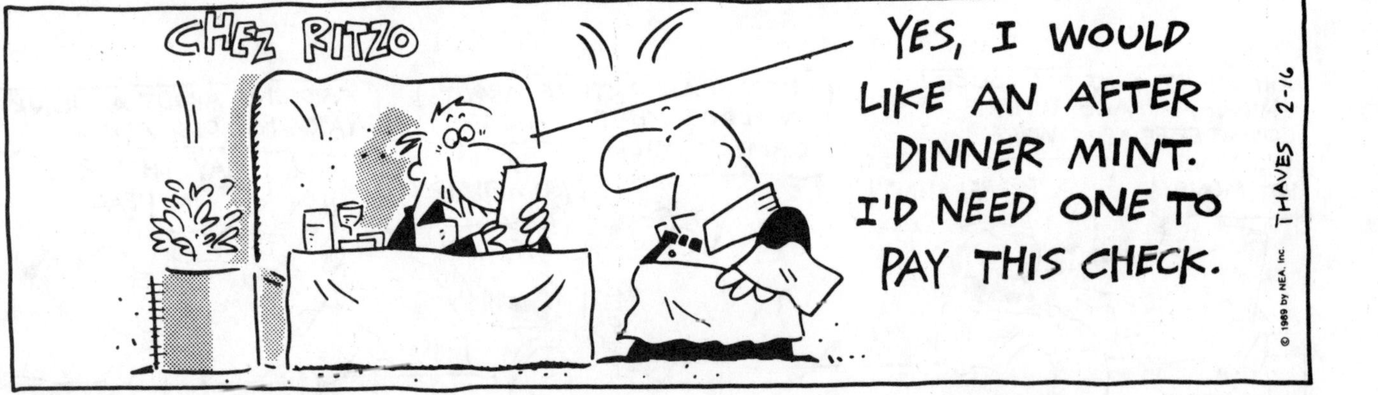
CHEZ RITZO
YES, I WOULD LIKE AN AFTER DINNER MINT. I'D NEED ONE TO PAY THIS CHECK.
THAVES 2-16
© 1989 by NEA, Inc.

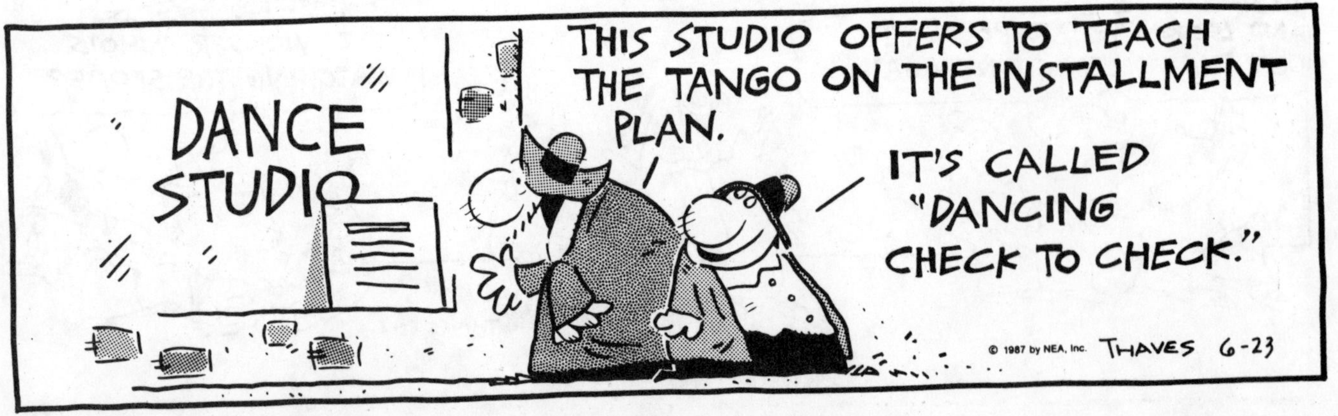
DANCE STUDIO
THIS STUDIO OFFERS TO TEACH THE TANGO ON THE INSTALLMENT PLAN.
IT'S CALLED "DANCING CHECK TO CHECK."
© 1987 by NEA, Inc.
THAVES 6-23

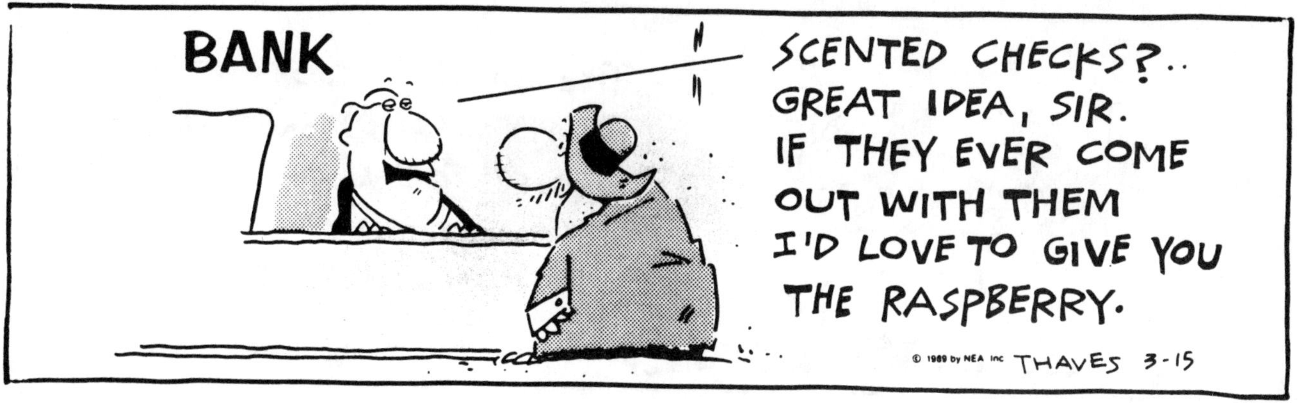
BANK
SCENTED CHECKS?.. GREAT IDEA, SIR. IF THEY EVER COME OUT WITH THEM I'D LOVE TO GIVE YOU THE RASPBERRY.
© 1989 by NEA Inc THAVES 3-15

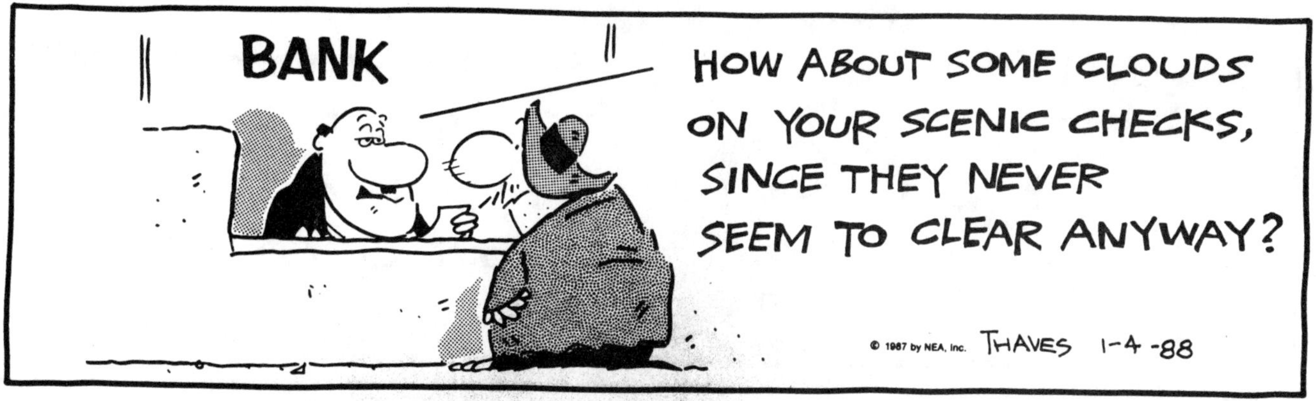
BANK
HOW ABOUT SOME CLOUDS ON YOUR SCENIC CHECKS, SINCE THEY NEVER SEEM TO CLEAR ANYWAY?
© 1987 by NEA, Inc. THAVES 1-4-88

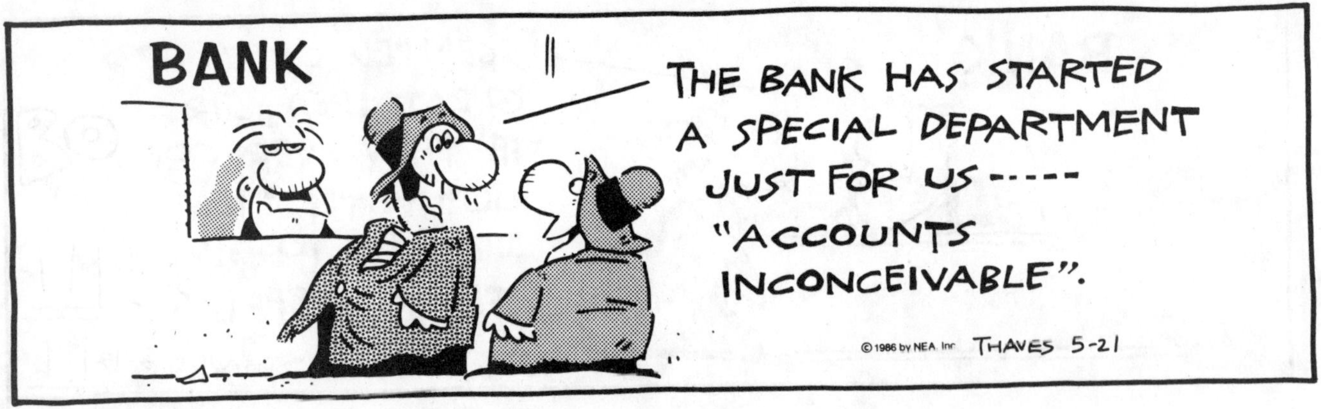
BANK
THE BANK HAS STARTED A SPECIAL DEPARTMENT JUST FOR US ----- "ACCOUNTS INCONCEIVABLE".
© 1986 by NEA, Inc THAVES 5-21

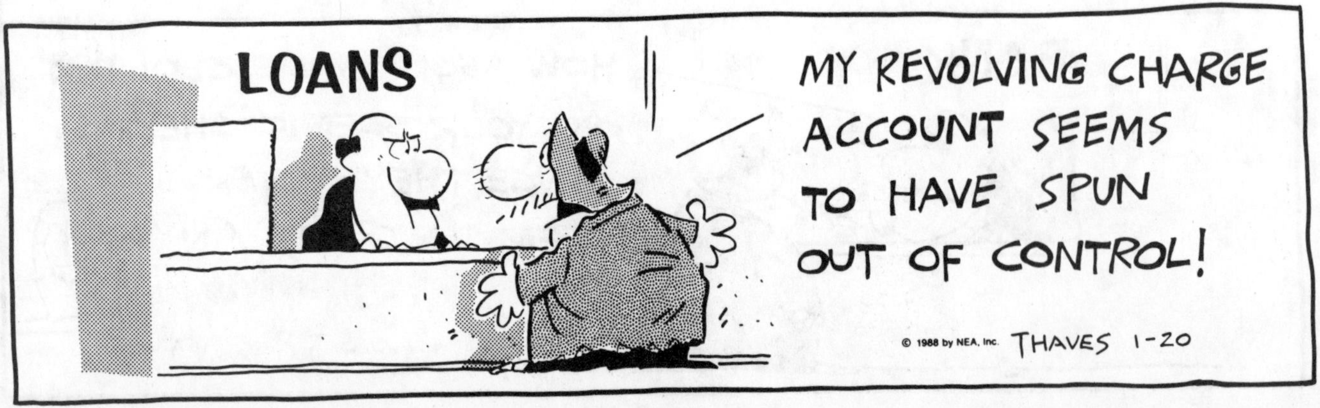
LOANS
MY REVOLVING CHARGE ACCOUNT SEEMS TO HAVE SPUN OUT OF CONTROL!
© 1988 by NEA, Inc. THAVES 1-20

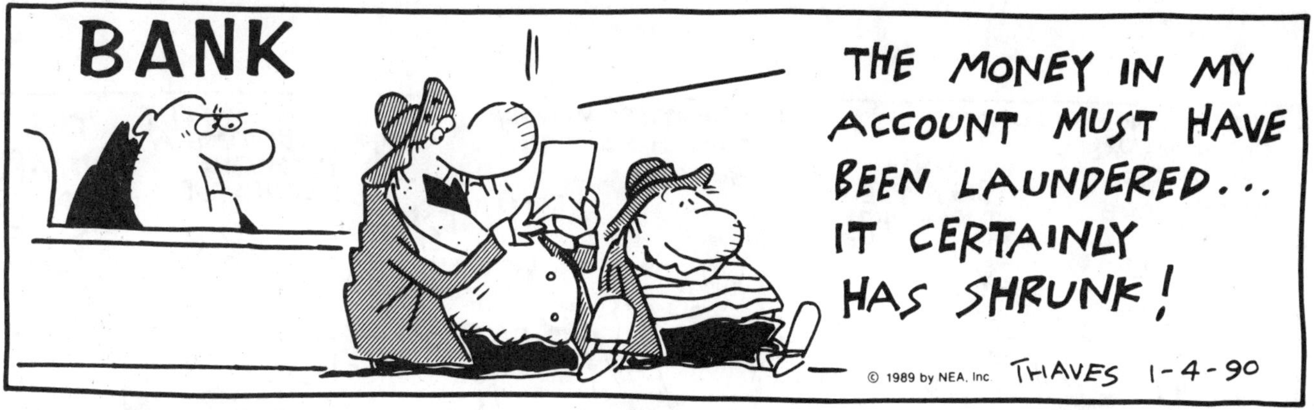
BANK
THE MONEY IN MY ACCOUNT MUST HAVE BEEN LAUNDERED... IT CERTAINLY HAS SHRUNK!
© 1989 by NEA, Inc. THAVES 1-4-90

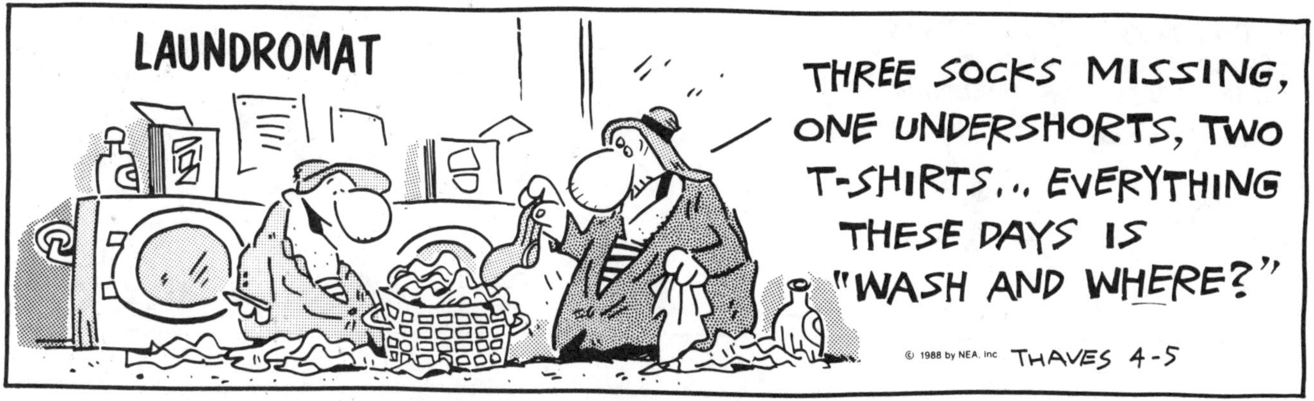
LAUNDROMAT
THREE SOCKS MISSING, ONE UNDERSHORTS, TWO T-SHIRTS... EVERYTHING THESE DAYS IS "WASH AND WHERE?"
© 1988 by NEA, Inc. THAVES 4-5

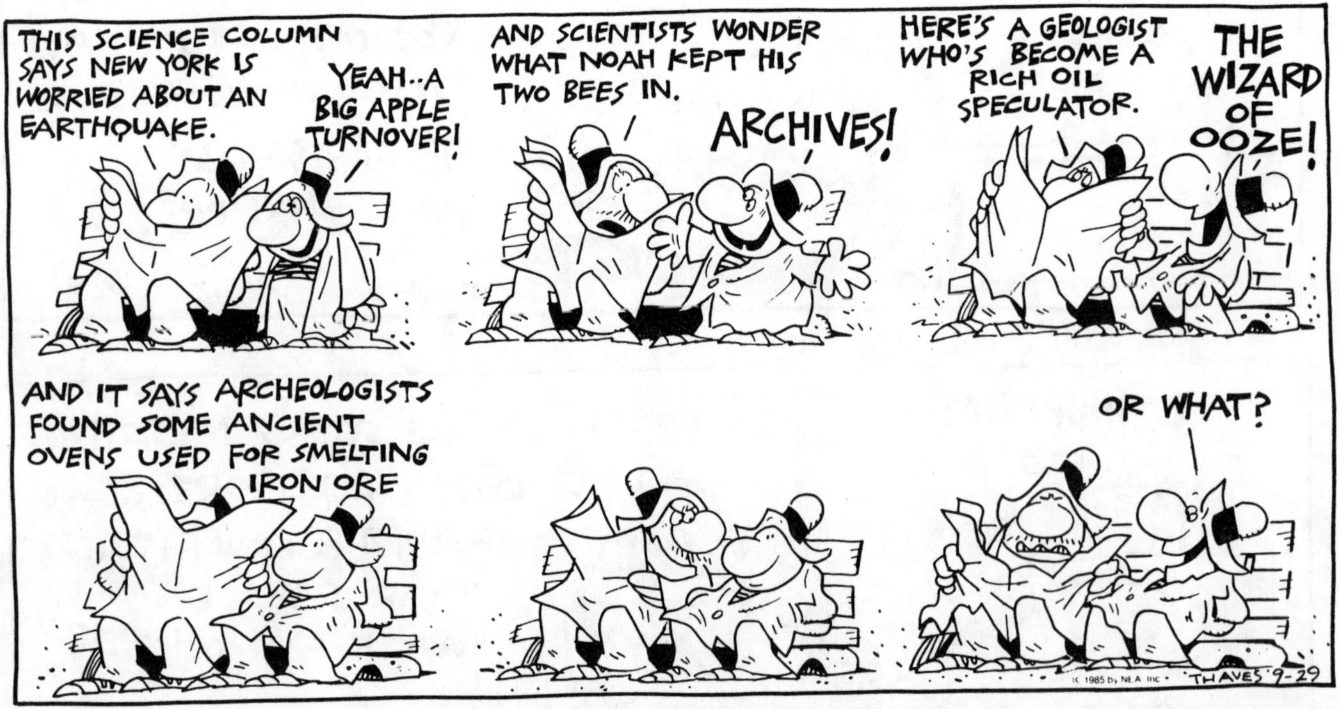
THIS SCIENCE COLUMN SAYS NEW YORK IS WORRIED ABOUT AN EARTHQUAKE.
YEAH..A BIG APPLE TURNOVER!
AND SCIENTISTS WONDER WHAT NOAH KEPT HIS TWO BEES IN.
ARCHIVES!
HERE'S A GEOLOGIST WHO'S BECOME A RICH OIL SPECULATOR.
THE WIZARD OF OOZE!
AND IT SAYS ARCHEOLOGISTS FOUND SOME ANCIENT OVENS USED FOR SMELTING IRON ORE
OR WHAT?
© 1985 by NEA, Inc.
THAVES 9-29

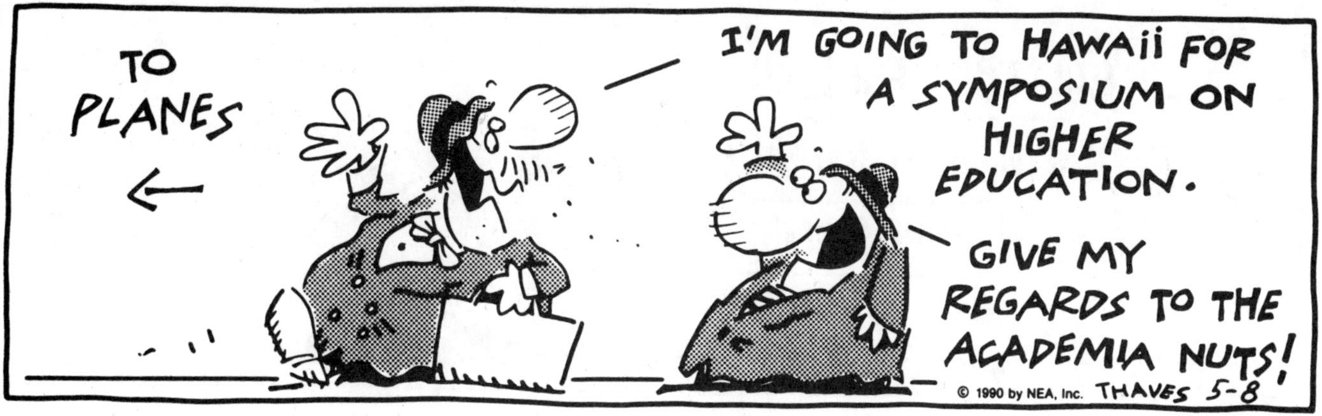
TO PLANES
I'M GOING TO HAWAii FOR A SYMPOSIUM ON HIGHER EDUCATION.
GIVE MY REGARDS TO THE ACADEMIA NUTS!
© 1990 by NEA, Inc. THAVES 5-8

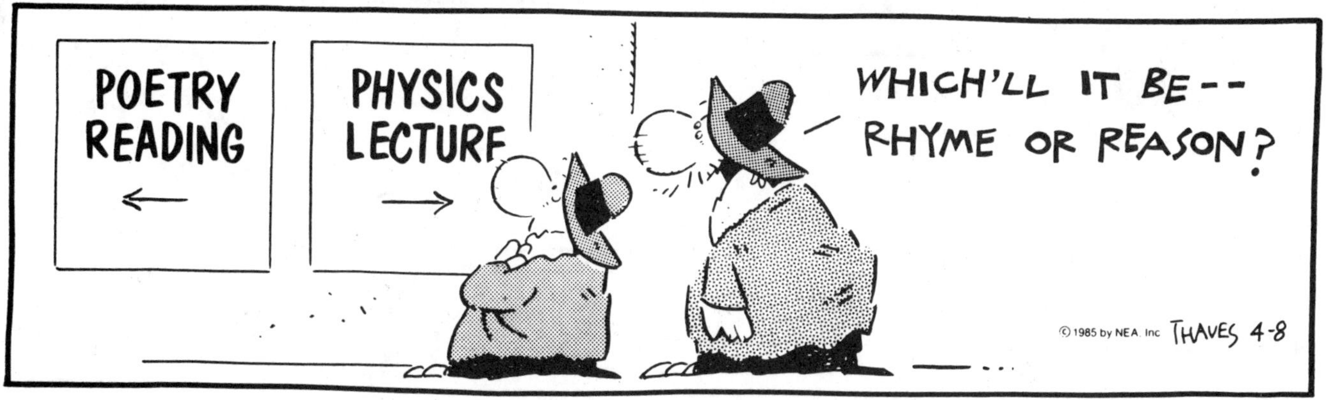
POETRY READING
PHYSICS LECTURE
WHICH'LL IT BE-- RHYME OR REASON?
© 1985 by NEA, Inc THAVES 4-8

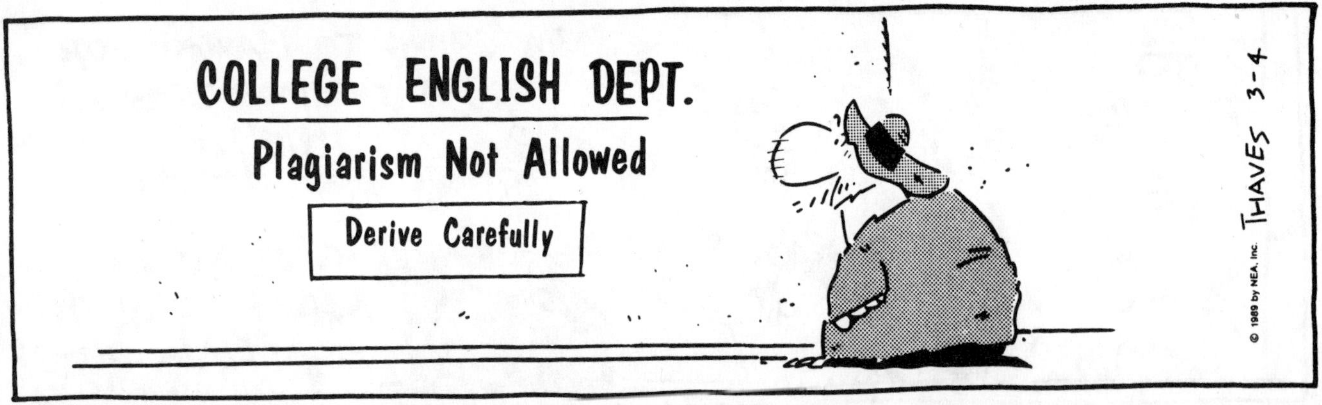
COLLEGE ENGLISH DEPT.
Plagiarism Not Allowed
Derive Carefully
THAVES 3-4
© 1989 by NEA, Inc.

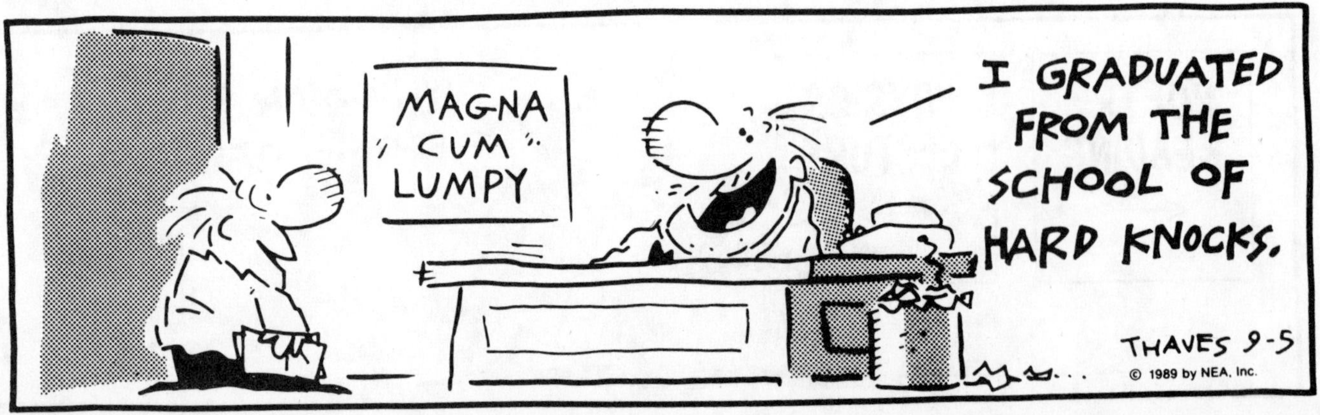
MAGNA CUM LUMPY
I GRADUATED FROM THE SCHOOL OF HARD KNOCKS.
THAVES 9-5
© 1989 by NEA, Inc.

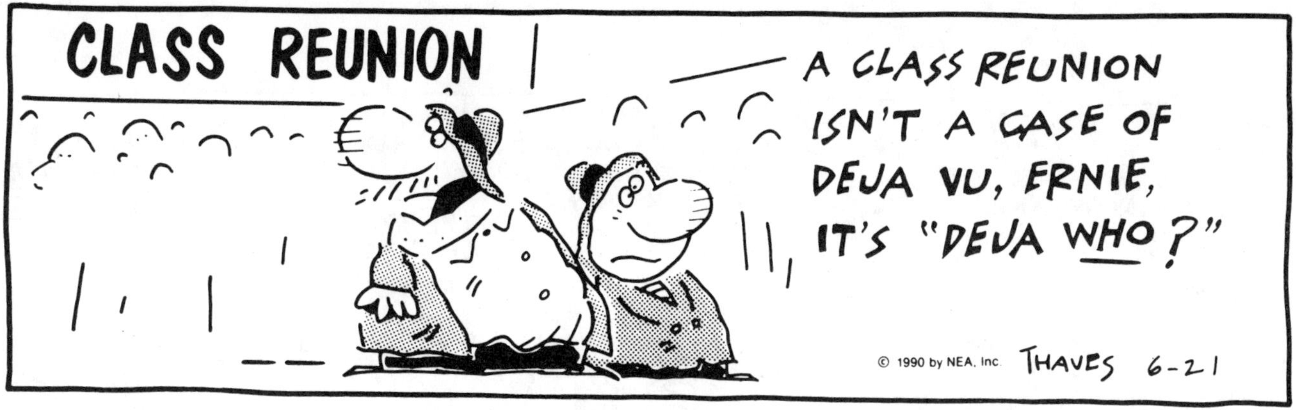
CLASS REUNION
A CLASS REUNION ISN'T A CASE OF DEJA VU, ERNIE, IT'S "DEJA WHO?"
© 1990 by NEA, Inc. THAVES 6-21

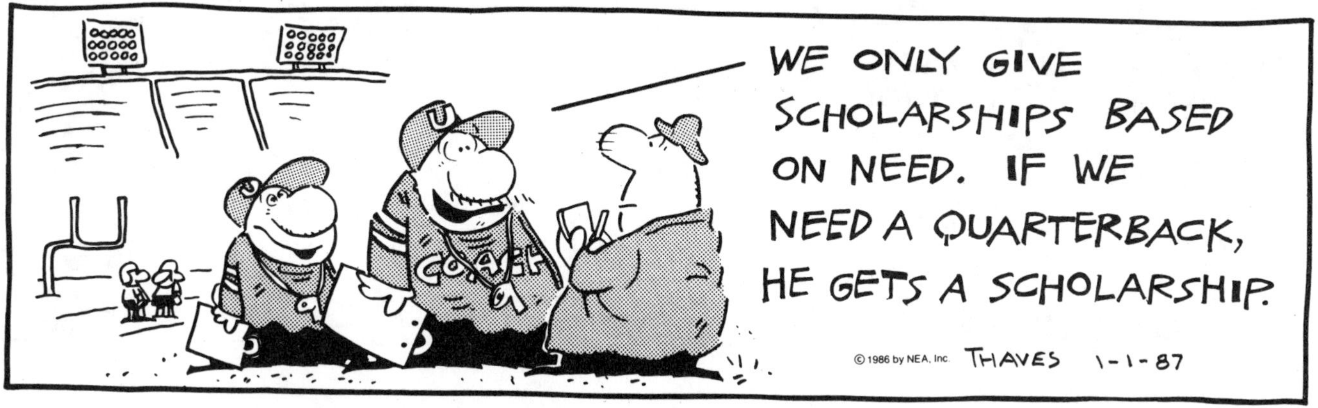
WE ONLY GIVE SCHOLARSHIPS BASED ON NEED. IF WE NEED A QUARTERBACK, HE GETS A SCHOLARSHIP.
COACH
© 1986 by NEA, Inc. THAVES 1-1-87

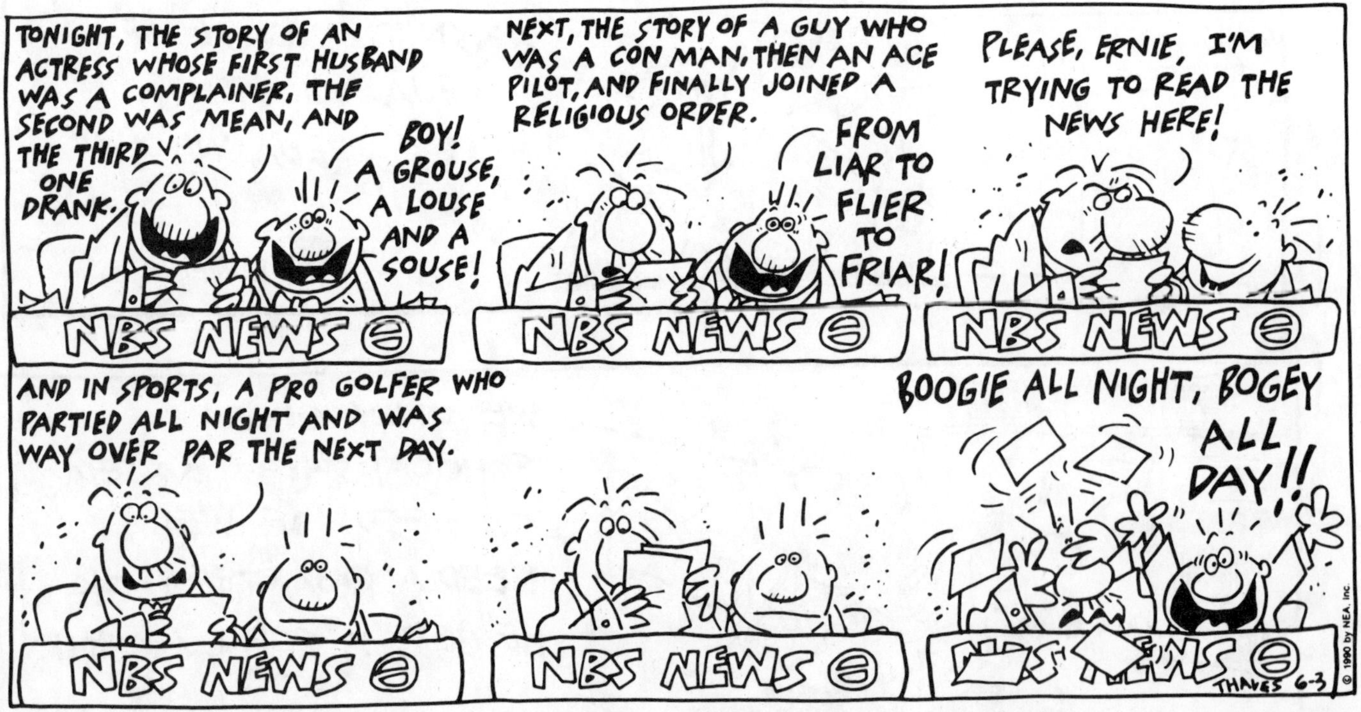
TONIGHT, THE STORY OF AN ACTRESS WHOSE FIRST HUSBAND WAS A COMPLAINER, THE SECOND WAS MEAN, AND THE THIRD ONE DRANK.
BOY! A GROUSE, A LOUSE AND A SOUSE!
NBS NEWS
NEXT, THE STORY OF A GUY WHO WAS A CON MAN, THEN AN ACE PILOT, AND FINALLY JOINED A RELIGIOUS ORDER.
FROM LIAR TO FLIER TO FRIAR!
NBS NEWS
PLEASE, ERNIE, I'M TRYING TO READ THE NEWS HERE!
NBS NEWS
AND IN SPORTS, A PRO GOLFER WHO PARTIED ALL NIGHT AND WAS WAY OVER PAR THE NEXT DAY.
NBS NEWS
NBS NEWS
BOOGIE ALL NIGHT, BOGEY ALL DAY!!
THAVES 6-3
© 1990 by NEA, Inc.

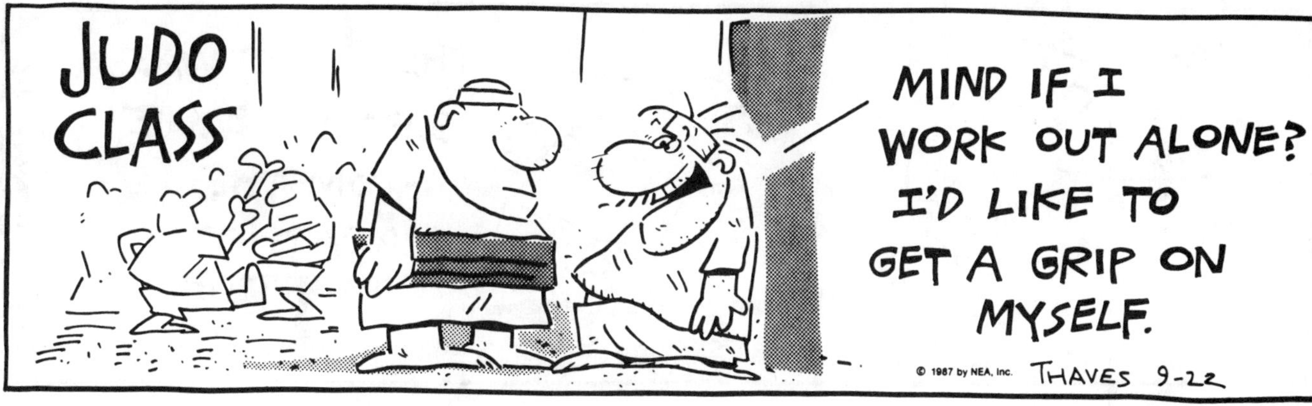
JUDO CLASS
MIND IF I WORK OUT ALONE? I'D LIKE TO GET A GRIP ON MYSELF.
© 1987 by NEA, Inc.
THAVES 9-22

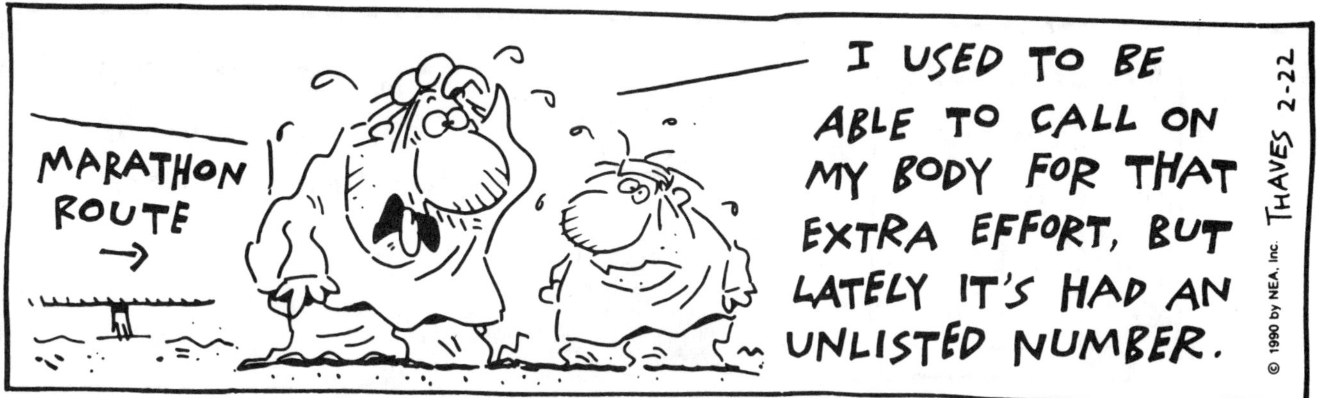
MARATHON ROUTE →
I USED TO BE ABLE TO CALL ON MY BODY FOR THAT EXTRA EFFORT, BUT LATELY IT'S HAD AN UNLISTED NUMBER.
© 1990 by NEA, Inc.
THAVES 2-22

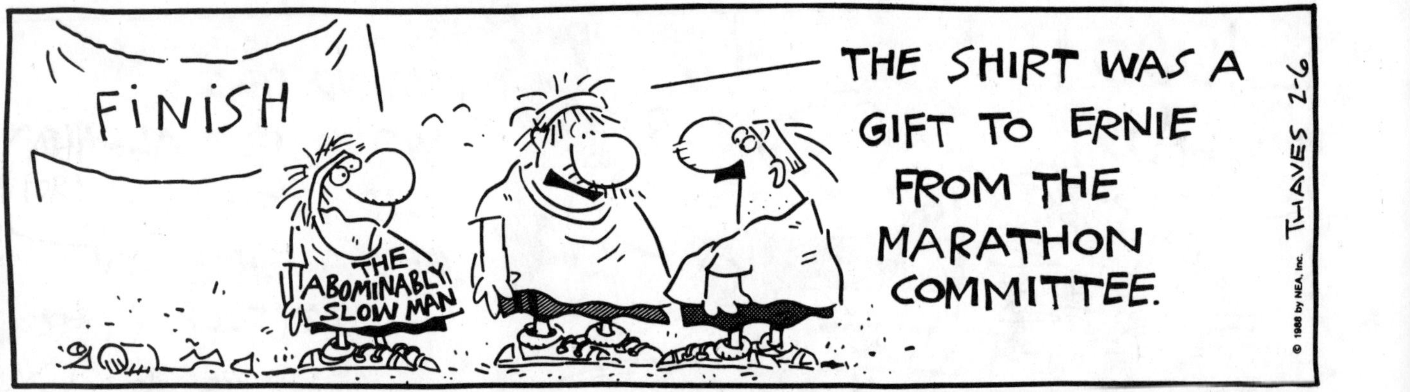
FINISH
THE ABOMINABLY SLOW MAN
THE SHIRT WAS A GIFT TO ERNIE FROM THE MARATHON COMMITTEE.
THAVES 2-6
© 1988 by NEA, Inc.

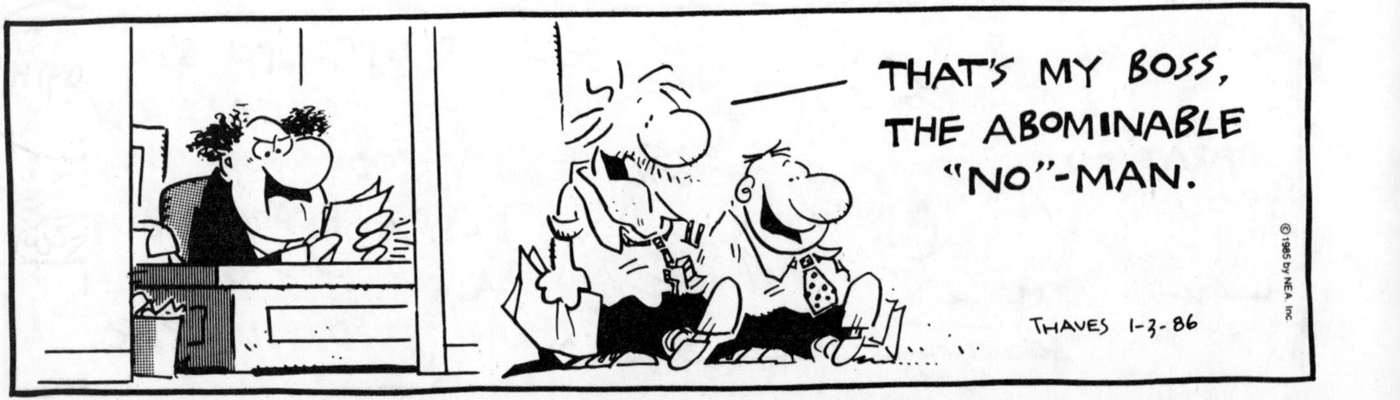
THAT'S MY BOSS, THE ABOMINABLE "NO"-MAN.
THAVES 1-3-86
© 1985 by NEA, Inc.

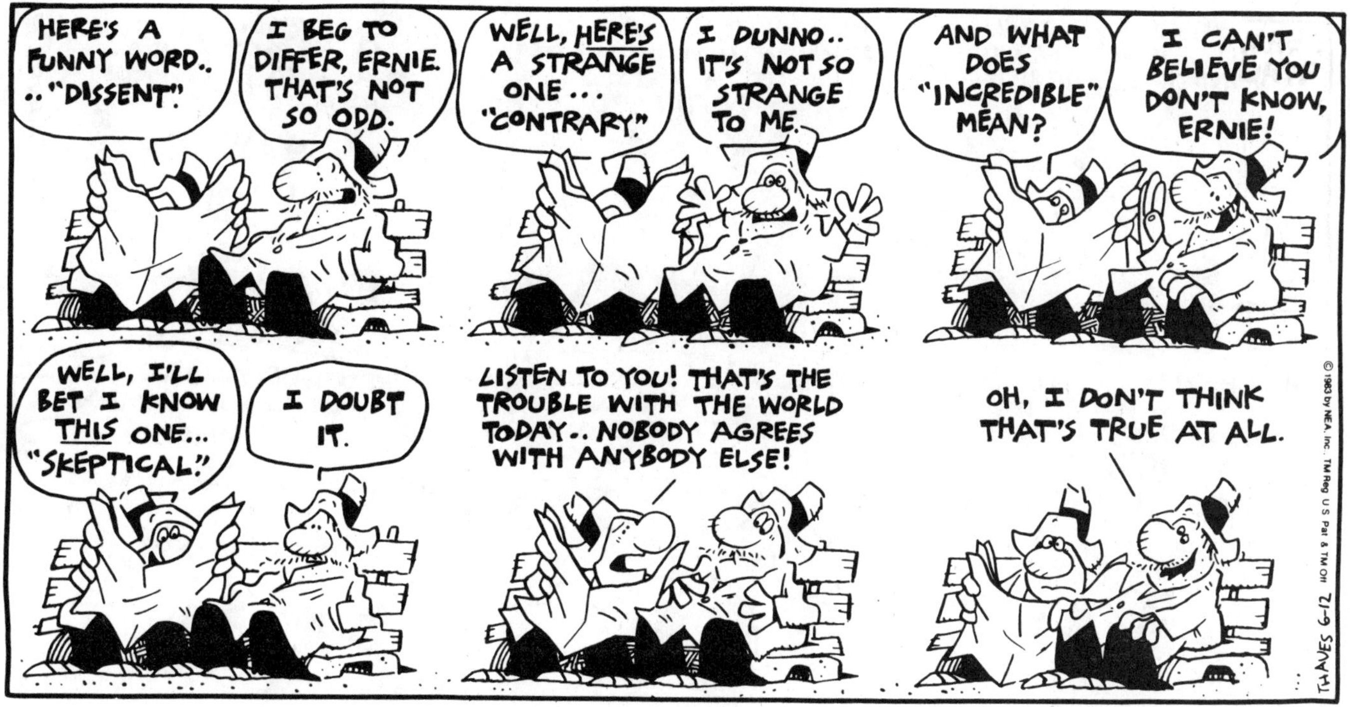
HERE'S A FUNNY WORD.. .."DISSENT."
I BEG TO DIFFER, ERNIE. THAT'S NOT SO ODD.
WELL, HERE'S A STRANGE ONE... "CONTRARY."
I DUNNO.. IT'S NOT SO STRANGE TO ME.
AND WHAT DOES "INCREDIBLE" MEAN?
I CAN'T BELIEVE YOU DON'T KNOW, ERNIE!
WELL, I'LL BET I KNOW THIS ONE... "SKEPTICAL."
I DOUBT IT.
LISTEN TO YOU! THAT'S THE TROUBLE WITH THE WORLD TODAY.. NOBODY AGREES WITH ANYBODY ELSE!
OH, I DON'T THINK THAT'S TRUE AT ALL.
THAVES 6-12
© 1983 by NEA, Inc. TM Reg U.S. Pat & TM Off

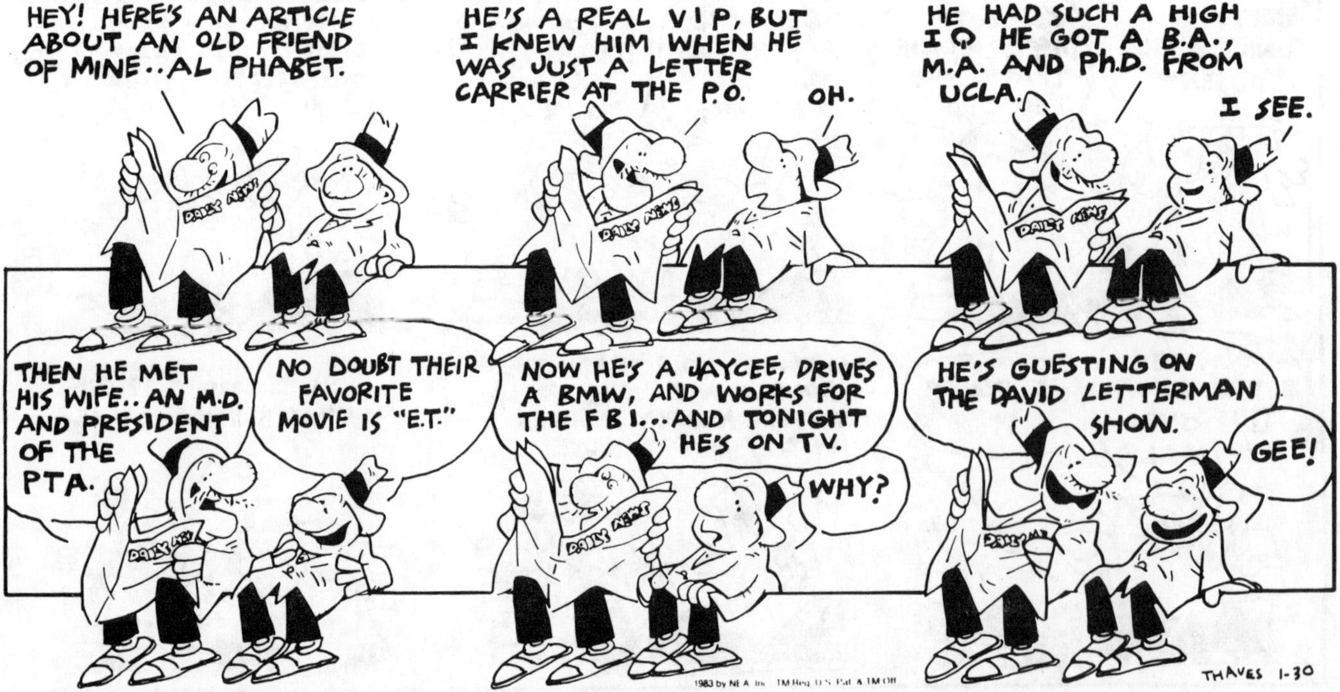
HEY! HERE'S AN ARTICLE ABOUT AN OLD FRIEND OF MINE..AL PHABET.
HE'S A REAL V I P, BUT I KNEW HIM WHEN HE WAS JUST A LETTER CARRIER AT THE P.O.
OH.
HE HAD SUCH A HIGH I Q HE GOT A B.A., M.A. AND Ph.D. FROM UCLA.
I SEE.
THEN HE MET HIS WIFE..AN M.D. AND PRESIDENT OF THE PTA.
NO DOUBT THEIR FAVORITE MOVIE IS "E.T."
NOW HE'S A JAYCEE, DRIVES A BMW, AND WORKS FOR THE F B I...AND TONIGHT HE'S ON T V.
WHY?
HE'S GUESTING ON THE DAVID LETTERMAN SHOW.
GEE!
THAVES 1-30

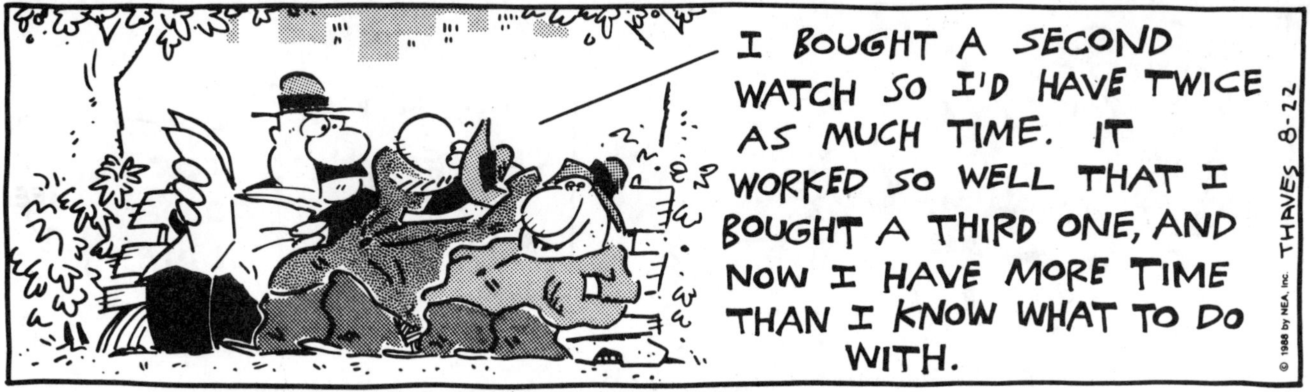
I BOUGHT A SECOND WATCH SO I'D HAVE TWICE AS MUCH TIME. IT WORKED SO WELL THAT I BOUGHT A THIRD ONE, AND NOW I HAVE MORE TIME THAN I KNOW WHAT TO DO WITH.
© 1988 by NEA, Inc. THAVES 8-22

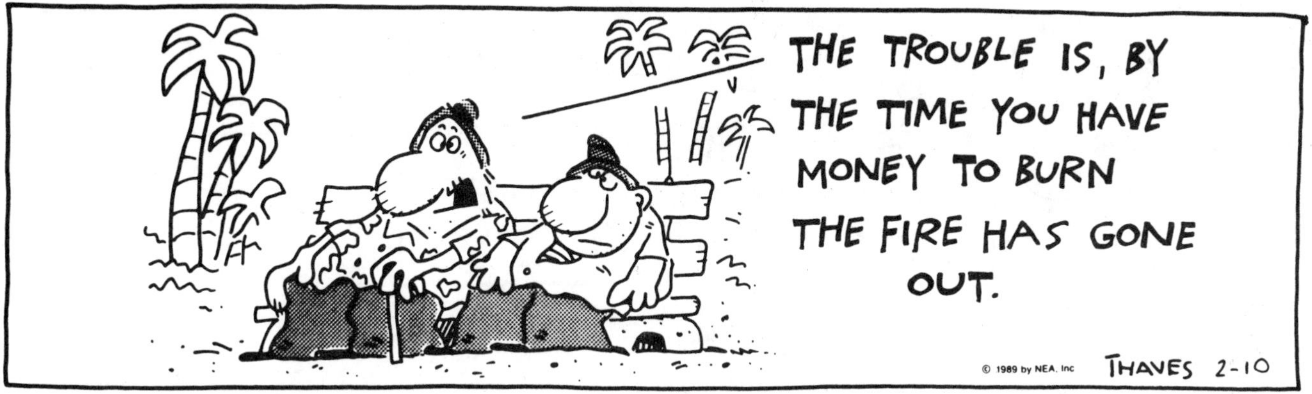
THE TROUBLE IS, BY THE TIME YOU HAVE MONEY TO BURN THE FIRE HAS GONE OUT.
© 1989 by NEA, Inc THAVES 2-10

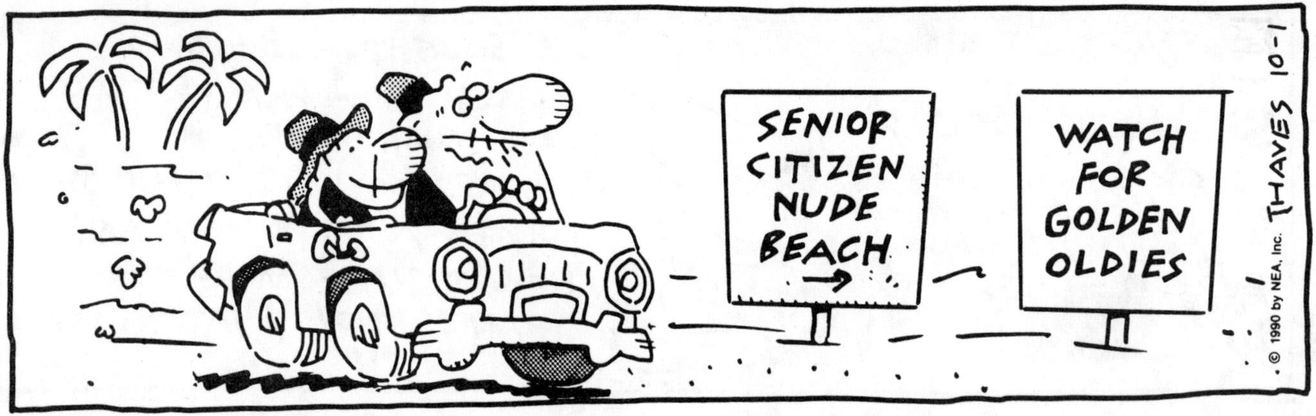
SENIOR CITIZEN NUDE BEACH →
WATCH FOR GOLDEN OLDIES
THAVES 10-1
© 1990 by NEA, Inc.

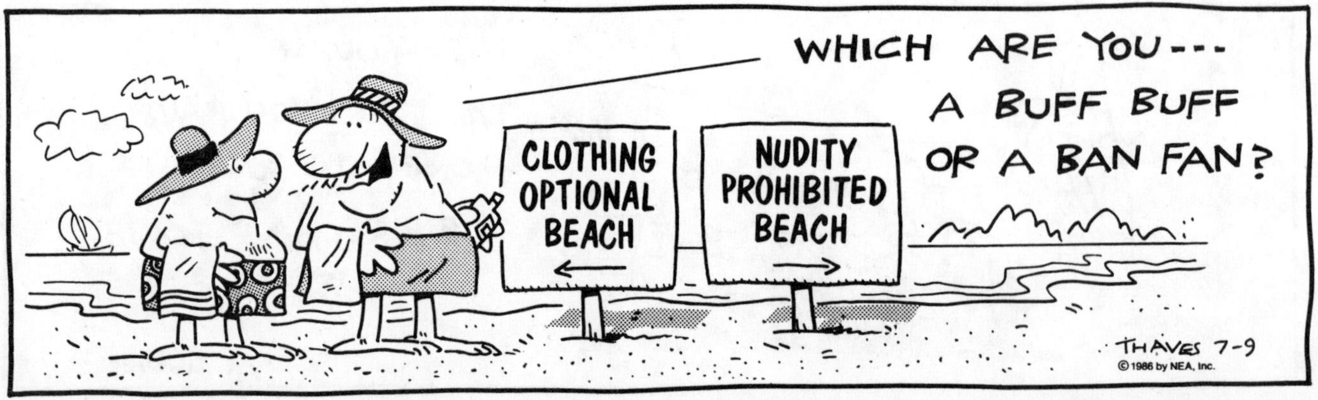
WHICH ARE YOU--- A BUFF BUFF OR A BAN FAN?
CLOTHING OPTIONAL BEACH ←
NUDITY PROHIBITED BEACH →
THAVES 7-9
© 1986 by NEA, Inc.

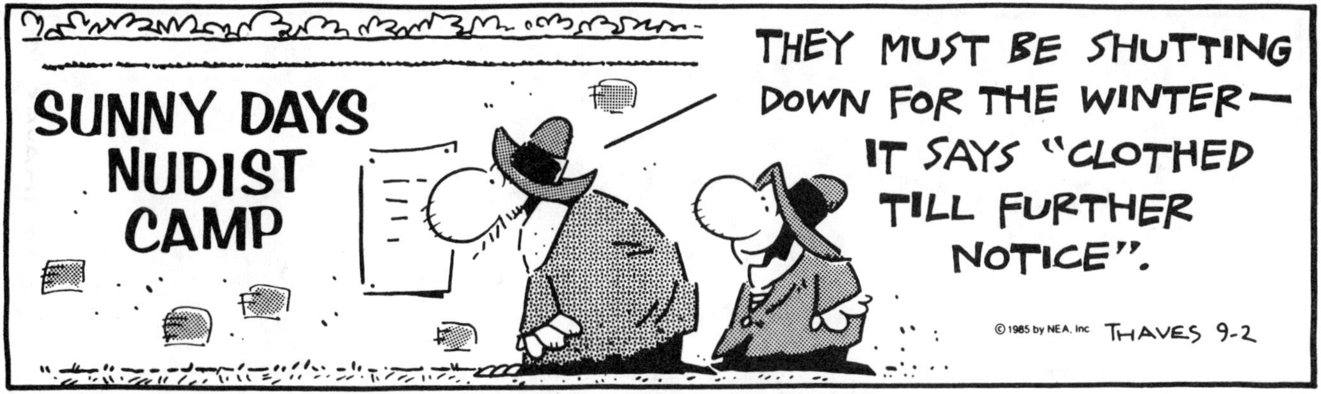
SUNNY DAYS NUDIST CAMP
THEY MUST BE SHUTTING DOWN FOR THE WINTER— IT SAYS "CLOTHED TILL FURTHER NOTICE".
© 1985 by NEA, Inc.
THAVES 9-2

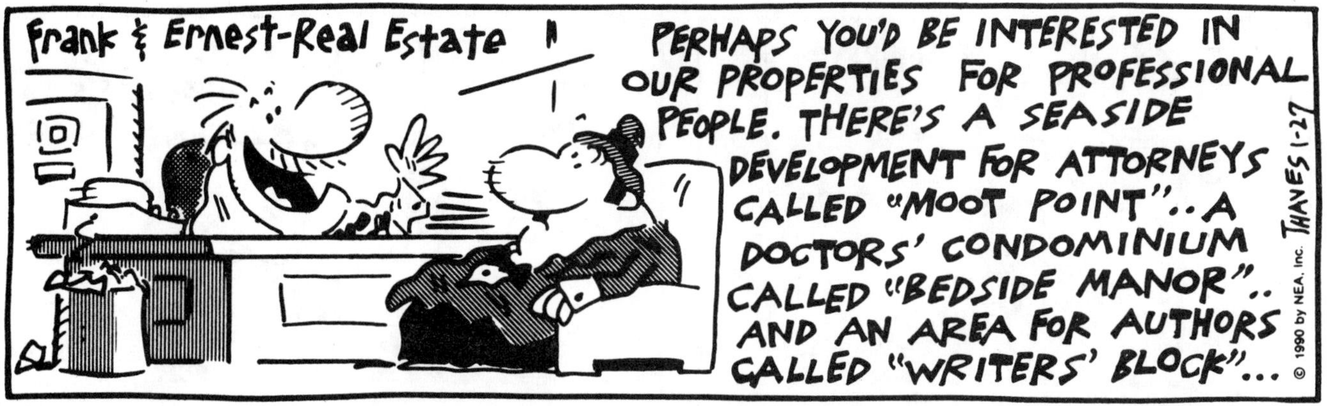
Frank & Ernest-Real Estate
PERHAPS YOU'D BE INTERESTED IN OUR PROPERTIES FOR PROFESSIONAL PEOPLE. THERE'S A SEASIDE DEVELOPMENT FOR ATTORNEYS CALLED "MOOT POINT".. A DOCTORS' CONDOMINIUM CALLED "BEDSIDE MANOR".. AND AN AREA FOR AUTHORS CALLED "WRITERS' BLOCK"...
THAVES 1-27
© 1990 by NEA, Inc.

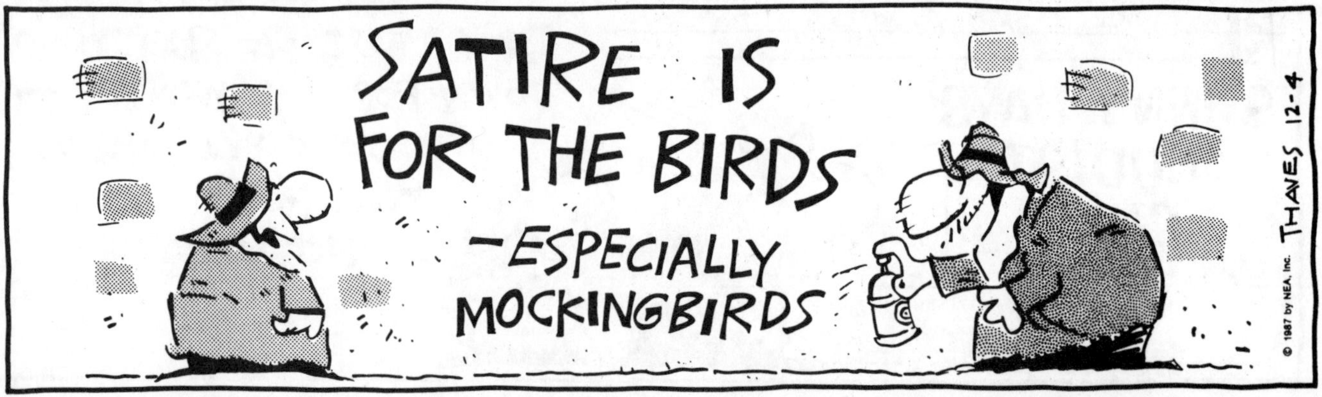
SATIRE IS FOR THE BIRDS
—ESPECIALLY MOCKINGBIRDS
THAVES 12-4
© 1987 by NEA, Inc.

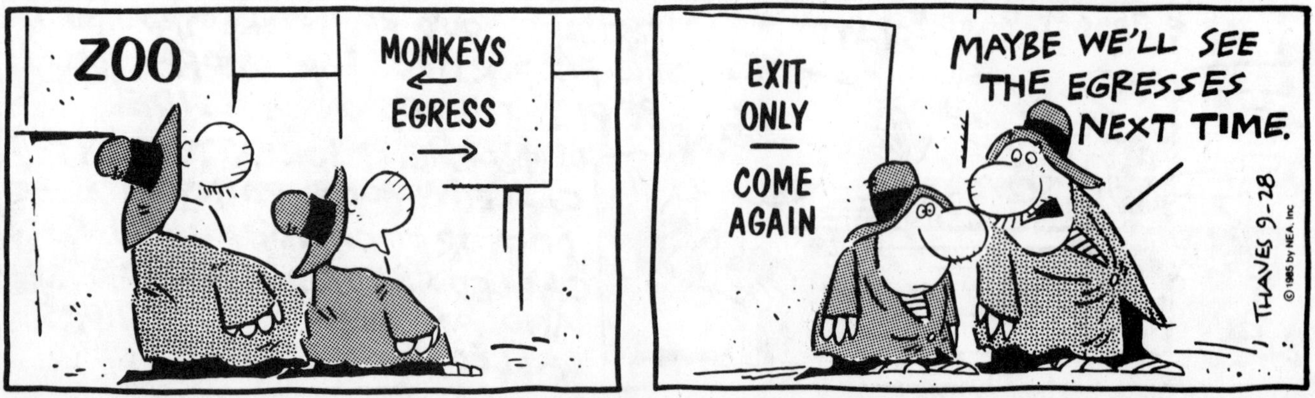
ZOO
MONKEYS ←
EGRESS →
EXIT ONLY
COME AGAIN
MAYBE WE'LL SEE THE EGRESSES NEXT TIME.
THAVES 9-28
© 1985 by NEA, Inc.

READ ANY GOOD BOOKS LATELY ?

_____ **ARE WE THERE YET? A Frank and Ernest History of the World.** A collection of cartoons by Bob Thaves. **$5.95**

_____ **FRANK AND ERNEST CAREER ADVICE How to Make Your Job Work For You.** Inspirational self-help for those seeking personal and professional fulfillment. By Tom Greening, Ph.D. Illustrated with Frank and Ernest cartoons by Bob Thaves. **$7.95**

_____ **ASSEMBLE THE HYENAS I Feel a Pun Coming On!** Selected Frank and Ernest cartoons featuring the best of Bob Thaves' word-play. **$6.95**

_____ **TOTAL BOOKS** (Please add .50 per book for postage and handling.)

My check for $_______________ is enclosed.
Ship to:

____
Name

____
Address

____
City, state, zip

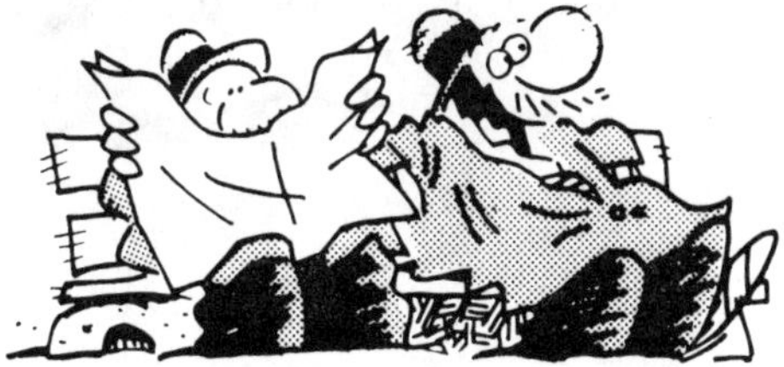

Return this coupon with your payment to: Sales Dept., Pharos Books, 200 Park Avenue, NY NY 10166.
Please allow 4-6 weeks for delivery.

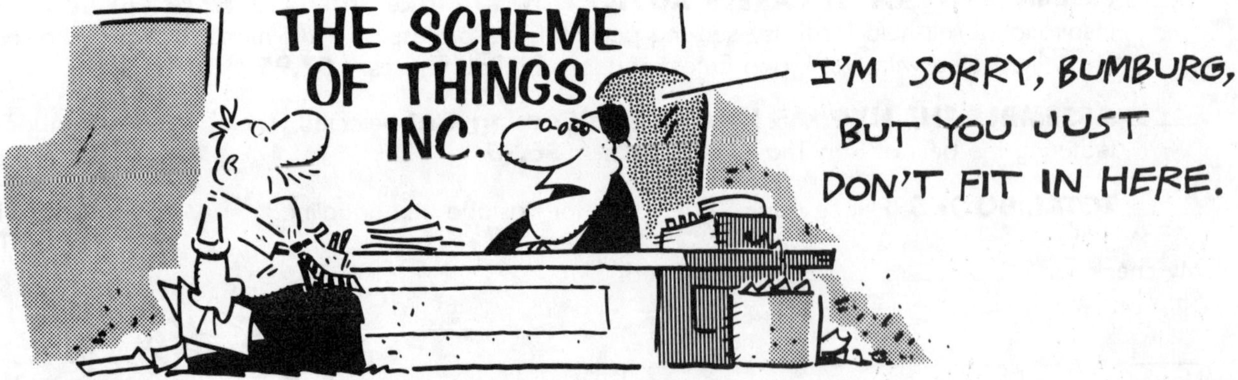
THE SCHEME OF THINGS INC.
I'M SORRY, BUMBURG, BUT YOU JUST DON'T FIT IN HERE.